After Crime and Punishment

Pathways to offender reintegration

Edited by

Shadd Maruna and Russ Immarigeon

WILLAN
PUBLISHING

Published by

Willan Publishing
Culmcott House
Mill Street, Uffculme
Cullompton, Devon
EX15 3AT, UK
Tel: +44(0)1884 840337
Fax: +44(0)1884 840251
e-mail: info@willanpublishing.co.uk
website: www.willanpublishing.co.uk

Published simultaneously in the USA and Canada by

Willan Publishing
c/o ISBS, 920 NE 58th Ave, Suite 300,
Portland, Oregon 97213-3786, USA
Tel: +001(0)503 287 3093
Fax: +001(0)503 280 8832
e-mail: info@isbs.com
website: www.isbs.com

First published 2004

ISBN 1-84392-057-3 (paper)
ISBN 1-84392-058-1 (cased)

British Library Cataloguing-in-Publication Data

A catalogue record for this book is available from the British Library

Project management by Deer Park Productions, Tavistock, Devon
Typeset by GCS, Leighton Buzzard, Beds
Printed and bound by T.J. International Ltd, Padstow, Cornwall

Contents

List of figures and tables

Figures

Tables

Foreword

Belief that prison confinement is a critical contingency in the lives of offenders who experience it is shared by analysts across the political spectrum. Seen from the left, it dehumanizes and diminishes individuals, leaves them less capable of finding a satisfying conventional niche and, more likely therefore, to break the law. Those on the right argue the contrary. As they see it, a taste of 'the joint' is an effective nostrum for turning offenders and others away from the path of transgression; put simply, it gives the former and all who witness their misfortune something to think about. But while imprisonment is a commonplace occurrence in the lives of street criminals, empirical interest in its long-term and cumulative effects has rarely sustained for long the attention of investigators. Until recently, remarkably few bothered even to consider its potential significance for their own work.

The reasons for this oversight can be seen in context of developments in late-twentieth-century domestic and global economic relationships, in criminal justice and in criminological thought. In the USA, this period saw prolonged wage stagnation for working citizens, deindustrialization of central cities, a significant shift of tax burdens to middle-income families and small businesses, and increasing income inequality between the wealthiest and poorest segments of the population. As for criminal justice, the crime control net was widened, its mesh was thinned and, increasingly, it was cast in the imagery and rhetoric of warfare. The list of specific changes in criminal justice is a long one but it includes a fundamental restructuring of sentencing laws, resurrection of the death penalty, a near five-fold increase in the rate of imprisonment, privatization of new expanses of policing and corrections, and appellate judicial decisions ratifying more repressive crime control measures. And all this ignores the emergence and spread of new surveillance technologies, both electronic and behavioural.

Historic transformations of this magnitude inevitably must be interpreted and justified by an equally profound shift in the way crime and criminals are understood. Consequently, the rightward turn in practice was underpinned by a refashioned image of street offenders. No longer were they and their crimes seen as products of dysfunctional criminogenic circumstances. Instead, neoconservative analysts pressed the claim that whatever the so-called 'root causes' of crime might be, they necessarily operate through the calculus of decision-making. And since the former were said to be largely beyond the reach of public policies, the new focus should be on criminal decision-making and policies that constrain it. Spurred by and finding justification in these suggestions, many political leaders and policy analysts quickly came to see street criminals as rational actors, albeit deficient in self-control or infected with a newly discovered virus of 'criminality'.

'Career criminals' and the criminal career perspective occupied centre stage. Employing conceptual inventions and distinctions of uncertain merit, the criminal career paradigm was built on pessimistic and over-deterministic assumptions about offenders. Less concerned with theory than policy, its proponents assumed and focused on *persistence* in offending. Their confidence was based largely on descriptive analyses of official and archival crime data since they showed little interest in first-hand knowledge of the lives and careers of offenders. Unreluctant volunteers in the movement to identify, convict and confine high-rate offenders, academics and policy-makers animated by notions of career criminals were not particularly interested in the potentially deleterious consequences of the new crime control.

It was not a time either for squeamish civil libertarians or any who wanted to explore close up any casualties of the new criminal justice; deliverance from crime would come through faith and perseverance. Nevertheless, the corpus of empirical research into the lives and careers of street offenders, while it was not voluminous, was sufficient in quality and consistency to raise serious questions about the picture of career criminals and criminal careers on which it rested. As opposed to the notion of career continuity and a constant rate of criminal participation, for example, research by Daniel Glaser and his students three decades earlier had shown that when viewed over time many offenders display a zig-zag pattern of criminality. Career continuity in their sample of men released from federal prisons was the exception.

Due in no small measure to its demonstrated shortcomings, the criminal career paradigm lost much of its lustre, and in its place we have seen the ascendance of developmental and life-course approaches to offenders' lives and crimes. This book and similar work by others in recent years are signs that neglect of offenders once they enter the prison has come to an end. Not only in North America but in Europe and Asia as well a growing number of investigators have turned their attention to the longitudinal dynamics of criminal careers. Informed by knowledge and perspectives from several disciplines, life-course investigators work with a stock of concepts that includes *risk factors, cycles, turning points, transitions* and *trajectories*. Much of their work is focused on offenders' early years, but there has been a rekindling of interest in the tail end of criminal careers also. The focus now spans decades, from childhood to dotage. Justification for these developments is grounded in the fact that few men and women past the age of 40 or so – it is difficult to be precise about these things – regardless of how serious their criminal records might be, continue showing up in police stations, courts and prisons. *Desistance* is the label that has come to be applied to this statistical relationship between ageing and participation in serious street crime. The concept admittedly is presumptive; when applied to individuals, it is clear that the break with crime is not always clean cut and final. In real life, desistance frequently is gradual, drawn out over years and interrupted by occasional relapse, at least in the short run. In place of the one-sided and distorted emphasis on criminal continuity characteristic of the criminal career approach, life-course investigators have demonstrated in offenders' lives positive changes and a turning away from earlier habits.

Desistance research clearly offers an opportunity to correct the theoretically incomplete and disingenuous policy approach to crime control characteristic of recent years. Justified by a theory of crime as choice, the harsher criminal justice was aimed almost exclusively at increasing the risk of criminal participation. This, however, ignores the theoretically obvious: offenders can be and are changed not only by manipulating threat but also by increasing their legitimate oppor-tunities. It is poor science and poor public policy to ignore this fact. To do so is to ensure that policy-makers are not presented with the full range of options, some of which certainly are more effective and efficient than others. Investigations of desistance hold great potential for correcting this one-sided concern with the effects of risk by widening the analytic focus to the entire array of forces that cause men and women to turn away from serious criminal participation.

Few areas of criminological investigation show a wider range or more impressive integration of materials and findings than life-course theory and research. Everything from life history to secondary analyses of archived data sets has found application. Those of statistical bent have brought to bear new or refashioned analytic techniques suitable for examination of complex, long-term and incremental change. Grounded ethnographic research has taught us a great deal about the options available to and the calculus of ex-offenders. This style of research also humanizes offenders and thereby balances or corrects assumptions developed far from first-hand experience with the subject-matter. At a time when increasing numbers of investigators know offenders only as coded categories in electronic data sets, the value of first-hand knowledge of them and their lives is considerable.

Like the range of objectives and methodologies represented in desistance theory and research, the chapters in this book are diverse. Maruna and Immarigeon are interested in more than sterile theoretical issues. Some chapters are focused on testing sociological theories of individual change, but others are conceptual or normative. Still others have a policy focus. Throughout, the contributors challenge and humanize the narrow and overly technical perspectives on desistance common among contemporary investigators.

Taken together, a number of chapters show unmistakably that return to the free world can be exceedingly difficult to manage for many men and women. These chapters shed light on an array of consequences of imprisonment, from abrogation of citizenship rights to difficulties securing legitimate employment. There can be little doubt that, whatever positive impact the experience of imprisonment may have on offenders, most who pass through the contemporary prison will find it a complicating factor in their efforts to make something of themselves and accomplish something in life. Confinement disrupts and may even obliterate any progress prisoners may have made towards identifying and settling into conventional channels. It is not recommended either for increasing or enhancing social capital.

Crime control policies rationalized by caricatures of career criminals and 'super-predators' were not limited only to increasing the risk of imprisonment, however; probationers, parolees and others permitted to serve all or part of their sentence in the community also were objects of more repressive crime control policies. Intensive supervision, drug testing, electronic monitoring and mandatory fees for 'service' are some measures that found adoption. As important, the new crime control ideology freed parole administrators of the restraint embedded in earlier notions of crime control that parole violation represented failure. This is one reason why parole bureaucracies today are returning their charges to prison in record numbers. There is no shortage of fodder. The imprisonment binge of the past three decades ensures that each year thousands of prisoners are disgorged from America's bloated prison systems.

The fact that these men and women are among us has given rise belatedly to new policy interest in them and their fortunes. Thus the new interest in desistance extends far beyond academics and their theoretical concerns. Some of this interest presumably is fuelled by fear, another part by policy concerns and the remainder by the availability of funds for examining desistance. Although there is much yet to learn about the post-imprisonment lives of men and women who have tasted one of the most severe sanctions employed by the state, it would be a mistake to ignore the substantial and solid evidence already available, both in earlier research and in this book. This collection of essays sheds revealing and critical light on desistance, a process that has been ignored by policy makers for too long.

Neal Shover
University of Tennessee

Notes on contributors

Gordon Bazemore is Professor of Criminology and Criminal Justice and Director of the Community Justice Institute at Florida Atlantic University. His primary research interests include community and restorative justice, juvenile justice, youth policy, victimology, corrections and community policing. Dr Bazemore's recent publications appear in *Justice Quarterly, Crime and Delinquency, Annals of the American Academy of Political and Social Sciences, Justice System Journal* and the *International Journal of Victimology*. He has completed two books, *Restorative Juvenile Justice: Repairing the Harm of Youth Crime* (co-edited with Lode Walgrave, Criminal Justice Press 1999) and *Restorative and Community Justice: Cultivating Common Ground for Victims, Communities and Offenders* (co-edited with Mara Schiff, Anderson 2001), and is currently principal investigator of a national study of restorative justice conferencing funded by the National Institute of Justice and the Robert Wood Johnson Foundation and a state-wide evaluation of restorative juvenile justice programmes in Vermont.

Angela Behrens is a recent graduate of the University of Minnesota and a student at the University of Minnesota Law School. Her interests are in the areas of criminal and constitutional law.

Leana Allen Bouffard is an assistant professor of criminal justice at North Dakota State University. She received her PhD and MA in criminology from the University of Maryland and her BS in psychology from Duke University. Her primary area of research interest is life-course theory and military service, particularly how the relationship between military service and criminal behaviour has changed over time. Her other research interests also include violence against women, gender and crime, police behaviour and correctional treatment programmes. Dr Bouffard has published articles in such journals as *Criminology*, *Criminal Justice and Behavior*, *Journal of Crime and Justice* and *International Journal of Offender Therapy and Comparative Criminology*. She has also written chapters in *Battle Cries on the Home Front: Violence in the Military Family*, *Essays in Criminology* and *Advances in Criminological Theory. Volume 12. Control Theories of Crime and Delinquency* (Transaction 2003).

Robert Brame received his PhD at the University of Maryland in 1997 and he teaches in the Department of Criminology and Criminal Justice at the University of South Carolina. His research interests include the study of criminal activity over the lifespan and methodological problems related to the study of crime and criminal justice.

Ros Burnett, DPhil (University of Oxford), is a research fellow at the University of Oxford Centre for Criminological Research and Deputy Head of its Probation Studies Unit. She has previous employment experience as a probation officer and a relationship counsellor. Her publications include books and articles on interpersonal relationships, probation practice, and recidivism and desistance. Her most recent book, with Caterine Appleton, is *Joined-up Youth Justice* (Russell House 2003).

Shawn D. Bushway is an assistant professor of criminology in the Department of Criminology and Criminal Justice at the University of Maryland and a fellow with the National Consortium of Violence Research. He received his PhD in public policy analysis and political economy in 1996 from the H. John Heinz III School of Public Policy and Management at Carnegie Mellon University. His current research focuses on understanding the process of desistance and disparity in sentencing outcomes.

James M. Byrne is a professor at the University of Massachusetts–Lowell in the Department of Criminal Justice. Dr Byrne is an expert in sentencing, corrections and organizational issues. He is a consultant to many different adult and juvenile justice system-examining organizational and management issues. He is the author of many scholarly articles in such journals as *Crime and Delinquency*, *Journal of*

Research in Crime and Justice and so on. He specializes in work on treatment issues for offenders and sentencing.

Carsten Erbe is a project co-ordinator with the Balanced and Restorative Project in Ft Lauderdale, FL. In this capacity he has worked on two national research projects identifying juvenile conferencing across the USA. He has also aided in the development of neighbourhood accountability boards in the state of Florida. Previous to joining the project he worked with community-based restorative justice programmes in the Yukon Territory and Australia.

Stephen Farrall (BSc, MSc, DPhil) is a research fellow in the Department of Criminology, Keele University. He has previously worked at the Centre for Criminological Research, Oxford University and in the Law Department, University of Sheffield. He is the author of *Rethinking What Works with Offenders* (Willan Publishing 2002). His current research revolves around the long-term impacts of probation supervision. He is currently working on a project funded by the Leverhulme Trust to retrace members of the sample referred to in his contribution to this book. He has recently finished writing an essay on theories of desistance with Shadd Maruna to be published in the *Kölner Zeitschrift für Soziologie und Sozialpsychologie*.

Russ Immarigeon, MSW, is the editor of *Offender Programs Report* and *Women, Girls and Criminal Justice*, published by the Civic Research Institute (CRI). He also edits *VOMA Connections*, the quarterly newsletter of the Victim–Offender Mediation Asociation. In addition, he contributes regular policy and literature review columns for *Community Corrections Report, Crime Victims Report* and *Corrections Managers Report*, all published by CRI. He is co-editor, with Meda Chesney-Lind, of the *Women, Crime and Criminology* series published by the State University of New York Press. His research interests include community corrections, decarceration and alternatives to imprisonment, gender and prison abolition, and the relationship between social work and criminal justice practices. His publications include *Women's Prisons: Overcrowded and Overused* (National Council on Crime and Delinquency 1992).

Janet Jamieson, BA, MPhil, is a lecturer in the Department of Applied Social Science, Lancaster University. Her current research interests include youth and offending, youth justice, and community and crime. Recent publications have appeared in the *British Journal of Community Justice* and *Youth Justice*.

Richard S. Jones is an associate professor of sociology at Marquette University. He was incarcerated at the Minnesota Correctional Facility, Stillwater (maximum security prison) for possession of marijuana with intent to distribute. His research on the male and female prison experience has been published in *The Prison Journal*, *Journal of Contemporary Criminal Justice*, *Perspectives on Social Problems*, *Women and Criminal Justice*, *Symbolic Interaction* and the *Journal of Contemporary Ethnography*. His most recent work includes *Doing Time: Prison Experience and Identity* (JAI Press 2000), with Thomas J. Schmid.

John H. Laub is a professor of criminology and criminal justice at the University of Maryland, College Park, and an affiliated scholar at the Henry A. Murray Center at the Radcliffe Institute for Advanced Study at Harvard University. He is currently President of the American Society of Criminology. Dr Laub's areas of research include crime and deviance over the life course, juvenile delinquency and juvenile justice, and the history of criminology. He has published widely including *Crime in the Making: Pathways and Turning Points through Life* (Harvard University Press 1993), co-authored with Robert Sampson. Also with Robert Sampson he has recently completed a book entitled *Shared Beginnings, Divergent Lives: Delinquent Boys to Age 70* (Harvard University Press 2003), which analyses longitudinal data from a long-term follow-up study of juvenile offenders from a classic study by Sheldon and Eleanor Glueck.

Thomas P. LeBel is a PhD student in the School of Criminal Justice of the University at Albany, State University of New York, and the 2003 recipient of the Eliot Lumbard Award for Outstanding Academic Excellence from that programme. He is the author or co-author of numerous recent and forthcoming articles and book chapters on the topic of prisoner reintegration. His dissertation research will examine the impact of stigma on the lives of former prisoners.

Jeff Manza is an associate professor of sociology and political science and a faculty fellow at the Institute for Policy Research, Northwestern University. His research is in the area of political sociology, social stratification and public policy. In addition to his collaborative work with Uggen on felon disenfranchisement, he is the co-author (with Clem Brooks) of *Social Cleavages and Political Change: Voter Alignments and US Party Coalitions* (Oxford University Press 1999), which received a distinguished book prize from the political sociology section of the American Sociological Association.

Shadd Maruna joined the Institute of Criminology at the University of Cambridge in 2001. Prior to that he had been an assistant professor at the School of Criminal Justice at the University of Albany, State University of New York. His research focuses on issues of offender reintegration, reconciliation, exclusion and forgiveness. In 2001 he was awarded the Michael J. Hindelang Award for Outstanding Contribution to Criminology by the American Society of Criminology for his book *Making Good: How Ex-convicts Reform and Rebuild their Lives* (American Psychological Association Books 2001).

Gill McIvor is Director of the Social Work Research Centre at the University of Stirling. She has a PhD in psychology and is a qualified social worker but, for the last 17 years, has undertaken research on various aspects of the criminal justice system in Scotland. Her research interests include community sentences, women and crime, and youth crime, and her current research projects include the evaluation of pilot drug courts in Scotland, victims' experiences of the police, drugs throughcare for short-term prisoners and a comparative analysis of women's experiences after prison. She is co-author of *Understanding Offending among Young People* (HMSO 1999), editor of *Women who Offend* (Jessica Kingsley forthcoming) and co-editor of *Managing Sex Offender Risk* (Jessica Kingsley forthcoming).

Cathy Murray is a lecturer in social policy in the Department of Applied Social Science, University of Stirling. She has researched and published in the field of young people and offending, including the Scottish Children's Hearings system. She teaches on undergraduate and postgraduate courses, including honours options on the 'Sociology of youth and young people, crime and society'. She is currently completing a PhD on young people's resistance and early desistance from offending.

Raymond Paternoster is Professor in the Department of Criminology and Criminal Justice at the University of Maryland. He is editor of *Criminology*, the official journal of the American Society of Criminology. His research interests include criminal offending over the life course, quantitative methods, criminological theory and issues related to capital punishment.

Alex R. Piquero is an associate professor of criminology at the University of Florida, member of the National Consortium on Violence Research and network associate with the MacArthur Foundation's

Research Network on Adolescent Development and Juvenile Justice. He received his PhD in Criminology from the University of Maryland in 1996. His research interests include criminal careers, criminological theory and quantitative research methods. He recently co-authored an essay on the current state of criminal career research in Volume 30 of *Crime and Justice: A Review of Research* (University of Chicago Press 2003). In addition to having published over 80 articles, he has co-edited four books, including *Life-course Criminology* (Wadsworth Thomson Learning 2001).

Stephen C. Richards is an associate professor of sociology and criminology at Northern Kentucky University. He is former federal prisoner having done time in maximum-security penitentiaries, medium-security correctional institutions and minimum-security camps for conspiracy to distribute marijuana. Richards has a BS in sociology (University of Wisconsin-Madison 1986), an MA in sociology (University of Wisconsin–Milwaukee 1989) and a PhD in sociology (Iowa State University 1992). His work has appeared in the *Journal of Contemporary Criminal Justice, Critical Criminology, Social Justice, Journal of Prisoners on Prisons, Policy Studies Journal* and *Criminology and Public Policy.* His most recent books include *Behind Bars: Surviving Prison* (Alpha 2002) and *Convict Criminology* (Wadsworth 2003), with Jeffrey Ian Ross. He is currently writing *USP Marion: The First Super Max Penitentiary.* Richards is a Soros Senior Justice Fellow and member of the American Society of Criminology National Policy Committee.

Faye S. Taxman is Director of BGR and an associate professor in the Department of Criminology and Criminal Justice at the University of Maryland, College Park. Dr Taxman is the PI for NIDA's Criminal Justice Drug Abuse Treatment Studies (CJ-DATS) Coordinating Center. She is also the PI for a two-site randomized experiment testing the efficacy of a seamless system of drug treatment services for offenders (NIDA). She has completed randomized studies and quasi-experimental designs on efficacy of jail-based drug treatment services, seamless system models of drug treatment services for probationers and parolees, and drug courts. Her expertise has resulted in work with the Office of National Drug Control Policy, Center for Substance Abuse Treatment, Correctional Program Office, Drug Court Program Office, Bureau of Justice Assistance and the National Institute of Justice, and other federal and state agencies. Dr Taxman has conducted invited talks and trainings in over 30 states, particularly on the topic of effective treatment for offenders, seamless systems and systems of care. Her articles on 'Unraveling what works in drug treatment for offenders' (1999) and 'Recidivism reduction' (1998) are frequently cited by practitioners as a guide to improving practice. In 2002 she was awarded the University of Cincinnati Award from the American Probation and Parole Association for contributions to the field of supervision.

Christopher Uggen is an associate professor of sociology, Life Course Center affiliate and McKnight Presidential Fellow at the University of Minnesota. He studies crime, law and deviance, with current projects involving felon voting rights, responses to sexual harassment and desistance from crime in the transition to adulthood. With Jeff Manza, he is co-author of *Locked Out: Felon Disenfranchisement and American Democracy* (Oxford University Press forthcoming).

Douglas Young is a senior research scientist at the Bureau of Governmental Research at the University of Maryland, College Park. After spending more than 15 years with the Vera Institute of Justice, Young joined BGR in 2000, where he manages the juvenile justice studies. He is involved with several studies aimed at developing new methods for assessing the integrity of programmes and for employing research findings to advance programme design and implementation within the justice and public health systems. His current work involves working with the juvenile justice system to utilize valid risk tools to structure decision-making and to develop case plans. He has spent most of the past 15 years conducting research in substance abuse, corrections and the courts. He has recently directed studies on the effectiveness of coerced treatment and courts' use of new treatment alternatives, pro-gramme evaluations of New York's system of alternative to incarceration programmes, prison treatment and La Bodega de la Familia, an innovative demonstration that aims to reduce drug-related harms by working with families of crime-involved drug abusers. His work includes development of a psychometric tool to measure coercion and a risk tool for juvenile justice populations. He is the author of many scholarly articles, many in the area of coercion and system issues.

Part 1
Desistance Theory and Reintegration Practice

Chapter I

Ex-offender reintegration: theory and practice

*Shadd Maruna, Russ Immarigeon and
Thomas P. LeBel*

Jazz saxophonist Sonny Rollins was 21 years old when his addiction to heroin threatened to end his budding musical career, just at a point when he was breaking in with the top jazz players of the day, including Charlie Parker, Dizzy Gillespie and Thelonious Monk. In 1951, many of these now famous composers and musicians were less well known and they would sit around small clubs, like Minton's in Harlem, playing what they knew, what they felt and what came to them. They were fashioning their careers and their legacies, but some of them were addicted to heroin. Indeed, heroin and other drugs were rampant in the jazz community in those years, so addictive behaviours were not viewed with much derision and addicts were typically not excluded from the community of jazz musicians.

But Sonny Rollins, like a few others, was deeper into the consequences of addiction. He committed a few strong-armed robberies and, subsequently, he spent some time on Rikers Island, New York City's jail. When on release, the threat of parole revocation shadowed his days and nights. He continued his drug use but he knew that one day he would be caught, returned to prison and left to an uncertain future.

Rollins found himself in great conflict. On the one hand, he was being welcomed into a talented circle but, on the other hand, he was seen as disreputable, especially by nightclub owners who booked musicians. According to jazz biographer Eric Nisenson (2000), Rollins recognized his conflict most ostensibly in the facial expressions of Charlie Parker, who was also a heroin user. One evening in 1951, Nisenson relates, Parker and Rollins were playing together at a recording session held only a few weeks after Rollins had been released on parole from Rikers.

Rollins tells the story like this:

> At the time of this session, I was on parole but I knew that I was probably headed back to Rikers Island because I was still getting high. Charlie Parker asked me something like, 'Well, are you okay now?' or something of that nature – 'Have you straightened yourself out?' – because he was always a very avuncular figure to me. That's when I told him, 'Oh, yeah, I'm straight now.' But there was somebody on the date with whom I had just been getting high before the date, and he spilled the beans to Bird [Charlie Parker] … After Bird found that out he became very cold to me. Not just cold to me, I could see in his face that once again he had been confronted with the fact that all of his young protégés were messed up on drugs. So once again this was in front of him. I could see that in him at that session and I got the realization of how he must really feel about it. I realized then that I really wanted to get off drugs. I thought, 'Okay, this is the impetus to get off drugs and I'm going to come back one day and show Bird that I actually did get off drugs. And this time it will be true.' I saw the pain in his face that day. And then it all made sense to me. (Nisenson 2000: 51–2)

Kicking heroin addiction, like breaking out of other entrenched behaviour patterns, is no easy thing. Despite his revelation during the session with Parker, it was another few years, and other close calls, before Rollins voluntarily entered a federal drug treatment programme in Lexington, Kentucky, where he began a successful recovery process. Rollins re-emerged in Chicago at the end of 1955 as a member of the Clifford Brown–Max Roach Quintet, and soon established himself as a master of thematic improvisation. In 1957, he won the prestigious *Down Beat* magazine Critics' Poll as 'New Star' of the tenor saxophone, and the rest, as they say, is history (for those interested in this history, see Kirschner 2000).

Sonny Rollins' escape from criminality and drug addiction is a story of desistance from crime. Of course, Rollins' contributions to the world of jazz – jazz critic Gary Giddens (1992: 164) has called him 'the world's greatest living saxophonist' – make him one of the most successful ex-convicts in recent history. Yet the processes of interpersonal reintegration and recovery from addiction he underwent are increasingly familiar ones. Indeed, the topic of ex-offender reintegration has become among the most important issues in criminology and related disciplines.

Reintegration (or 're-entry' as it is sometimes called) is both an event and a process. Narrowly speaking, re-entry comes the day a prisoner is released from confinement. In its own way, the time (or timing) of a prisoner's release offers challenges and conflicts that may or may not be managed by corrections officials or criminal justice agents. For instance, shortly before he became better known, the cult leader Charles Manson was an average prisoner being released from San Quentin into the San Francisco Bay area. In one version of the events of this day (see Emmons 1986), Manson hitched a ride just outside the gates of the prison from a delivery truck driver who almost immediately offered him a marijuana cigarette. Manson, not unreasonably, was startled that drugs were so readily available so close to the prison and wondered what was happening to the society that had kept him in isolation for a significant amount of time. Other, less notorious ex-offenders tell similar stories of being delivered from a prison to an inner-city bus station in the middle of the night, with $40 in gate money, nowhere to go and no one except drug dealers waiting for them in the station. What impact do such episodes have for a person newly released from confinement? At present, answers are more readily available from biographical accounts of prisoner life than from social science research, although this is changing (see, e.g. Travis *et al.* 2001; Chapter 9 this volume).

More broadly, re-entry is also a long-term process, one that actually starts prior to release and continues well afterwards. It is fashionable among some British resettlement workers to suggest that the re-entry process should begin as soon as the individual is taken into custody. That is, everything that is done to a convicted person should be serving the cause of preparing the individual for success after release. By this larger definition (the one most of the contributors to this book will be concerned with), reintegration encompasses many aspects of processes that go by names such as 'corrections,' 'rehabilitation,' 'treatment' and the like. In fact, the UK Association of Chief Officers of Probation recently defined 'resettlement' as:

A systematic and evidenced-based process by which actions are taken to work with the offender in custody and on release, so that communities are better protected from harm and re-offending is significantly reduced. It encompasses *the totality of work with prisoners*, their families and significant others in partnership with statutory and voluntary organisations. (Cited in Morgan and Owers 2001: 12, emphasis added)

Essentially, then, reintegration involves everything – from literacy training to electronic monitoring – that is intended to reduce recidivism after release from prison. As such, public and governmental interest in successful re-entry is, of course, of longstanding vintage.

Still, the topic has never been more urgent than it is today. At the time of writing, in the USA, around 600,000 men and women (over 1,600 per day) will be released from prisons, compared to around 170,000 in 1980 (see especially Travis and Petersilia 2001). Criminological research suggests that many of them, perhaps even the majority of them in some states, will not achieve anything resembling successful reintegration into society. For instance, of the 459,000 US parolees who were discharged from community supervision in 2000, 42 per cent were returned to incarceration – 11 per cent with a new sentence and 31 per cent in some other way (Bureau of Justice Statistics 2001). In a recent study of 272,111 state prisoners released in 1994, 67.5 per cent were rearrested within three years, as compared to an estimated 62.5 per cent in a similar study of 1983 releases (Langan and Levin 2002).

In fact, re-entering society seems to be more difficult and precarious a transition than ever before. In 1980, 27,177 released ex-offenders were returned to state prisons in the USA. In 1999, this number was 197,606. As a percentage of all admissions to state prison, parole violators more than doubled from 17 per cent in 1980 to 35 per cent in 1999 (in California, a staggering 67 per cent of prison admissions were parole failures). Between 1990 and 1999 the number of parole violators rose by 50 per cent while the number of new court commitments rose by only 7 per cent (Hughes et al. 2001). This indicates that the re-entry problem is not only a product of the 1990s' incarceration boom in the USA but was actually a leading cause of the boom as well.

Arguably, the situation for ex-offenders in the UK is less dire. Certainly, Britain has a longer and more substantive history of addressing the housing, employment and counselling needs of released prisoners (Haines 1990). Still, the UK prison population has jumped from around 40,000 in 1992 to over 68,000 today, and may reach as high as 90,000 in the near future (Grove et al. 1999). Moreover, substantial difficulties remain for returning ex-convicts (see Hagell et al. 1995; Metcalf et al. 2001; Niven and Olagundaye 2002). In fact, 57 per cent of all prisoners in England and Wales discharged in 1996 were reconvicted for a standard list offence within two years of their release (Home Office 2001). In a joint thematic review on resettlement issues, HM Inspectorates of Prisons and Probation conclude 'The resettlement needs of many prisoners are being severely neglected' because of the lack of an overall strategy for reintegration (Morgan and Owers 2001: 1).

It is no wonder that, in the USA, the re-entry issue has been described by former Attorney General Janet Reno as 'one of the most pressing problems we face as a nation' (2000). The importance of improving the prison release and re-entry process may be one of the few issues on which Reno agrees with the current Attorney General, John Ashcroft. In July 2002, Ashcroft announced that 68 different jurisdictions will share $100 million in grant funds through the new 'Serious and violent offender reentry' initiative, a reworking of the 'Young offender reentry' initiative originally proposed during Reno's term in office. The purpose of the much-touted new initiative is 'to ensure public safety and reduce victimization by helping returning offenders become productive members of their communities' (OJP 2002).

Similarly, in the UK there have been numerous recent calls for the development of a 'National rehabilitation strategy' or system-wide resettlement agenda for HM Prison Service for England and Wales (Morgan and Owers 2001; Social Exclusion Unit 2001; Home Office 2002). Among the proposals being advocated include a 'going straight contract' to be signed by prisoners and prison staff, the creation of 'rehabilitation governors' in every prison; and the development of resettlement performance targets to which every prison will be held accountable. In the USA, some state and local prison systems are gradually integrating 'release planning' into their standard custodial functions.

The promise of desistance theory

Some projects under development in the UK and the USA are incredibly exciting new efforts that involve multiple agencies and detailed planning. Yet these new initiatives hardly represent a new paradigm in reintegration practice. Criminologist James Austin (2001) argues that even though 're-entry' has become 'the new buzzword in correctional reform' the term is often 'simply another word for parole supervision, which many have tried to discredit and dismantle' (p. 314). Certainly, its not an unfamiliar habit for the corrections industry to dress up a failed old policy as a seemingly new, exciting paradigm shift simply by changing a few agency names (see Cohen 1985). As a buzzword, 're-entry' appears to connote something similar to previous terms such as 'prisoner aftercare' (Haines 1990), 'throughcare' (McAllister et al. 1992), 'discharged prisoners' aid' (Soothill 1974), 'reintegration', 'integration', 'parole' and the currently preferred term in Britain, 'resettlement' (see Morgan and Owers 2001).

A legitimate paradigm shift would require, among other things, a new understanding of the process of reintegration – in a word, new theory – on top of the new buzzwords and taskforce names. Unfortunately, for the most part, current reintegration practices seem to be operating in a theoretical vacuum, with no clear explanation for how the process is supposed to work (see especially Simon's 1993 history of parole). Maloney *et al.* (2001: 24) quip: 'If there is an intervention theory in use, it is generally based on the rather bizarre assumption that surveillance and some guidance can steer the offender straight.' Ed Rhine (1997: 74) concludes that the lack of a 'plausible narrative of community-based supervision' is 'the most pressing and vexing problem facing probation and parole administrators today'.

Much of the blame for this predicament has to be laid at the feet of corrections officials and policy-makers who are too wedded to the status quo and too fearful of appearing 'soft on crime' to experiment with innovations that might improve life opportunities for ex-offenders. Practitioners also share some blame. Practitioners need to bring the everyday realities of offenders' lives to the attention of policy-makers as well as academic researchers. Notably, they must identify key service delivery concerns that establish greater acceptance for the use of community-based interventions. In the course of several decades of a 'nothing works' mindset, practitioners have largely refrained from speaking – loudly at least – about 'what works' in this way.[1]

Finally, academic criminologists most certainly cannot escape the blame for the apparent void in reintegration theory. As Frank Cullen (2002: 283) writes: 'Although criminology is rich in contemporary theories of crime, true theories of correctional intervention are in short supply. One searches in vain in mainstream criminology journals and textbooks for new systematic theories of intervention and for empirical tests of these perspectives.' Like others, Cullen blames this lack of theoretical innovation on the legacy of the 'nothing works' challenge to the practice of rehabilitation: 'Developing theories of effective intervention seemed ill advised if there was, in essence, no "treatment effect" to be explained.' (2002: 283). There are exceptions, of course. Cullen rightly cites the principles of rehabilitative practice developed by Canadian researchers Don Andrews and James Bonta (1998) and Paul Gendreau (1996). Likewise, Joan Petersilia's (2003) recent book *When Prisoners Come Home* articulates a clear and refreshing vision for the reform of the US system of ex-offender release and re-entry (for a similar British effort, see Farrall 2002). None the less, these works of reintegration theory remain aberrant exceptions in a research field that is dominated by descriptive and atheoretical evaluative research. That is, we often ask 'what works,' but too rarely ask 'how' or 'why?' (Palmer 1994).

With this volume we hope to make the case that there is, in fact, a rich, largely untapped resource of criminological theory and research already in existence that potentially could be drawn upon in the development of theories for reintegration practice: namely, the literature concerning 'desistance' from crime (see also McNeill 2003). The study of crime desistance emerged out of the criminal career literature in the 1980s and 1990s (e.g. Farrington 1986; Paternoster 1989; Moffitt 1993; Sampson and Laub 1993; Sommers *et al.* 1994; Graham and Bowling 1995; Shover 1996; Warr 1998) and, although still relatively new, has in recent years come of age as a field of scholarly research (see the important recent review by Laub and Sampson 2001).

This book represents the first edited collection of original essays on the topic of desistance from crime from an international cast that includes most of the top scholars in the field. Our hope is that, taken together, the chapters in this volume also contain the raw material for the beginnings of a theory-driven approach to ex-offender reintegration.

In many ways our project parallels a shift that is taking place in the related field of addiction studies, where 'recovery' is gradually replacing 'treatment' as its focus of inquiry. In an influential recent essay, William White (2000) argues that treatment (e.g. professional work with addicts) should be understood as a minor aspect of the larger process of recovery:

> Professionally-directed addiction treatment may or may not be a factor in [the recovery process] and, where treatment does play a role, it is an important but quite time-proscribed part of the larger, more complex, and more enduring process of recovery. Treatment was birthed as an adjunct to recovery, but, as treatment grew in size and status, it defined recovery as an adjunct of itself. The original perspective needs to be recaptured. Treatment institutions need to once again become servants of the larger recovery process and the community in which that recovery is nested and sustained. Treatment is best considered, not as the first line of response to addiction, but as a final safety net to help heal the community's most incapacitated members. The first avenue for problem resolution should be structures that are natural, local, non-hierarchical and non-commercialized.

Likewise, we argue that criminal justice policies meant to help reintegrate, reform or rehabilitate ex-offenders are best understood when situated within the larger context of crime desistance and the known correlates of this process. Social intervention does not preclude desistance, and in fact is often part of the process of desistance. Similarly professional intervention does not preclude community, familial or voluntary interventions or self-change processes. Still, it is important to acknowledge that neither professional intervention nor self-help is a guarantee of successful re-entry or reintegration. Sonny Rollins, when all was said and done, found both self-directed and professionally co-ordinated interventions helpful in his voyage from criminality and drug abuse to respectability and stature within the community. Understanding how the larger voyage works may be the best strategy for understanding how and when to intervene.

Desistance and reintegration: strange bedfellows?

Basic social science research is often criticized, not unfairly, because of its apparent distance or removal from matters of public policy or programme practice. Accordingly, it is often asked, again not unfairly, 'Of what use is this for policy or practice?' A central dilemma, of course, is that researchers are usually not experienced or trained in public policy or programme practice, and those with public policy or programme experience and training are similarly disadvantaged about the implementation and utility of research design and methodology. So, a bridge is necessary, and we as editors (we ourselves are a mix of researcher, practitioner and former prisoner), hope to provide one in this brief introduction.

Research on the topic of desistance from crime focuses on understanding why and how former offenders avoid continued involvement in criminal behaviour. Re-entry policy and practice are intended to improve public safety by insuring that former offenders avoid continued involvement in criminal behaviour. As such, the two areas seem a natural fit. This appearance may be deceiving, however. There are numerous reasons, beyond the usual distance between academia and the 'real world' for the lack of cross-fertilization between desistance theory and re-entry practice.

To practitioners and policy-makers, even the word 'desistance' may seem like the latest addition to academia's apparently never-ending quest to make well-known social behaviours more complicated and scientific than they really are. To them, more familiar terminology, like 'going straight,' 'straightening up one's hand' or 'cleaning up one's act' have always sufficed. Essentially, desisting from crime is what practitioners in the field of offender programming and treatment have always wanted for their clients. Still, desistance, as it is typically used, is definitely not a synonym and may even be an antonym for words like 'rehabilitation' or 'reform' (for a historical overview of desistance research, see Farrall 2000).

The study of desistance, in fact, originally emerged out of something of a *critique* of the professionally driven 'medical model' of corrections. To explore desistance was to study those persons who change *without* the assistance of correctional interventions. Thus, one either 'desists' on one's own accord or else one is 'rehabilitated' through formal counselling or treatment. There is an important medical metaphor at work here. In medicine, persons with illnesses who are able to recover without treatment are said to have experienced 'spontaneous remission' or a 'natural recovery'. Likewise, the term desistance (originally deemed 'spontaneous desistance') is intended to distinguish the self-change process undergone by an offender who was perhaps never caught and punished from the process experienced by someone who was formally reformed.

As such, some observers interpret the growing body of criminal career research – which demonstrates how widespread spontaneous desistance is in the life course of young offenders – as providing a rationale for shifting attention away from rehabilitation practice. Nettler (1974: 114), for instance, writes: 'Since most offenders "mature out", it is questionable whether "the war on crime" should attempt to reduce criminality by correcting predators.' Indeed, although this fact has been largely misinterpreted, the infamous 'nothing works' finding never suggested that criminals cannot change their ways. Just the opposite; the familiar null findings central to the 'nothing works' claim suggested only that members of the 'no treatment' control groups tended to reform themselves at the same rate as members of the treatment groups. As Hans Toch (1997: 97) states, the 'most salient finding in therapeutic research is that the control group members tend to improve too'. The problem, Toch (2002) more recently joked, was never so much that 'nothing works,' but that almost 'everything works'. Although this can be a happy prospect for rehabilitators willing to employ substandard self-evaluation designs (they can always make exaggerated claims of success for clients who would have improved even without their services), it also presents a considerable threat to rehabilitation supporters (who are always under political threat anyhow). After all, why throw money at rehabilitation if offenders are going to naturally mature out of crime on their own?

This inherent conflict between research on spontaneous recovery and the applied world of treatment has been even more profound in the addiction field. Peele (1990: 7) writes: 'One of the best-kept secrets in the addiction field is that people often quit drugs or alcohol without entering treatment or support groups like AA. The treatment industry repeatedly and erroneously claims that no such self-curers exist.' Indeed, even though it is known that anywhere from 80 to 90 per cent of smokers beat their addiction without formal treatment, research that suggests that alcoholics and other addicts can do the same is routinely dismissed and heavily criticized (see Sobell *et al.* 2000). Chiauzzi and Liljegren (1993: 303) describe natural recovery from addiction as a 'taboo topic in addiction treatment' that threatens to diminish the many gains made by the drug treatment movement over the last 50 years. In their 'defence' from such research, treatment professionals and advocates have even resorted to the ingenious tautology that 'an ability to cease addictive behaviors on one's own suggests that the individual was not addicted in the first place' (1993).

A truce and marriage proposal

We see no reason why desistance and official intervention (reintegration, treatment, rehabilitation and so forth) should be understood in opposition to one another, nor do we believe that the frequency of desistance in the life course of offenders should be seen as a reason to neglect rehabilitation work. Indeed, recent research in psychology has begun to blur the illusory distinction between those who change with the help of support groups, on the one hand, and 'self-curers' who change 'without any assistance' on the other. The processes of change employed by the former group (e.g. consciousness raising, contingency management and counter-conditioning) appear to be almost identical to the processes used by persons in the latter group, who change without the help of professional therapy (Prochaska and DiClemente 1992). In short, desistance (self-change) and rehabilitation (change through intervention) might best be understood, for all practical purposes, as the same thing, or at least part of the same process.

Persons who change while in treatment are still 'self-changers.' Individuals spend only a tiny fraction of their daily lives undergoing formal treatment or counselling, so most of the hard work involved in changing one's sense of self takes place *outside* therapy or other formal, professional interventions. Successful treatment clients frequently reiterate the truism that, at the end of the day, 'you rehabilitate yourself'.

Whether or not one is undergoing professional treatment, change still feels like an agentic, individual pursuit to those undergoing it. Equally, can it really be true that members of the control group really receive 'no assistance'? (Peele 1990) Try telling that to the parents, friends, partners and children of ex-offenders and recovering addicts. No person is an island. So-called 'spontaneous self-changers' seek out and receive tremendous amounts of outside support, help and advice. Whether it is from a trained therapist, a friend or a family member, this is still 'intervention'.

Behavioural change follows a multi-level, rather than a single, track. Rarely does real change occur simply because someone like Sonny Rollins simply decides to 'straighten up and fly right' or even as a direct result of enrolling in a treatment programme (as Rollins did when he went to Lexington). Both tracks – self-determination and professional intervention – are part of a larger process of change. This process also involves a third, often unacknowledged track involving informal help, social support and social control from friends, acquaintances, family members, neighbours and significant others (see especially Farrall 2002; Warr 2002). For instance, in her study of women prisoners transitioning to the community, Patricia O'Brien (2001: 119–20) describes the multi-level relationships the women built and maintained as essential to successful reintegration:

> [A key] aspect of relationship building had to do with the willingness of the women to elicit assistance through their relationships with professionals, recovering people, ex-inmates, and peers for the information, support, and skills they needed to normalize some of the initial feelings of alienation. These mentors reflected a rootedness in reality and exemplified survival and growth as a possibility to the women. The women also looked for such support to decrease their sometimes overwhelming sense of powerlessness in handling the challenges during various points of the transition.

Although the social aspects of the desistance process (Warr 2002) are often overlooked in traditional treatment practices, innovative, new interventions such as family group conferencing (a restorative justice intervention based on Maori *whanau* or extended family practices) explicitly seek to capitalize on the social influence of these intimate groups in the change process (see Chapter 2 this volume).

Like so many other phrases that have been appropriated from the field of medicine, phrases like 'spontaneous remission' or 'natural recovery' do something of a disservice to the understanding of criminal behaviours. In the medical world, these terms refer to persons who physically recover from illnesses without the benefit of treatment, so it is clear why one would be tempted to apply them to the field of criminal justice, where we also talk about 'treatments' for offenders. But our treatment is different from their treatment. In the medical sense, treatment implies the systematic application of some particular remedy for a measurable and well defined symptom (Schneider 1999: 206).

Whatever correctional intervention is, it isn't that. Consider the following comment from a successfully desisting ex-offender interviewed as part of the Liverpool Desistance Study (Maruna 2001):

> *Maruna:* Have you ever received counselling or treatment for crime and drug issues?
> *Desister:* Eh, I done community hours. I got this thing one time, it was like community hours, but you were in every day. You had to go every day, morning and afternoon, and you sat down. It was probation people and you sat down and you talked. But I didn't do it very long. After three weeks I went to court and got jail and I never went back. (Maruna, unpublished fieldnotes)

So, would the speaker, now reformed, qualify as a spontaneous desister or is he a treated desister? Would it matter if he said he had some conscious 'moment of clarity' during his three weeks of counselling when he realized he wanted to stop offending? Would it matter if he said he had sat through three *years* of talking with probation officers rather than three weeks of it? Would it matter if he said the talks he had were with a community volunteer rather than with 'probation people'?

While words like 'treatment' and 'correctional interventions' conjure pictures of scientists in white lab coats curing passive patients, Toch (1997: 89) argues: 'No rehabilitators see their job as "coercing change", and rehabilitators who think they are in the disease-curing business exist only in sociology texts.' Similarly, practitioners interviewed as part of a fieldwork study by Maruna *et al.* (forthcoming) said that they thought they could offer assistance, guidance, support, structure, training or counselling for those who wanted to change, but they insisted that it was 'up to the individual' whether he or she was really going to succeed. Schneider (1999) suggests that instead of being seen as a 'treatment', psychotherapy is better understood and modelled as a *relationship*, with all the dynamics common to such complex social interactions. The same could be said for criminal justice interventions, such as the interactions between a parole officer and a parolee, or even restorative justice conferencing.

If this is the case, then the distinction between receiving professional treatment and not receiving treatment is less important than understanding the quality of the actual experiences, processes and pathways that desisting persons experience (Farrall 2002). Just as William White (2000) argues that treatment is only an adjunct of the larger process of recovery, professionally driven rehabilitation, re-entry or reintegration should be understood as a crucial, but relatively minor part of the larger process of desistance from crime. As Farrall (1995: 56) accurately summarizes: 'Most of the research suggests that desistance "occurs" away from the criminal justice system. That is to say that very few people actually desist as a result of intervention on the part of the criminal justice system or its representatives.' This should not be surprising, nor should it be seen necessarily as an attack on the criminal justice system. Research suggests that the average US parole officer has a caseload of 69 parolees and is able to make around 1.6 face-to-face contacts with each per month (Camp and Camp 1997). On the other hand, the major correlates of desistance from crime identified in research by Sampson and Laub (1993) and others – marriages and steady employment – involve ongoing, interactive relationships that can take up most of an individual's waking life during adulthood. It is difficult to imagine the 1.6 meetings with a parole officer competing with such forces.

As such, the quasi-experimental lens that focuses on programmes and programme outcomes (success or failure) may be missing what is really important in terms of desistance from crime. Again, the field of drug addiction research can provide lessons here. Research in the addictions field is shifting from a focus on evaluating individual treatment outcomes to a focus on 'drug treatment careers', which understands cycles of treatment in terms of the natural history of the person's life. Hser and his colleagues (1997: 544) write: 'While it is important to determine outcomes for any single intervention, a research approach that evaluates patterns and outcomes of multiple, sequential interventions provides a fuller understanding of the effectiveness of treatment over time.' By modelling recovery as a long-term, cyclical process involving a series of different interventions, this research is able to identify life-course 'successes' (i.e. people who recover) who might appear to be 'failures' after exiting a particular treatment programme. Alternatively, evaluation methodologies that put too much weight on programmes instead of individual lives are more likely to find that 'nothing works' (Lewis 1991).

What this means for policy-makers and applied researchers is that it may be time to broaden our focus from the always important question of 'what works' to 'how it works' (see Lin 2001). Robert Martinson (1976: 189), in one of his more colourful attacks on the rehabilitative ideal, laid out this challenge to treatment supporters in no uncertain terms:

> But what specifically is the method? Probation-like placement? Small caseloads? Unadulterated love? What is it? What is the actual process that takes place by which 'recidivism' is reduced? If [one of the rehabilitation supporters] knew which 'element' or 'dimension' of [the treatment] was having whatever effect he thinks he has found, he surely would not keep it such a secret. He would patent it, sell it around the country to our administrators, be given the Congressional Medal of Honor, and retire to the Bahamas, an honored and wealthy man. [The average rehabilitation supporter] can talk for twenty pages in the special language we all know so well, but he cannot bring himself to say in plain English to my neighbors, who are waiting with bated breath, just what this process is.

We feel the place to start asking 'how' is the emerging field of desistance research (see especially Laub and Sampson 2001; Giordano *et al.* 2002; Warr 2002). To some degree, of course, the process of desistance from crime will always be a mystery. We will never fully know how Sonny Rollins transformed from a junkie and petty offender to the jazz world's greatest living improviser. Yet this is no reason not to try to understand. Moreover, his transformation, aided by not just his friends in the jazz world but also the most medical of medical model treatments (at Lexington he was prescribed the drug dolophine to help him overcome the withdrawl symptoms associated with kicking a heroin habit), should hardly be seen as evidence that formal treatment practices should be abandoned. To us, the lesson of desistance research is not that ex-offenders should be left alone to get on with the business of self-change. The process of spontaneous desistance takes far too long and leaves too many victims in its wake. The lesson of desistance research is that correctional interventions should recognize this 'natural' process of reform and *design interventions that can enhance or complement these spontaneous efforts* (e.g. Prochaska and DiClemente 1992). Toch (1997: 97) states this eloquently: 'The line between treatment and nontreatment must be drawn around interventions that work in partnership with self-restorative forces where these exist.'

Again, a parallel can be taken from the medical world that may be appropriate to consider. Within the immune system, the body has regenerative powers that can naturally fight off a variety of infections and complications. Faith healing, non-traditional medicine and the more pedestrian practice of prescribing 'two aspirins and call me in the morning' are all founded on the fact that the body itself works to heal many ills. Yet our white blood cells and other protectors can be slow warriors, sometimes allowing annoying or painful symptoms to persist beyond the point that we can tolerate. We therefore turn to professional help to boost or speed up this process. The antibiotics that we are frequently prescribed are intended to *work in partnership* with our bodies' natural, self-restorative functions, not over-ride them. Although we sometimes mistakenly credit our own recoveries to pharmaceutical treatment, in fact we were doing the work ourselves with some assistance. We argue that that a similar model is an appropriate way to understand how 're-entry' can work.

Defining desistance

This book, we hope, helps prepare grounds for the development of theoretical understanding about how the reintegration process might best be designed, facilitated and implemented by exploring what is known about the 'natural' process of desistance. Yet, what do we mean by desistance? Typically, desistance has been defined (and modelled) in criminological research as the 'termination point' at which offending ceases. This understanding has been widely criticized (see Bushway *et al.* 2001; Laub and Sampson 2001), perhaps most noisily by Maruna (2001) who argues that the termination of offending occurs all the time in a so-called 'criminal career.' All the persons we describe as 'offenders' go days, months, even years between offences. As such, it is impossible to know when offending has finally ended until the person is dead. Even if we were only interested in understanding dead people's desistance, however, this definition still seems unhelpful. Maruna (2001: 23) gives the example of a purse-snatcher who stops offending:

> Suppose we know conclusively that the purse-snatcher (now deceased) never committed another crime for the rest of his long life. When did his desistance start? Is not the ... concluding moment the very instant when the person completes (or terminates) the act of theft? If so, in the same moment that a person becomes an offender, he also becomes a desister. That cannot be right.

In an inventive response to such criticisms, Laub and Sampson (2001) distinguish between what they call 'termination' (the outcome) and 'desistance' (the process) in their important reformulation of desistance. They write: 'Termination is the time at which criminal activity stops. Desistance, by contrast, is the causal process that supports the termination of offending.' Desistance, according to this reformulation, is the process that 'maintains the continued state of nonoffending' (p. 11) beginning prior to termination but carrying on long after. Likewise, Le Blanc and Loeber (1998) describe a process of desistance that is composed of the four subprocesses of deceleration (a reduction in the frequency of offending before cessation); de-escalation (committing less serious offences); reaching a ceiling (remaining at or below a level of offending without any escalation into more serious offending); and specialization (in types of offending). In brief, any diminution in the level, seriousness or heterogeneity of criminal activity may mark a step in the process that will lead to the cessation of criminality. For this reason, it is argued that desistance is a process that occurs over time, rather than as a switch that comes on or goes off (see Chapter 4 this volume for an empirical framework for the analysis of desistance as a process).

Although this represents a significant improvement over past working definitions of desistance, by defining desistance as the 'causal process that supports the termination of offending', Laub and Sampson (2001) add new confusion by conflating the causes of desistance with desistance itself. The verb 'to desist' means to abstain from doing something. As such, in criminology, desistance is almost always used to mean 'the continued state of non-offending' – not the factors that lead to it. Suppose, for instance, that deterrence is identified as a major 'causal process' in the 'outcome' of termination. The Laub and Sampson definition would seem to suggest that when an individual steals a purse, then is engaged in the process of being deterred (i.e. getting busted), he is actively involved in desisting from crime. The definition still ends up confusing criminality with its opposite. Like other efforts to define desistance as a 'process,' this approach also confounds desistance with the process of 'de-escalation' or the slowing down of criminal behaviours that sometimes happens over time. De-escalation may (or may not) eventually build into fully-fledged desistance, but there is no reason to force the two, perfectly understandable processes to share the same name. It seems to us that de-escalation should remain de-escalation, and desistance should remain desistance.

We think this misunderstanding can be clarified by pilfering from the literature on criminal aetiology. A half century ago, Edwin Lemert (1948:

27) introduced considerable clarity into the debate on the origins of deviance by differentiating between two 'sharply polarized or even categorical phases' in this developmental process: primary deviation and secondary deviation. Primary deviation involved the initial flirtation and experimentation with deviant behaviours. Secondary deviation, on the other hand, is deviance that becomes 'incorporated as part of the "me" of the individual' (Lemert 1951: 76). Lemert's argument was that 'criminal careers are fashioned in the time of personal identity' and that 'to deviate over time is to assume a self-understanding consistent with the behavior' (2000: 5).

This two-pronged understanding of deviance allowed Lemert (1951: 75) to avoid 'the fallacy of confusing original causes with effective causes':

> Primary deviation can arise from a wide variety of 'causes' … Each theory may be a valid explanation … Thus, it can be freely admitted that persons come to drink alcoholic liquors excessively for many different reasons: death of loved ones, exposure to death in battle,… inferiority feelings, nipple fixation, and many others. (Lemert 1948: 57)

Freed from what he saw as a 'burdensome' debate around initial aetiology, Lemert focused on why some primary deviants underwent a symbolic reorganization at the level of their self-identity and others did not.

This same framework might clarify some issues in the study of desistance. Perhaps there are (at least) two, distinguishable phases in the desistance process: primary and secondary desistance. Primary desistance would take the term desistance at its most basic and literal level to refer to any lull or crime-free gap in the course of a criminal career (see West 1961, 1963; Chapter 5 this volume). Because every secondary deviant experiences a countless number of such pauses in the course of a criminal career, primary desistance would not be a matter of much theoretical interest. The focus of desistance research, instead, would be on secondary desistance: the movement from the behaviour of non-offending to the assumption of the role or identity of a 'changed person'. In secondary desistance, crime not only stops but 'existing roles become disrupted' and a 'reorganization based upon a new role or roles will occur' (Lemert 1951: 76). Indeed, recent research (Shover 1996; Maruna 2001; Giordano *et al.* 2002) provides compelling evidence that long-term desistance does involve identifiable and measurable changes at the level of personal identity or the 'me' of the individual.

Layout of the book

Of course, effecting change at this level has been a traditional (although sometimes maligned) goal of offender rehabilitation. The findings of rehabilitation evaluation research, although not as negative as is often portrayed (see McGuire 1995), demonstrate at least how difficult it is to engineer this sort of change in the face of all the other obstacles in the lives of even suitably motivated ex-offenders. The premise of this volume is that reintegration policy can be improved by learning from success, and modelling the re-entry process on what is known about desistance.

The chapters in the volume's first part, 'Desistance theory and reintegration practice,' make this case most directly. In Chapter 2, Gordon Bazemore and Carsten Erbe focus on informal social control, probably the best developed theoretical tradition in desistance research (e.g. Sampson and Laub 1993), and discuss the implications of this research for restorative justice practice in the reintegration process. Next, Stephen Farrall (Chapter 3) outlines his findings from an important new, longitudinal study of desistance, in which he specifically tested the relationship between probation practices and the social capital of ex-offenders. Farrall concludes this part of the book by arguing that the probation and parole establishment may be better off shifting their traditional focus from 'offending-related behaviours' to 'desistance-focused behaviors' (see also McNeill 2003).

Appropriately, the next part, 'Methodological considerations,' pauses to reflect on some important empirical concerns involved in making the link between basic and applied reintegration research. In Chapter 4, Shawn Bushway, Robert Brame and Raymond Paternoster argue that, although the two areas of research have developed independently, desistance research and programme outcome evaluation research share much common ground. They posit that combining the methodological innovations of both fields allows for a powerful framework in which to understand and to model the reintegration process. Alex Piquero (Chapter 5) rounds out this part with a useful reminder that criminal careers are remarkably intermittent in nature and that a vast terrain exists 'somewhere between persistence and desistance'. Piquero provides a useful methodological discussion for taking the many stops, starts and missteps in criminal careers into account when investigating the reintegration process.

The book's third part, 'Applied research on desistance,' takes up some of the methodological challenges inherent in trying to study desistance with a distinct focus on the policy implications of this new work. In

Chapter 6, Leana Allen Bouffard and John Laub systematically review a number of studies to determine if the experience of military service facilitates desistance from crime. Just as importantly, they consider 'how' such service could act as a reintegrative agent. Ros Burnett (Chapter 7) describes the key findings from the Oxford University 'Dynamics of recidivism study,' a longitudinal inquiry into the lives of 130 prisoners for up to two years after their release. Finally, in Chapter 8, Gill McIvor, Cathy Murray and Janet Jamieson introduce the often-neglected issue of gender differences in the experience and process of desistance from crime.

We close the book by turning from policy-focused desistance research to 'Desistance-focused reintegration research', or studies of ex-offenders that are theoretically informed and grounded in an understanding of desistance. The first of these, by Stephen Richards and Richard Jones (Chapter 9), draws on a recent study of the experiences of released prisoners in Iowa but, importantly, also represents the perspective of 'convict criminology'. The 'convict criminologists' are a growing group of former prisoners now employed as criminology and criminal justice faculty members at different universities (see Ross and Richards 2002; Terry 2003). Here, Richards and Jones define the convict perspective as 'the experience of captivity, ethnographic research, and the need to give voice to the men and women who live behind prison walls'. In Chapter 10, Faye Taxman, Douglas Young and James Byrne provide a first glimpse into one of the most exciting of the experimental, new re-entry projects – the re-entry partnership initiative – framing their analysis in the context of the literature on informal social control. Finally, Christopher Uggen, Jeff Manza and Angela Behrens conclude by considering just how possible social reintegration can be when ex-offenders are denied the rights of full citizenship.

A point about context: throughout, we draw on work from both the UK as well as the USA. Although others have argued that there is increasing convergence between these two countries in terms of crime problems and criminal justice responses (see especially Garland 2001; Newburn and Sparks 2003), there are of course significant differences between the two jurisdictions, just as there is enormous diversity within each country. Still, the process of desistance from crime seems to be a largely universal one, as is the difficulty experienced by returning offenders (compare Social Exclusion Unit 2001 to Travis and Petersilia 2001, for instance). As such, it is important to represent a range of research from a diversity of settings.

Additionally, the contributors to this book come from a variety of different academic disciplines and theoretical traditions. They use diverse research methods, and describe new research findings from populations as diverse as adolesescent delinquents in Scotland to adult ex-offenders in Iowa. Each of the authors, however, has either tried to look at the topic of desistance from an applied perspective or else to address the topic of reintegration from a theoretically grounded position, drawing on what is known about desistance in critiquing re-entry practice. Our final product is not a magic bullet for the urgent problem of improving ex-offender reintegration. However, as a collection, we think this volume demonstrates the potential of using criminological theory and research in the development of reintegration practice. If not, we hope other academics and practitioners, preferably working together, will take up the call to try to better realize this ideal.

Note

1 Fortunately, this has been changing in recent years. Over the past decade, professional groups such as the American Probation and Parole Association, the Community Service Sentencing Association and, especially, the International Community Corrections Association, have examined issues pertaining to the implementation of successful community reintegration programmes, thereby re-establishing the importance of social intervention in the criminal justice process.

References

Andrews, D.A. and Bonta, J. (1998) *The Psychology of Criminal Conduct.* Cincinnati, OH: Anderson.

Austin, J. (2001) 'Prisoner reentry: current trends, practices, and issues', *Crime and Delinquency*, 47 (3): 314–34.

Bureau of Justice Statistics (2001) *Probation and Parole in the United States, 2000 – Press Release* (NCJ 188208). Washington, DC: US Department of Justice.

Bushway, S.D., Piquero, A., Broidy, L., Cauffman, E. and Mazerolle, P. (2001) 'An empirical framework for studying desistance as a process', *Criminology*, 39: 491–515.

Camp, C. and Camp, G. (1997) *The Corrections Yearbook.* South Salem, NY: Criminal Justice Institute.

Chiauzzi, E.J. and Liljegren, S. (1993) 'Taboo topics in addiction treatment: an empirical review of clinical folklore', *Journal of Substance Abuse Treatment*, 10: 303–16.

Cohen, S. (1985) *Visions of Social Control.* Cambridge: Polity Press.

Cullen, F. (2002) 'Rehabilitation and treatment programs', in J.Q. Wilson and J. Petersilia (eds) *Crime: Public Policies for Crime Control* (2nd edn). Oakland, CA: ICS Press.

Emmons, N. (1986) *Manson in his Own Words*. New York, NY: Grove Press.

Farrall, S. (1995) 'Why do people stop offending?', *Scottish Journal of Criminal Justice Studies*, 1: 51–9.

Farrall, S. (ed.) (2000) *The Termination of Criminal Careers*. Burlington, VT: Ashgate/Dartmouth.

Farrall, S. (2002) *Rethinking What Works with Offenders*. Cullompton: Willan Publishing.

Farrington, D.P. (1986) 'Age and crime', in N. Morris and M. Tonry (eds) *Crime and Justice. Vol. 7*. Chicago, IL: University of Chicago Press, 189–250.

Garland, D. (2001) *The Culture of Control*. Chicago, IL: University of Chicago Press.

Gendreau, P. (1996) 'Offender rehabilitation: what we know and what needs to be done', *Criminal Justice and Behavior*, 23: 144–61.

Giddens, G. (1992) *Faces in the Crowd: Players and Writers*. New York, NY: Oxford University Press.

Giordano, P.C., Cernkovich, S.A. and Rudolph, J.L. (2002) 'Gender, crime and desistance: toward a theory of cognitive transformation', *American Journal of Sociology*, 107: 990–1064.

Graham, J. and Bowling, B. (1995) *Young People and Crime*. Home Office HORS 145. London: HMSO.

Grove, P.G., Godfrey, D.A. and McLeod, J.F. (1999) *Long Term Prison Population Projection: Operational Research Unit Model 1999*. London: Home Office RDSD.

Hagell, A., Newburn, T. and Rowlingson, K. (1995) *Financial Difficulties on Release from Prison*. London: Policy Studies Institute.

Haines, K. (1990) *After-care Services for Released Prisoners: A Review of the Literature*. London: Home Office.

Home Office (July 2002) *Breaking the Circle: A Report of the Review of the Rehabilitation of Offenders Act*. London: Home Office.

Hser, Y.-I., Anglin, M.D., Grella, C., Longshore, D. and Prendergast, M.L. (1997) 'Drug treatment careers: a conceptual framework and existing research findings,' *Journal of Substance Abuse Treatment*, 14: 543–58.

Hughes, T.A., Wilson, D.J. and Beck, A.J. (2001) *Trends in State Parole, 1990–2000*. Washington, DC: US Department of Justice, Bureau of Justice Statistics.

Kirschner, B. (ed.) (2000) *The Oxford Companion to Jazz*. New York, NY: Oxford University Press.

Langan, P.A. and Levin, D.J. (2002) *Recidivism of Prisoners Released in 1994* (NCJ 193427). Washington, DC: US Department of Justice, Bureau of Justice Statistics.

Laub, J. and Sampson, R. (2001) 'Understanding desistance from crime', *Crime and Justice: A Review of Research*, 28: 1–70.

Le Blanc, M. and Loeber, R. (1998) 'Developmental criminology updated', in M. Tonry (ed.) *Crime and Justice: A Review of Research. Vol. 23.* Chicago, IL: University of Chicago Press, 115–98.

Lemert, C.C. (2000) 'Introduction,' in C.C. Lemert and M.F. Winter (eds) *Crime and Deviance: Essays and Innovations of Edwin M. Lemert.* Lanham, MD: Rowman & Littlefield.

Lemert, E.M. (1948) 'Some aspects of a general theory of sociopathic behavior', *Proceedings of the Pacific Sociological Society. Research Studies, State College of Washington,* 16: 23–9.

Lemert, E.M. (1951) *Social Pathology: Systematic Approaches to the Study of Sociopathic Behavior.* New York, NY: McGraw-Hill.

Lewis, D.A. (1990) 'From programs to lives: a comment', *American Journal of Community Psychology,* 18: 923–6.

Lin, A.C. (2001) *Reform in the Making.* Princeton, NJ: Princeton, University Press.

Maloney, D., Bazemore, G. and Hudson, J. (2001) 'The end of probation and the beginning of community justice', *Perspectives,* 25(3): 24–30.

Martinson, R. (1976) 'California research at the crossroads', *Crime and Delinquency,* 22: 180–91.

Maruna, S. (2001) *Making Good: How Ex-convicts Reform and Rebuild their Lives.* Washington, DC: APA Books.

Maruna, S., LeBel, T.P., Naples, M. and Mitchell, N. (forthcoming) 'Pygmalion in the reintegration process: desistance from crime through the looking glass', *Psychology, Crime and Law.*

McAllister, D., Bottomley, K. and Liebling, A. (1992) *From Custody to Community: Throughcare for the Young.* Aldershot: Ashgate.

McGuire, J. (ed.) (1995) *What Works: Effective Methods to Reduce Re-offending.* Chichester: Wiley.

McNeill, F. (2003) 'Desistance-focused probation practice', in W.H. Chui and M. Nellis (eds) *Moving Probation Forward: Evidence, Arguments and Practice.* Harlow: Pearson Longman.

Metcalf, H., Anderson, T. and Rolfe, H. (2001) *Barriers to Employment for Offenders and Ex-offenders.* London: Department for Work and Pensions Research.

Moffitt, T.E. (1993) 'Adolescence-limited and life-course-persistent antisocial behavior: a developmental taxonomy', *Psychological Review,* 100: 674–701.

Morgan, R. and Owers, A. (2001) *Through the Prison Gate. A Joint Thematic Review by HM Inspectorates of Prisons and Probation.* London: Her Majesty's Inspectorate of Prisons.

Nettler, G. (1974) *Explaining Crime.* New York, NY: McGraw-Hill.

Newburn, T. and Sparks, R. (eds) (2003) *Criminal Justice and Political Culture.* Cullompton: Willan Publishing.

Nisenson, E. (2000) *Open Sky: Sonny Rollins and his World of Improvisation.* New York, NY: St Martin's Press.

Niven, S. and Olagundaye, J. (2002) *Jobs and Homes: A Survey of Prisoners Nearing Release.* London: HMSO.

O'Brien, P. (2001) *Making it in the 'Free World': Women in Transition from Prison.* Albany, NY: SUNY Press.

Office of Justice Programs (2002) 'Attorney General Ashcroft announces nationwide effort to reintegrate offenders back into communities.' Press release, 15 July.

Palmer, T. (1994) *A Profile of Correctional Effectiveness and New Directions for Research.* Albany, NY: SUNY Press.

Paternoster, R. (1989) 'Decisions to participate in and desist from four types of common delinquency: deterrence and the rational choice perspective', *Law and Society Review*, 23: 7–40.

Peele, S. (1990) 'Cures depend on attitudes, not programs', *Los Angeles Times*, 14 March: B7.

Petersilia, J. (2003) *When Prisoners Come Home: Parole and Prisoner Reentry.* Oxford: Oxford University Press.

Prochaska, J.O., and DiClemente, C.C. (1992) 'Stages of change in the modification of problem behavior', in M. Hersen *et al.* (eds) *Progress in Behavior Modification. Vol. 28.* Sycamore, IL: Sycamore, 184–214.

Reno, J. (2000) *Remarks of the Honorable Janet Reno on Reentry Court Initiative*, John Jay College of Criminal Justice, New York, 10 February 10 (accessed 2 December 2000, at http://www.usdoj.gov/ag/speeches/2000/doc2.htm).

Rhine, E.E. (1997) 'Probation and parole supervision: In need of a new narrative', *Corrections Management Quarterly*, 1 (2): 71–5.

Ross, J.I. and Richards, S.C. (2002) *Convict Criminology.* Belmont, CA: Wadsworth.

Sampson, R.J., and Laub, J. (1993) *Crime in the Making: Pathways and Turning Points through Life.* Cambridge, MA: Harvard University Press.

Schneider, K.J. (1999) 'Clients deserve relationships, not merely "treatments"', *American Psychologist*, 54: 206–7.

Shover, N. (1996) *Great Pretenders: Pursuits and Careers of Persistent Thieves.* Boulder, CO: Westview Press.

Simon, J. (1993) *Poor Discipline: Parole and the Social Control of the Underclass, 1890–1990.* Chicago, IL: University of Chicago Press.

Sobell, L.C. Ellingstad, T.P. and Sobell, M.B. (2000). 'Natural recovery from alcohol and drug problems: methodological review of the research with suggestions for future directions', *Addiction*, 95: 759–64.

Social Exclusion Unit (2001) *Reducing Re-offending by Ex-prisoners.* London: Home Office.

Sommers, I., Baskin, D.R. and Fagan, J. (1994) 'Getting out of the life: crime desistance by female street offenders', *Deviant Behaviour*, 15 (2): 125–49.

Soothill, K. (1974) *The Prisoner's Release: A Study of the Employment of Ex-prisoners.* London: Allen & Unwin.

Terry, C. (2003) *The Fellas: Overcoming Prison and Addiction.* Belmont, CA: Wadsworth.

Toch, H. (1997) *Corrections: A Humanistic Approach.* Guilderland, NY: Harrow & Heston.

Toch, H. (2002) 'Everything works', *International Journal of Offender Therapy and Comparative Criminology*, 46: 119–22.

Travis, J. and Petersilia, J. (2001) 'Reentry reconsidered: a new look at an old question', *Crime and Delinquency*, 47: 291–313.

Travis, J., Solomon, A.L. and Waul, M. (2001) *From Prison to Home: The Dimensions and Consequences of Prisoner Reentry.* Washington, DC: Urban Institute.

Warr, M. (1998) 'Life-course transitions and desistance from crime', *Criminology*, 36: 183–215.

Warr, M. (2002) *Companions in Crime.* Cambridge: Cambridge University Press.

West, D.J. (1961) 'Interludes of honesty in the careers of persistent thieves.' Unpublished paper.

West, D.J. (1963) *The Habitual Prisoner.* London: Macmillan.

White, W. (2000). 'Toward a new recovery movement: historical reflections on recovery, treatment and advocacy.' Paper presented at the Center for Substance Abuse Treatment, Recovery Community Support Program conference, Alexandria, Virginia, April.

Chapter 2

Reintegration and restorative justice: towards a theory and practice of informal social control and support

Gordon Bazemore and Carsten Erbe

Introduction

> The problem of crime cannot be simplified to the problem of the offender. (Leslie Wilkins 1991)

> Worse still, we fear that even when something does work, it is seen to do so only in the eyes of certain professionals, while 'outside' the system ordinary citizens are left without a role or voice in the criminal justice process. (Braithwaite and Mugford 1994)

Parole and aftercare practice has been stymied historically by an insular focus on the needs and risks of offenders. Having identified these needs and risks, intervention professionals then proceed to develop supervision plans that gear levels of surveillance to the documented levels of threat presented by the offender. In some jurisdictions, and especially in juvenile justice agencies, these professionals also conduct offender needs assessments and attempt to match offenders with appropriate services and treatment or remedial programmes designed to address the deficit in question. Though various aftercare models talk about community-based agencies, and occasionally about the role of work and educational institutions, the parole/aftercare enterprise is in essence a highly individualized one.

The new popularity of the concept of *reintegration* implies a recognition that returning offenders to the community raises larger issues than those associated with offender surveillance and service. Indeed, reintegration has always been as much about the community as the offender. Yet the traditional literature of parole and aftercare remains devoid of broader policy visions and of theory that places the offender in the context of community and gives specific consideration to the role of neighbourhood organizations, local socializing institutions or citizen supporters in the reintegration process.[1] Though some aftercare/ reintegration discourse has recently begun to attend to the *human capital* issues of employment and education (Travis and Petersilia 2001), with few exceptions (Clear *et al.* 2001) the field has failed to address how community *social capital* (Putnam 2000) can be an important intervening factor aimed at increasing the likelihood of offender transition to conventional life. The risk management and service needs focus limits debate about re-entry practice to alternative means of applying varying amounts of government intervention to bring about offender change while typically failing to address community transformation. Moreover, current approaches seem disconnected from research based on normative data that demonstrate successful negotiation of desistance pathways throughout the life course of offenders – independent of the influence of correctional intervention (Sampson and Laub 1993; Elliot 1994).[2]

Despite concerns about the 'trendiness' of the new reintegration focus after years of prison crowding due in part to the elimination of parole (Austin 2001), optimistically, this new policy lens offers an opportunity to give strategic consideration both to the community role in re-integrating offenders and to the impact of offender re-entry on com-munities. The purpose of this chapter is to outline a different framework for reintegration grounded in the principles of *restorative justice* (Zehr 1990). Broadly conceptualized as a new way of thinking about crime that gives emphasis to the harm caused by offences, restorative justice seems to provide an opportunity to move beyond the individualizing tendencies of offender-focused treatment and punishment paradigms (Bazemore *et al.* 2000). Such a broader focus may open doors to what Sampson and Wilson (1995: 54) refer to as 'a community-level perspective ... [that] lead[s] away from a simple 'kinds of people' analysis to a focus on social characteristics of collectivities that foster violence (and crime)'. Though somewhat marginal to mainstream criminal justice practice and often limited in its scope to the micro level of intervention, we argue that restorative justice practice can be effectively linked to the issue of offender reintegration through the related concepts of informal *social control* (Hunter 1985) and *social support* (Cullen 1994).

First, we briefly outline a normative theory of restorative justice and then consider how core principles that form the foundation of this theory and of restorative practice may be used to guide intervention aimed at strengthening networks of informal control and social support. We then provide some general components of an intervention theory of re-integration grounded in naturalistic neighbourhood processes using the concept of relationship-building as a core linking intermediate outcome of the reintegration effort.

Restorative principles for a normative theory of intervention

> communities should not measure the success of any [community-based initiative] based upon what happens to offenders. The impact of community based initiatives upon victims, upon the self-esteem of others working [in the community justice process], on strengthening family, building connections within the community, on enforcing community values, on mobilizing community action to reduce factors causing crime – and ultimately on making the community safer – while not readily visible, these impacts are, in the long run, significantly more important than the immediate impact on an offender's habits. (Stuart 1995: 6)

When crime is viewed primarily as a violation of individuals, com-munities and relationships, 'justice' must be seen as more than punishing or treating those found guilty of law-breaking. Because offences 'create obligations to make things right' (Zehr 1990: 181), restorative justice can therefore be described as including 'all responses to crime aimed at doing justice by repairing the harm, or "healing the wounds", crime causes' (Bazemore and Walgrave 1999: 26).[3] Defining 'harm', and determining what should be done to repair it, is best accomplished with input from crime victims, citizens and offenders. Restorative justice advocates therefore promote practices such as victim–offender mediation or dialogue, family group conferencing and a range of other informal decision-making processes aimed at developing reparative agreements that allow offenders to 'make things right' with victims and the community. Restorative justice also includes these decision-making processes, those obligations or sanctions that make up such reparative plans and a variety of policies and practices designed to meet the individual and collective needs of victim, offender and com-munity as primary 'stakeholders' in the justice process (see Table 2.1).

Three 'big ideas' provide the basis for a normative theory of restorative justice. These core principles – *repairing harm, stakeholder involvement* and *the transformation of community and government roles* in

Table 2.1 Restorative justice practice, location and objectives

Objective/focus	Practice	Location
Conflict resolution, prevention, peacemaking	Community conferencing and mediation; alternative dispute resolution; school and neighbourhood conferencing; victim awareness education; youth development	Schools; neighbourhoods; churches; civic groups
Provide decision-making alternative to formal court or other adversarial process for determining obligations for repairing harm	Victim–offender dialogue; family group conferencing circles; reparation boards; other restorative conferencing	Police and community diversion; court diversion; dispositional/sentencing alternatives; post-dispositional planning; residential alternative discipline; conflict resolution; post-residential re-entry
Victim and community input to court or formal decision-making	Written or oral impact statement to court or other entity	Court, probation, residential
Provide reparative sanctions or obligation in response to crime or harmful behaviour	Restitution; community service; service to victims; service for surrogate victims; payment to victim service funds	Diversion, court sanction, probation condition, residential programme, post-incarceration
Offender treatment/ rehabilitation/ education	Victim impact panels; victim awareness education; MAD panels; community service learning project designed to build offender competency and strengthen relationships with law-abiding citizens	Probation, residential facilities, diversion programme; jails
Victim services and support groups	Counselling; volunteer support groups; faith community groups	Multiple settings
Parole and aftercare	Re-entry circles and conferences; offender and victim support groups; service opportunities for the offender; use of natural helpers	Neighbourhood and community
Community-building	Family support and discussion groups	Neighbourhood and community

the response to crime (Van Ness and Strong 1997) – most clearly distinguish restorative justice from other orientations, and define the core outcomes, processes, practices and structural relationships that characterize restorative models (Bazemore and Walgrave 1999).

Principle 1: repairing the harm of crime

The first and most important principle of the restorative perspective is that justice requires that we work to heal victims, offenders and communities that have been injured by crime or other harmful behaviour. Restorative justice responses to intervention therefore begin with a focus on identifying, and then repairing, the damage caused by the actions of offenders and are driven in each case by the needs of these primary stakeholders in the justice process.

Restorative justice also demands vigilance in seeking, first, to *avoid doing additional harm,* and to think more critically about the ways in which even the most well intended criminal and juvenile justice intervention can itself make things worse for victim, offender, or community (Rose and Clear 1998). Focused on multiple and collective objectives, the effort to repair is first concerned with the crime victim and victimized communities. Regarding victim needs, 'repair' may mean restitution or other forms of reparation, information about the case, the opportunity to be heard and (ideally) vindicated, the chance to provide input into the case and, generally, expanded choices about opportunities for involvement and influence (Achilles and Zehr 2001). In the re-entry context, as Herman and Wasserman (2001) point out, providing such opportunities first requires avoidance of stereotypes of victims as vengeful or unable to control their emotions, as well as openness to the idea of a positive role for the victim in ensuring safe and successful reintegration. When multiple options are provided for participation based on the assumption of differences in the experience of each victim, victims may become a vital resource in reintegrating offenders because 'they have a common interest in initiatives designed to prevent recidivism … [and thus] can contribute to reentry successes in significant ways' (2001: 429, 432). For the community, restorative justice offers the promise of reduced fear and safer neighbourhoods, accountability for harmful behaviour, a more accessible justice process and increased neighbourhood efficacy. Restorative justice also implies an obligation for citizens to begin to take ownership over and participate in decisions about sanctioning crime, reintegrating offenders and crime prevention. From the perspective of the offender, the idea of repair focuses our attention first on the most important obligation that incurs when a crime is committed: taking responsibility for making amends to individual victims and victimized communities, rather than simply taking one's punishment as a form of accountability to the state, or obeying supervision rules as accountability to the court or to corrections officials. For offenders who seek to meet these obligations, or 'earn their redemption', there is in turn an opportunity to develop new competencies, social skills, new relationships and the capacity to avoid future crime (Maloney 1998).

The appeal and meaning of repair: though repair is an important objective in its own right, it receives sequential priority in a restorative justice model because it is viewed as a prerequisite for achieving other justice objectives – public safety, fairness, victim satisfaction and accountability in sanctioning, rehabilitation and, most importantly, reintegration. The obligation to repair what one has damaged seems in this sense to be part of a more naturalistic attitude towards crime, the offender and reintegration that, according to citizen surveys, appears to be widely supported by the general public (Pranis and Umbreit 1992; Schwartz 1992). The notion of someone who has hurt another citizen or the community getting help or service without making amends for what has been damaged flies in the face of virtually universal norms of fairness, and is therefore a barrier to meaningful offender reintegration. Unlike corrections models focused only on offender rehabilitation, restorative approaches by contrast 'move away from the principle of entitlement to the principle of social exchange' (Levrant *et al.* 1999: 22). By addressing reciprocity in this way, restorative justice explicitly engages the community and victim side of the reintegration equation that has been missing from standard correctional treatment and aftercare models (e.g. Andrews and Bonta 1994). Though offender reintegration is never guaranteed, the notion of community acceptance of the offender who has 'made it right' with those harmed seems much more likely, and public support for restorative justice may well be linked to such commonsense understandings of crime and justice.

Based on current practice, it is possible to identify five primary dimensions of repair. These dimensions include repair as *compensation* to individuals and communities for loss and damages or more direct efforts to 'fix what was broken' (for example, by paying restitution or completing service to victims or community); repair as *stakeholder satisfaction* (generally assessed by surveys/interviews with participants in restorative processes about feelings, reductions in fear, etc.); repair as *norm affirmation,* or community and victim expression of harm and disapproval; repair as *relationship-building,* or the extent to which the process leads to mutual respect and connections between individuals and their communities; and repair as *crime prevention* (assessed in this context, for example, by reductions in recidivism, but also by building community capacity to prevent and control crime generally). Though restorative practice may at times be concerned exclusively or primarily with one dimension, generally the nature of harm in most crimes, and the desire to take account of the needs of each stakeholder, requires consideration of all five dimensions (Van Ness and Strong 1997).[4] Doing so may well be part and parcel of what restorative practitioners have meant for some time in using the general phrase 'making things right'.

Principle 2: stakeholder involvement

Viewed through the restorative 'lens,' questions of guilt, law-breaking and how to punish (or treat) the offender are incomplete and one-dimensional. In a restorative justice process, participants are therefore concerned with three very different questions: what is the nature of the harm resulting from the crime? What needs to be done to 'make it right' or repair the harm? And who is responsible for this repair? (Zehr 1990). Because harm cannot be understood in a vacuum, repair cannot be achieved in the absence of input from those most affected by crime. These questions are therefore best answered with input from crime victims, citizens and offenders in a decision-making process that maximizes their input into the case. This approach therefore defines the 'case' not simply as the offender, or 'the client,' but rather as a three-dimensional problem presented by the needs and interests of three stakeholders in the aftermath of crime. Hence, the second core principle of restorative justice – that victims, offenders and community members be provided with opportunities for input and participation in the justice process as early and as often as possible (Van Ness and Strong 1997) – follows logically from the principle of repair. Because the structure and formal procedures of courts and other formal criminal justice agencies present a barrier to meaningful input, problem-solving, expression of emotions and creative dialogue (Stuart 1996), in much of the world today, Principle 2 is being operationalized through 'restorative conferencing' approaches that seek to provide more user-friendly, informal alternatives to adversarial decision-making processes (Bazemore and Umbreit 2001) (see Figure 2.1).

The appeal and meaning of stakeholder involvement: traditional intervention focused on treatment and/or punishment suffers from an insular and one-dimensional focus that fails to address the independent and mutual needs of the community, victim, offender and family. For most of the public, criminal justice intervention is largely incomprehensible. If support comes from understanding, and understanding

33

Figure 2.1 Some restorative decision-making processes

- *Victim–offender dialogue mediation*: trained mediators facilitate face-to-face discussion between offender and victim to allow for expression of feelings, discussion of harm and obligation, and arrive at agreement with offender to repair the harm.

- *Family group conferencing*: allows for community, victim and family input into the development of a restorative sanction for juvenile offenders in a process initiated by a trained facilitator usually known as a convener or co-ordinator.

- *Peacemaking circles/circle sentencing*: a sentencing and/or problem-solving process currently being implemented throughout Canada and several locations in Minnesota, Colorado and a limited number of other US jurisdictions usually facilitated by a community in the role of 'keeper' who manages dialogue by use of a talking piece. Circles are attended by victims, offenders and a variety of local citizens who both support and wish to develop a local resolution of the crime.

- *Community reparative boards*: currently being widely implemented in Vermont, Arizona and parts of California and Colorado, these citizen sentencing panels develop agreements with offenders that focus their probation on victim and community reparation, understanding of harm caused by their crime and avoiding future offending behaviour.

- *Merchant accountability boards*: local merchants volunteer their time to sit on reparative panels that hear cases of shoplifting, vandalism or other crimes committed by juveniles against city-centre businesses.

from involvement and participation, there should be little wonder that community attitudes about criminal justice often range from apathy to hostility.

Indeed, a core tenet of democratic decision-making is that citizens denied opportunities for meaningful participation may move from feelings of apathy, to distrust, to active opposition. The appeal of the principle of stakeholder involvement in justice decision-making is therefore not limited to citizens who are permitted direct input into processes that effect them personally as victims, offenders and community members. Offender service professionals also recognize that community participation not only increases support and understanding for the offender but may in addition spill over to expand involvement in other aspects of intervention – including rehabilitation programmes, prevention initiatives and victim services.

Typically, parole and aftercare practice have emphasized sanctions and surveillance with more progressive approaches adding the concern that treatment and other services receive equal emphasis (Altshuler and Armstrong 1994). Yet the limits of both treatment and punishment are in part due to the fact that neither seems capable of moving beyond the focus on professionals as the sole providers of intervention. As Maruna (2001: 28) observes, 'even the most extreme partisans' of both the 'medical model story' and the 'deterrence story' 'do not suggest that either state rehabilitation or punishment can account for most ex-offenders desisting in any consistent way'.

While traditional justice responses separate the parties in crime and conflict, and assume that their interests are mutually exclusive, the promise of a restorative justice process is the possibility of finding 'common ground'. Because conflict and distrust in formal justice decision-making results from an overemphasis on the needs and risks presented by the offender (Achilles and Zehr 2001; Bazemore and Umbreit 2001), the most important challenge in restorative justice decision-making is the search for a balance of victim, offender and community interests by giving consideration to the voices and roles of each stakeholder (Stuart 1996).

Principle 3: transformation in community and government roles and relationships

The third core principle in restorative justice stems from the conviction that there are limits on the role of government in the response to crime and trouble, and from the parallel view that communities have an essential role to play in this response. If crime is more than law-breaking – and if we wish to repair the harm of crime by actively involving those most effected in justice processes – we must, as Van Ness and Strong put it, 'rethink the relative roles and responsibilities of government and community. In promoting justice, government is responsible for preserving order, but the community is responsible for establishing *peace*' (1997: 25, emphasis added).

This core restorative justice principle suggests in essence that there are some things criminal justice systems and other government agencies do well, and some things not so well. Certainly, any of us who are falsely charged with committing a crime will insist on our due process rights. Most will also agree that some problems require application of pro-fessional expertise. However, Principle 3 reminds us that offenders grow up and live most of their lives in communities – not corrections programmes – and it is families, extended families, teachers, neighbours, ministers and others who provide both support and guidance in socialization and maturation processes. These 'natural helpers' accomplish the primary work of reintegration informally by identifying mentoring adults and community groups that help delinquent youths develop new skills, improve school performance and connect with other community organizations or small businesses who may provide employment opportunities as well as creativity and access to vital resources (Sullivan 1989).[5]

If the principle of stakeholder involvement can be viewed as defining the nature of a justice *process* focused on the goal of healing or reparation, Principle 3 defines the *organizational structure* or specific roles and responsibilities of justice systems and communities. The new relationship between professionals and citizens required to facilitate victim, offender and citizen participation in a restorative response is one of true collaboration in an effort to co-produce community safety, peace and justice by, first, healing the harms of crime. This relationship implies dramatic transformation in the role of the juvenile justice professional, from case management specialist or service provider, to facilitator of informal, problem-solving community responses to crime and mobilizer of community resources. In this new role, rather than making an 'end-run' around these community resources to provide direct services to the offender, these professionals, when asked, work through citizens and community groups, families, victim support groups and socializing institutions (e.g. school, work). In doing so, they seek to bring about positive change in the situation of both offenders and crime victims, primarily by strengthening the capacity of these natural helpers to continue to provide support and assistance (see Figure 2.2) (Perry and Gorsyk 1997).

In the reintegration context, where the professional role has been defined most narrowly as one of service broker at best, and rule enforcer at worst,[6] this transformation is probably one of the most difficult of any in the criminal justice system. Yet it is also one that is likely to achieve the most profound results because of the direct proximity to the community.

The goal of shifting the role of the criminal justice system from sole responder to crime to partner with the community occurs as citizens take on more responsibility and provide more input in an emerging collaborative process. As the justice system's relationship to the community evolves through these stages,[7] the professional's role becomes less one of direct provider and more one of catalyst for mobilizing community

Figure 2.2 Restorative justice: redefining the government's role

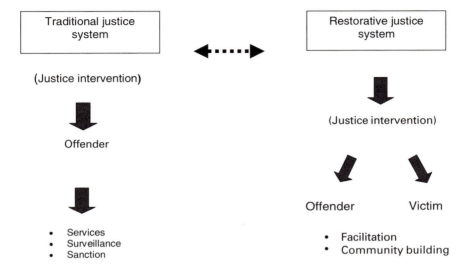

resources for reintegration through informal control grounded in an 'ecology of social support' (Cullen 1994).

The meaning and appeal of community empowerment: following the logic of Nils Christie's insight that crime is essentially conflict that has been 'stolen' from victims, offenders and communities (1977), many restorative justice advocates are concluding that citizens and community groups should take back these conflicts and rediscover their capacity to resolve them. More generally, there also appears to be something in the restorative frame of reference that addresses a realistic citizen anxiety about the loss of community capacity to address youth crime, trouble, conflict and other issues (Putnam 2000).

Perhaps the greatest barrier for most formal service and justice systems is the pejorative view of 'citizens as clients' (McKnight 1995) and the tendency of some professionals to dismiss the possibility of community as a partner, much less a driving force, in the response to crime (Pranis 1996). Here, the restorative justice ideal is consistent with emerging frameworks that challenge medical and public health perspectives focused on disease and deficiency in the community context. As McKnight suggests, the ascendancy of professional and service establishments may be associated with an expansion in the number of *clients* and a decline in the capacity and authority of *citizens*. Proponents of new community frameworks, however, emphasize the capacity, resiliency and strength of citizens and community *resources* at both individual and social ecological levels (Benson 1997).

Restorative justice and social capital: towards a theory of the community role in reintegration

The challenge of community involvement and the space for citizen efficacy

In the last three to four decades, as juvenile justice agencies and systems have expanded, they have taken on increasing responsibility for addressing problems once dealt with by families, neighbours, teachers, clergy and others at the neighbourhood level by these less formal means. As this has occurred, these local problems have begun to find their way into arrest files, court dockets and probation caseloads. Moreover, efforts to centralize, professionalize and expand generally the reach of criminal justice and social services seem, over time, to have sent destructive messages to community groups and neighbourhoods. While widening the *system net*, social service and juvenile justice agencies have often weakened historically stronger *community nets* and inadvertently undercut the role and responsibility of citizens, neighbourhood institutions and community groups in socialization and informal sanctioning (Braithwaite 1994; McKnight 1995). In addition, as Clear and Karp (1999: 38) observe:

> When agents of the state become the key problem solvers, they might be filling a void in community; but just as in interpersonal relationships, so in community functioning, once a function is being performed by one party it becomes unnecessary for another to take it on ... parents expect police or schools to control their children; neighbors expect police to prevent late night noise from people on their street; and citizens expect the courts to resolve disputes ... informal control systems may atrophy like dormant muscles, and citizens may come to see the formal system as existing to mediate all conflicts.

In this context, a revitalization of viable neighbourhood responses to crime will not be easy, as communities today may be resistant to taking on increased responsibility after being told for years to 'leave it to the experts'. Indeed, citizens and community groups who do not learn and regularly *practise* the art and techniques of norm affirmation, apology, forgiveness and mutual aid may become so deskilled that they are incapable of doing so (Moore 1994).[8] More optimistically, restorative practices appear to be creating the space for a kind of community learning process. Crime and barriers to offender reintegration can from this perspective be viewed not only as tragic features of modern life but also as an opportunity for transformative change (Stuart 1996: 8). Although there would appear to be clear limits on the capacity of restorative and community justice programmes to make a significant dent in crime rates citizen involvement in conflict resolution and problem-solving may have direct impact on community efficacy. Such enhancements in efficacy may in turn mobilize support for a vision and practice of community engagement in the justice process that could have important implications for crime prevention and control. To do so, however, restorative processes must be focused on achieving tangible collective outcomes and must connect with, revitalize and strengthen community-based processes of informal social control and support.

Social control

Sociologist Albert Hunter (1985) has suggested that there are three general types of social control. *Public controls* are those imposed by the state and generally implemented through the various agencies of the criminal justice system. *Private controls* are those informal constraints imposed by families and extended families. As previously discussed, public controls have begun to play a more dominant role as juvenile and criminal justice agencies have assumed much greater responsibility in the response to crime, conflict and trouble. In turn, both private social controls, and what have been called *parochial controls* – those exercised by community groups and institutions (Hunter 1985: 57) – have become substantially weaker, with often distressing consequences:

> *public controls can operate in the neighborhood without regard for private and parochial controls, although often not was well.* For instance, the police can do their jobs regardless of the state of the local PTA. Further, police can make the streets safe so residents can attend the local PTA meeting. They cannot, however, make residents want to attend that meeting. Only well-functioning private controls can manage that. (Rose and Clear 1998, emphasis added)

The weakening of 'village-level,' parochial controls that once supported adults in exercising informal sanctions over young people is perhaps most apparent. When present in communities, parochial control has been empirically associated with low rates of youth crime (Sampson *et al.* 1997). When dormant or weak, it may be viewed as a net loss in an essential form of neighbourhood social capital that some proponents of restorative justice ultimately wish to replenish. Families, schools and neighbourhood groups who refer their problem young people for professional help may in fact be replacing parochial control with public control. Similarly, parole and aftercare professionals who fail to mobilize and build on both private and parochial controls must rely even more on the relatively meager power of formal sanctioning and surveillance strategies. If restorative justice advocates wish to change this pattern – and ensure that citizens do not choose to 'mind their own business' in addressing crime and trouble – they may seek to fill the void in parochial and private controls with restorative decision-making processes that provide the space and tools necessary for adults to intervene firmly, and respectfully, in the lives of young people in trouble (Braithwaite 1994).

Specifically, restorative conferencing models (Bazemore and Umbreit 2001) are potentially well placed to summon the private controls of families and extended families in the broader context of the parochial control aimed at reinforcing behavioural and disciplinary norms. To the extent that such processes also continue to increase the skills and willingness of neighbourhood adults informally to censure destructive and harmful behaviour by young people, and reinforce other families in doing so, they will have expanded and strengthened what may be conceptualized as a kind of 'public safety social capital'.

Social support

Social support has been defined as the 'provision of affective and/or instrumental (or material) resources ... [through] *intimate or confiding relationships* ... [or] as a property of (cultural or structural) macro-level social units'. As such it is a potentially preventative and rehabilitative factor (inversely associated with crime in a variety of empirical studies, according to the Cullen *et al.* 1999: 190 definition) that seems to be fundamentally associated with one or more *social relationships* between the providers and recipients of such support. The quality and strength of such support are directly related to the connections young people develop – through kinship, friendship and instrumental affiliations – to individuals and social groups, and to the overall quality of the nurturing and socialization process, both of which are dependent upon the sustained affective commitment of one or more caring adults (Werner 1986).

Though most commentators have used the concept of social support to advocate for expanded social services and treatment programmes (Cullen *et al.* 1999), it is within informal community networks that social support has its most robust influence. At the micro, informal level, where reintegration and integration actually occur, personal relationships with 'natural helpers' (Annie E. Casey Foundation 2001) or 'community guides' (McKnight 1995) often act as bridge and buffer between the offender and the community. Social relationships smooth the way for the development of additional connections between the offender, law-abiding citizens and legitimate institutions – providing offenders with a legitimate identity and a 'link' to the conventional community based on commitments and opportunities (Polk and Kobrin 1972), as well as responsibilities and obligations (Cullen 1994: 543). This connection substantially increases the likelihood that they will make the transition from delinquent and deviant careers to conventional lifestyles (Hirschi 1969; Sampson and Laub 1993). As the strength and number of such relationships increase, offenders accrue the human capital needed to gain access to institutional roles (e.g. in work, education and community groups) and, in turn, social capital in neighbourhood networks is increased.

Restorative practices seem particularly well suited to strengthen what could be labelled *private social support*, for example, by engaging families in family group conferencing or family support groups. Such practices also strengthen *parochial social support* by, for example, engaging community members in reparative boards and in community service projects in which they work together with young people on initiatives that meet local needs. To the extent that restorative interventions actually do build or strengthen relationships between young people and law-abiding adults, they can indeed contribute to the reservoir of social capital needed to guide and nurture young people and reintegrate those in trouble. While others have proposed new theoretical frameworks suggestive of interventions that may be expected to strengthen informal social control (Rose and Clear 1998), we focus below on the idea of social support in outlining the components of an intervention theory of reintegration based on restorative justice principles.

Towards a naturalistic theory of reintegration: reciprocity, social support and the social relationship as integrating concepts

Indeed, researchers have recognized that a major limitation of even the empirically-driven, well-conceived and carefully executed treatments for serious antisocial behavior is that they address at best a small subset of the factors that contribute to the problems experienced by these youths across several social contexts. (Shoenwald *et al.* 1999)

It is easier to act one's way into better thinking than think one's way into better acting. (See 1996)

In an integrated restorative justice model, the reciprocity and social exchange value inherent in the obligation of offenders to make amends to victim and community, the moral condemnation of an act as harmful, and the community norm affirmation that accompanies informal restorative processes (Karp and Walther 2001) are all viewed as directly related to the likelihood of offender reintegration. Specifically, community forgiveness of the offender occurs as a process of 'earned redemption' (Bazemore 1998), and in turn makes possible informal social support while giving legitimacy to informal control. Indeed, support and control should be viewed as interdependent because, as Cullen (1994: 545) observes: 'social support often is a precondition for effective social control ... [and] because of investments in relationships, high levels of social support provide the social capital for guardianship.' Moreover, restorative conferencing processes provide one of the clearest illustrations of the interdependence of support and control in the effort to ensure that those who express to the offender the harm that his or her crime has caused are those with close personal ties whose opinions therefore matter (Braithwaite and Mugford 1994). Such participants in the informal sanctioning process are often those who have established some relationship of support with the offender, and/or will develop or strengthen these affective ties as part of the conferencing process. Moreover, such processes do not require an aggressive or authoritarian 'shaming' approach to ensure that offenders get the message: 'The testimony of the victims and the apologies (when they occur, as they often do) are sufficient to accomplish the necessary shaming of the evil of violence. But there can *never be enough* citizens active in the *reintegration* part of reintegrative shaming' (Braithwaite and Roche 2001, emphasis added).

It is important to note that one of the previously mentioned dimensions of repair, relationship-building, appears to be emerging as an important overarching indicator of intermediate success in much restorative justice practice (Van Ness and Strong 1997).[9] The importance of relationships in restorative processes, and in the context of reintegration, is grounded in a sense of community as interconnected networks of citizens who have tools and resources that can be mobilized collectively to promote healing and reintegration. At the micro level, processes such as restorative conferencing may help to connect or reconnect victims and offenders with their support networks, or to new sources of support in a kind of naturalistic ceremony of reintegration

(Braithwaite and Mugford 1994). At a more macro level, the idea of relationship-building outcomes also helps to connect restorative justice to propositions derived from extant theories of community and crime (Braithwaite 1989; Skogan 1990), as well as to emerging theories of intervention specific to restorative justice.[10]

Theory and practice

Treatment itself depends on a supportive relationship between the therapist or counsellor and client of service, and the effectiveness of treatment is in part a function of the quality of this relationship (Andrews and Bonta 1994). There are, however, practical limits to this professional relationship, and competing agendas that may weaken its impact, at least over sustained intervals. Although important, such professional relationships take on a different connotation because offenders know that treatment providers are paid to spend time with them. Moreover, the therapist/client relationship seldom allows an opportunity for the offender to move into roles that allow for the truly transformative experience of *giving* rather than simply receiving social support (Cullen 1994: 544).

Unfortunately, the current structural and cultural configuration of treatment programmes and social service organizations does not allow them easily to promote, develop and mobilize the informal support networks that are suggested to be important links in a theory of social support. Nor are treatment programmes geared towards the advocacy for change in the organizational dynamics of socializing institutions such as school and work that could develop and increase access to new roles for offenders and young people at risk (Polk 2001).

A naturalistic reintegrative strategy based on building meaningful relationships between young offenders and law-abiding adults includes two practical intervention components which should fit together as part of a seamless whole rather than as independent programmatic units. First, offenders need some minimal level of skill, or *human capital*, to develop and maintain strong, positive relationships. They need assets that allow them to take advantage of the 'connectedness' that can be experienced through good relationships with employers, teachers, friends, fellow church members, etc. (Benson 1997). These assets are not developed in a vacuum, and they are also unlikely to be fully developed in treatment or remedial programmes focused primarily on skill deficit reduction, or cognitive therapy aimed at correcting 'thinking errors'. Correctional programmes can provide an important piece of a more holistic asset-building strategy for many offenders. Yet when these interventions are not linked to institutional roles that allow offenders actively to *practise* and *demonstrate* skills in a way that strengthens a community connection, they run the risk of becoming yet another pathway that leads offenders towards what McKnight (1995) calls the 'dependency of serviced life'.

Secondly, a practical relationship-building strategy therefore requires a change in the context in which offenders are expected to develop assets. Such a change is needed to ensure that, in building competencies, they also build and are able to sustain connections. Offenders, like young people in general, are most likely to learn social and occupational skills in settings where they are linked organically to positive adults, and where the motivation for coming together with such guides or mentors is not premised primarily on the presumed need for remedial training or treatment. Rather, the relationship is about a mutual instrumental commitment to a common task, which in turn provides the opportunity for developing affective connections to others. The best historical examples are the classic apprenticeship models in craft and trade occupations, the master/student relationship in the arts and the extended family business, all of which provided for natural ties between young and old and offered a clear transition to adulthood, even for those young people already actively involved in criminal activity (Sullivan 1989). Because, with the limited exceptions of the arts and sports, such opportunities are largely unavailable to young people today, it is therefore important to think about new strategies for recreating such socialization contexts in the present political economy. One of the easiest and least exploited, for example, is the opportunity for meaningful service to others – in a setting where offenders work with community members on projects such as building Habitat for Humanity homes or doing chores for the elderly (Bazemore and Maloney 1994). Such service can also be part of a transition connected to a new kind of 'designed' paid work experience that is in turn linked to new career tracks (Bazemore 1991).

For the offender, such experiences tap into two important constructs rarely incorporated into the primary objectives of correctional programming and strangely missing from most discourse and research around control theory that purports to increase understanding of the 'bond' to others that keeps most of us from involvement in crime (Hirschi 1969). These are the sense of *usefulness* and the sense of *belonging*, which some writers in the more structural and developmental tradition of control theory have viewed as vital components of a 'legitimate identity' (Polk and Kobrin 1972). Unlike the more individually focused elements of the bond in recent statements of so-called 'internal control' theory (Hirschi and Gottfredson 1995), usefulness and belonging are established in the context of community. Instrumentally, the sense of belonging is often directly linked to usefulness, or the sense that one has something to contribute that is important to the happiness and well-being of others. Because usefulness and belonging are most strongly reinforced in activity in which the participant has an opportunity to contribute to the common good (Bellah *et al.* 1985), the best interventions are those that allow offenders to make meaningful and visible assistance to neighbourhood improvement or relief efforts, social causes or individuals in need (Bazemore and Maloney 1994; Maruna 2001). Such demonstrations send a message to the community that the offender is worthy of further support and investment in his or her reintegration, and to the offender that he or she has something to offer that is value to others. Service to community or those in need also implies a role change that requires the offender to take responsibility for others in a context of support, whether in work, family or other informal as well as institutional settings. In the intervention context, it has been the logic of such a shift in external expectations of these new roles that appears to lie behind a variety of mutual support programmes. When effective, interventions such as the 12-step programmes in essence promote behaviour change in the form of sobriety and non-criminal lifestyles through informal pressure on the deviant actor to 'live up to' the demands of a new role in which one's conforming behaviour is directly linked to the well-being of others (see Trice and Roman 1970).[11]

The cycle of support: social relationships and reintegration

As Figure 2.3 suggests, the traditional treatment and/or remedial focus on removing deficits offers an overly simplistic approach much akin to the 'receptacle model' of education that depicts students as passive vessels waiting to be filled up with knowledge. In this remedial model, which seems all too typical of many current cognitively based correctional treatment programmes, reintegration is depicted as a linear two-step path to social adjustment in which remedial or therapeutic intervention is viewed as the 'independent' variable, and relationship-building is left to chance.

In contrast, Figure 2.4 suggests that the social relationship, in conjunction with opportunities to earn one's redemption and contribute to

Figure 2.3 Treatment/remedial model

| Offender (deficits and dysfunction) | ➡ | Remedial or therapeutic intervention | ➡ | Offender adjustment (desistance from crime) |

Figure 2.4 Restorative/relational model

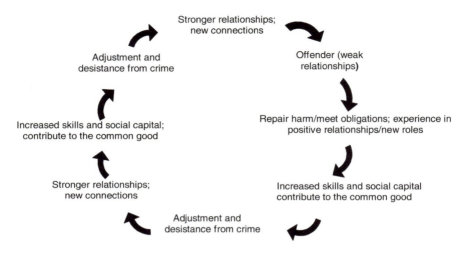

the common good, may be depicted as the catalyst that provides the necessary context both for ongoing social support and asset-building. New assets, in turn, lead to more support and connections and, hence, to stronger relationships, a greater repertoire of skills and still more connections (and the opportunities these provide) through a cyclical process. In this non-recursive model, anticipated feedback loops between skill-building, service to others, relationship building, access to positive roles and offender adjustment are associated with a gradual reduction in criminal behaviour until at some point the life space of the offender is simply too committed to conventional lines of action to make offending an attractive or practically feasible prospect.

In this model, the social relationship is the primary vehicle for engaging both formal and informal community social support and social control. This in turn provides the affective or emotive components of offender attachment to conventional groups as well as the basis for instrumental commitment to conventional behaviour through experiences in roles that provide opportunities for offenders to demonstrate their potential value as resources to communities. An intervention model aimed at maximizing this attachment and commitment must focus on the creation of new institutional roles, as well as informal and quasi-formal support networks for building connections to facilitate reintegration and *integration* of offenders (Polk and Kobrin 1972). Because relationship building is more complex than simply creating new intervention programmes, we have argued elsewhere for the development of new models of reintegration and rehabilitation based essentially on strengthening offender competencies, and building connections between offenders, law-abiding adults and socializing institutions (Bazemore 1998, 2000).

Discussion

This chapter has proposed a general approach to reintegration that envisions new spaces for relationship-building at the individual/ interpersonal, institutional (e.g. school, work) and community levels. Such spaces provide a context for connecting offenders to conventional groups and individuals using strategies that tap into the strengths of offenders, victims and the communities surrounding them to mobilize new structures for informal social support and control. Ultimately, we suggest that intervention based on restorative justice principles is essentially about accelerating naturalistic processes of desistance by creating new connections that build human capital in offenders and social capital in the communities where they will be reintegrated (Maruna 2001).

Although evaluation of restorative practices is in its relative infancy,[12] the proposed approach builds on a large body of empirical research studies of resiliency among children and young people, which demonstrates the need for committed, sustained relationships between at-risk youth and adults with a long-term interest in their well-being and successful development (Rutter 1985). Similarly, life-course research on desistance (Sullivan 1989; Sampson and Laub 1993) suggests that connections that flow from the transitions offenders make to conventional roles in work, family and community – coupled with creating a new self-identity based on new role expectations (Maruna 2001) – ultimately lead to maturational reform. Finally, at a social ecological level, what is being demonstrated by the Chicago studies of collective efficacy (Sampson *et al*. 1997) is that the impact of informal sanctions and social support may reduce community crime rates despite the presence of other risk factors (e.g. poverty) associated with underclass neighbourhoods.

At a minimum, making progress towards the vision of restorative justice, as suggested in the previous discussion of restorative justice Principle 3 (transformation in community and government roles and relationships), requires a significant revamping of organizational and interorganizational responsibilities and professional roles in order to facilitate the even more difficult activation or reactivation of the community role in the reintegration process. Moreover, the naturalistic emphasis of the model outlined in this chapter does not mean 'naturally occurring', nor does it suggest specifically that desistance and re-integration occur through an 'ontogenic' or 'ageing out' process (see Maruna 2001: ch. 5 for a critique). In fact, there is much agency and strategic action involved in the restorative/relational approach. Despite emphasis on the importance of actions by citizens and community groups rather than professionals, this focus is not a call for an abandonment of the government role or a prescription for a roll-back in social services. Rather, it means a different and more relevant role for justice organizations and justice professionals that, in the view of some restorative justice advocates, must be supported by a strong and generous social welfare state (Braithwaite 2000).[13] Working in favour of the vision of restorative justice proponents is the fact that current initiatives are very much a part of a larger movement symbolized by such phrases as 'it takes a village', and by practice fuelled by a desire to recreate a new collective, informal, community response to crime and a variety of social problems (Schorr and Schorr 1989). Intentional efforts to rebuild now weakened informal networks of community social control and support for young people generally, and offenders specifically, are now taking the form of concrete policy and programmatic expressions, as seen for example in a new focus on the strengths and resources, rather than risks and deficits of young people and their communities (Benson 1997). Such experiential models of reform and transition seem to move almost inevitably towards building or rebuilding community capacity to fashion new roles for young people as resources in the context of much strengthened youth–adult relationships, while also recognizing the limits of an individually focused, case-driven, professionalized response unconnected to efficacious communities. Despite challenges to transcend traditional bureaucratic and functional boundaries that artificially compartmentalize responses to crime, it is possible to speculate about how restorative practices could contribute directly to community-building and 'collective efficacy' (Sampson et al. 1997) in the reintegration context. Such practices might even become a catalyst for a 'democratization of social control' whereby a kind of 'bubbling up' becomes possible as social justice issues are increasingly aired in community justice forums linked intentionally to what Braithwaite (1994) has described as a vibrant social movement politics. Indeed, restorative justice advocates may begin to use crime and issues of reintegration as an opening for rather ambitious forms of community organizing aimed as much at breaking down social distance and engaging the least powerful and most vulnerable community members – victims and offenders – in grassroots decision-making (Pranis 2001).

Notes

1   The more sophisticated parole and aftercare models (Altschuler and Armstrong 1994; Petersilia 1999) represent advances over the current state of affairs in which virtually no follow-up support is available for offenders re-entering the community. However, these models seem primarily focused on more rationalized approaches to co-ordinating treatment provider and criminal justice agencies to ensure that offenders are provided with services and supervision. Indeed, an important indicator of the current state of the field is the fact that long-established, empirically grounded admonitions to focus at least as much on services as on surveillance, and to avoid overloading offenders with sanctions, are often viewed in these models as profound new insights.

2   For their part, social scientists – and especially criminologists focused on theory and research in the area of communities and crime – have not applied their work to intervention. As Cullen *et al.* (2000) suggest, this failure may be part of a more general non-interventionist or libertarian bias among criminologists who have been so distrustful of the criminal justice system that they have abandoned the intervention enterprise to those who, for reasons of political expediency, may have little use for thoughtful and productive social policy.

3   Broadly, modern restorative justice practice appears to have been directly influenced by new developments in the victims' rights movement and an expanded role for victims in a community justice process (Young 1995); the community and problem-oriented policing philosophy and movement (Goldstein 1990; Sparrow *et al.* 1990); and renewed interest in indigenous dispute resolution and settlement processes (Griffiths and Hamilton 1996). Some critics dismiss restorative justice as simply a restatement of the individual treatment perspective grounded firmly in *parens patriae* logic (Feld 1999), while others see it as a new form of the 'get tough' crime control perspective (Moon *et al.* 2000). Although restorative justice is in no way a 'lenient' approach, it is grounded in a strong critique of punishment generally, and retributive justice specifically (Zehr 1990).

4   Van Ness and Strong suggest a difference between 'reparative' and restorative approaches in which the latter are regarded as primarily focused on compensation in its various forms. Restorative justice may also be said to encompass strategies that seek to transform widely accepted criminal and juvenile justice goals that take the form of 'restorative approaches' to offender rehabilitation, community safety, victim assistance and sanctioning crime (Bazemore and Walgrave 1999).

5   'Community' in a restorative process is an emergent concept that is defined in a flexible way based on the impact of the crime on neighbourhood, church, school, workplace or extended family. Terms such as 'affected community' and 'community of care' are used to indicate that community is *not only a place* (McCold and Wachtel 1998), but also, more importantly, 'a

network of relationships where members share joy and pain' (Earle 1996: 8).

6   One result of the latter has been a steady increase in the past decade in the proportion of new prison admissions who are technical parole violators (see Austin 2001).

7   Beginning with the current 'expert' model (that essentially views the community as a nuisance), this evolution involves movement to intermediate stages of information-sharing and input-seeking and, ideally, on to a community-driven approach (Pranis 1996).

8   Indeed, the larger concern is that generations who do not practise the skills of conflict resolution and engage in informal support and control may become increasingly deficient in the competencies of citizenship itself.

9   Consistent with this focus, one approach to evaluating the short-term effectiveness of a restorative intervention might be to ask whether or not a specific process or programme created new positive relationships or strengthened existing ones; increased community skills in problem-solving and constructive conflict resolution; increased participants' sense of capacity and efficacy in addressing problems; increased individual awareness of and commitment to the common good; and created informal support system or 'safety nets' for victims and offenders (Pranis and Bazemore 2001).

10 Restorative justice has also been linked to other aetiological theories of crime including symbolic interaction theory and labelling, control theory and social disorganization theory (Bazemore 1998; Braithwaite 1998).

11 Regarding community-building and the development of social capital, restorative justice processes also allow community members to develop feelings of usefulness and belonging in problem-solving around crime (Hudson *et al.* 1996). Hence, the 'helper principle' of behaviour change is indeed quite apparent in its impact on community in restorative conferencing and, as Hudson *et al.* (1996: 3) suggest: 'Conferences can also be seen as an educational tool, a forum for teaching and practicing problem-solving skills. Family members can learn and practice these skills and learn about the strengths of (other) family members and the resources available to them.'

12 Though evaluation results cannot be fairly compared with those associated with the most effective, high-end, multi-modal treatment programmes (Andrews and Bonta 1994), these short-term restorative programmes perform significantly better than most other long-term treatment programmes in common use (Umbreit 1998), and unlike many clinical treatment programmes, no restorative programmes have demonstrated negative impacts on recidivism in empirical studies. Recidivism reduction effects are positive though not as strong in the case of restorative sanctions such as restitution and community service (Schneider 1990; Butts and Snyder 1991) and, unlike multi-model treatment programmes, the overall impact of restorative programme components (e.g. participating in a

restorative conference, completing community service, attending a victim impact session) has not been studied in evaluations that view these components collectively as part of a holistic rehabilitation approach (Bazemore *et al*. 2000).

13 Such a state would also ideally be supported by a full employment economy. Contrary to some recent misrepresentations in the literature (Delgado 2000), restorative justice advocates do not suggest that government abandon the justice process to community groups. Indeed, the formal system retains an important role in both peacemaking and maintaining order – while also functioning as a guardian of individual liberties in the face of possible tyranny of the community (Pranis 1996). The third restorative justice principle of transformation in community and government roles appears to presume that communities are willing and able to come forward and assume a primary leadership role in the response to crime. Although the empirical evidence drawn from the experience of community policing in some jurisdictions creates significant doubts about this willingness and capacity (Rosenbaum *et al*. 1998), what we have learnt from the restorative conferencing *experience* thus far seems to challenge the commonly accepted wisdom of an apathetic public (Hudson *et al*. 1996; Perry and Gorsych 1997; Bazemore 1997, 2000; Morris and Maxwell 2001).

References

Achilles, M. and Zehr, H. (2001) 'Restorative justice for crime victims: the promise, the challenge', in G. Bazemore and M. Schiff (eds) *Restorative and Community Justice: Repairing Harm and Transforming Communities*. Cincinnati, OH: Anderson.

Altschuler, D.M. and Armstrong, T. (1994) *Intensive Aftercare for High Risk Juveniles: Policies and Procedures*. Washington, DC: Office of Juvenile Justice and Delinquency Prevention.

Andrews, D. and Bonta, J. (1994) *The Psychology of Criminal Conduct*. Cincinnati, OH: Anderson.

Annie E. Casey Foundation (2001) *Walking our Talk in the Neighborhood: Partnerships between Professionals and Natural Helpers*. Baltimore, MD: Annie E. Casey Foundation.

Austin, J. (2001) 'Prisoner reentry: current trends, practices, and issues', *Crime and Delinquency*, 47(3): 314–34.

Bazemore, G. (1991) 'New concepts and alternative practice in community supervision of juvenile offenders: rediscovering work experience and competency development', *Journal of Crime and Justice*, 14 (2): 27–52.

Bazemore, G. (1998) 'Restorative justice and earned redemption: communities, victims and offender reintegration', *American Behavioral Scientist*, 41 (6): 768–813.

Bazemore, G. and Maloney, D. (1994) 'Rehabilitating community service: toward restorative service in a balanced justice system', *Federal Probation*, 58 (1): 24–35.

Bazemore, G., Nissen, L. and Dooley, M. (2000) 'Mobilizing social support and building relationships: broadening correctional and rehabilitative agendas', *Corrections Management Quarterly*, 4 (4): 10–21.

Bazemore, G. and Schiff, M. (eds) (2001) *Restorative and Community Justice: Repairing Harm and Transforming Communities*. Cincinnati, OH: Anderson.

Bazemore, G. and Umbreit, M. (2001) 'A comparison of four restorative conferencing models', *Juvenile Justice Bulletin*, Office of Juvenile Justice and Delinquency Prevention, Office of Justice Programs, US Department of Justice.

Bazemore, G. and Walgrave, L. (1999) 'Restorative juvenile justice: in search of fundamentals and an outline for systemic reform', in G. Bazemore and L. Walgrave (eds) *Restorative Juvenile Justice: Repairing the Harm of Youth Crime*. Monsey, NY: Criminal Justice Press, 45–74.

Bellah, R.N., Madsen, R., Sullivan, W., Swidler, A. and Tipton, M. (1985) *Habits of the Heart: Individualism and Commitment in American Life*. Berkeley, CA: University of California Press.

Benson, P. (1997) *All Kids are our Kids*. San Francisco, CA: Jossey-Bass.

Braithwaite, J. (1989) *Crime, Shame, and Reintegration*. New York, NY: Cambridge University Press.

Braithwaite, J. (1994) 'Thinking harder about democratizing social control', in C. Alder and Joy Wundersitz (eds) *Family Group Conferencing in Juvenile Justice: The Way Forward of Misplaced Optimism?*. Canberra, Australia: Australian Institute of Criminology.

Braithwaite, J. (1998) 'Restorative justice', in M. Tonry (ed.) *The Handbook of Crime and Punishment*. New York, NY: Oxford University Press, 323–44.

Braithwaite, J. and Mugford, S. (1994) 'Conditions of successful reintegration ceremonies: dealing with juvenile offenders', *British Journal of Criminology*, 34 (2): 139–71.

Braithwaite, D. and Roche, D. (2001) 'Responsibility and restorative justice', in G. Bazemore and M. Schiff (eds) *Restorative and Community Justice: Repairing Harm and Transforming Communities*. Cincinnati, OH: Anderson.

Butts, J. and Snyder, H. (1991) 'Restitution and juvenile recidivism.' Monograph. Pittsburgh, PA: National Center for Juvenile Justice.

Christie, N. (1977) 'Conflict as property', *British Journal of Criminology*, 17 (1): 1–15.

Clear, T. and Karp, D. (1999) *The Community Justice Ideal: Preventing Crime and Achieving Justice*. New York, NY: Western Press.

Clear, T., Rose, D. and Ryder, J. (2001) 'Incarceration and the community: the problem of removing and returning offenders', *Crime and Delinquency*, 47 (3): 335–51.

Cullen, F.T. (1994) 'Social support as an organizing concept for criminology. Presidential address to the Academy of Criminal Justice Sciences', *Justice Quarterly*, 11: 527–59.

Cullen, F.T., Wright, J.P. and Chamlin, M.B. (1999) 'Social support and social reform: a progressive crime control agenda', *Crime and Delinquency*, 45: 188–207.

Delgado, R. (2000) 'Goodbye to Hammerabi: concerns about restorative justice', *Stanford Law Review*, 52 (4): 751.

Diaz, J. (1997) 'Mission statement.' Florence, AZ: Pinal County Department of Juvenile Court Services.

Doble, J. and Immerwahr, S. (1997) 'Delawareans favor prison alternatives', in M. Tony and K. Hatlestad (eds) *Sentencing Reform in Overcrowded Times*. New York, NY: Oxford University Press.

Earle, R. (1996) 'Community justice: the Austin experience', *Texas Probation*, 11: 6–11.

Elliott, D. (1994) 'Serious violent offenders: onset, developmental course, and termination. The American Society of Criminology 1993 presidential address', reprinted from *Criminology*, 32 (1).

Feld, B. (1999) 'Rehabilitation, retribution and restorative justice: alternative conceptions of juvenile justice', in G. Bazemore and L. Walgrave (eds) *Restorative Juvenile Justice: Repairing the Harm of Youth Crime*. Monsey, NY: Criminal Justice Press.

Goldstein, H. (1990) *Problem-oriented Policing*. New York, NY: McGraw-Hill.

Griffiths, C.T. and Hamilton, R. (1996) 'Spiritual renewal, community revitalization and healing. Experience in traditional Aboriginal justice in Canada', *International Journal of Comparative and Applied Criminal Justice*, 20 (1): 285–310.

Herman, S. and Wasserman, C. (2001) 'A role for victims in offender reentry', *Crime and Delinquency*, 47 (3): 428–45.

Hirschi, T. (1969) *Causes of Delinquency*. Berkeley, CA: University of California Press.

Hudson, J., Galaway, B., Morris, A. and Maxwell, G. (1996) 'Introduction', in J. Hudson, B. Galaway, A. Morris and G. Maxwell (eds) *Family Group Conferences: Perspectives on Policy and Practice*. Monsey, NY: Criminal Justice Press, 1–17.

Hunter, A.J. (1985) 'Private, parochial and public social orders: the problem of crime and incivility in urban communities', in G.D. Suttles and M.N. Zald (eds) *The Challenge of Social Control: Citizenship and Institution Building in Modern Society*. Norwood, NJ: Aldex.

Karp, D. and Walther, L. (2001) 'Community reparative boards in Vermont', in G. Bazemore and M. Schiff (eds) *Restorative and Community Justice: Repairing Harm and Transforming Communities*. Cincinnati, OH: Anderson.

Levrant, S., Cullen, F., Fulton, B. and Wozniak, J. (1999) 'Reconsidering restorative justice: the corruption of benevolence revisited?', *Crime and Delinquency*, 45 (1): 3–27.

Maloney, D. (1998) 'The challenge of restorative community justice.' Address at the annual meeting of the Juvenile Justice Coalition, Washington DC, February.

Maruna, S. (2001) *Making Good: How Ex-convicts Reform and Rebuild their Lives.* Washington, DC: American Psychological Association.

Maxwell, G. and Morris, A. (1996) 'Research of family group conferencing in child welfare in New Zealand', in J. Hudson *et al.* (eds) *Family Group Conferences: Perspectives on Policy and Practice.* Monsey, NY: Criminal Justice Press, 88–111.

McCold, P. and Wachtel, B. (1998) *Restorative Policing Experiment: The Bethlehem Pennsylvania Police Family Group Conferencing Project.* Pipersville, PA: Community Service Foundation.

McKnight, J. (1995) *The Careless Society: Community and its Counterfeits.* New York, NY: Basic Books.

Moon, M., Sundt, J., Cullen, F. and Wright, J. (2000) 'Is child saving dead? Public support for rehabilitation', *Crime and Delinquency*, 46: 38–60.

Morris, A. and Maxwell, G. (2001) 'Restorative conferencing', in G. Bazemore and M. Schiff (eds) *Restorative and Community Justice: Repairing Harm and Transforming Communities.* Cincinnati, OH: Anderson.

Perry, J. and Gorcyzyk, J. (1997) ' Restructuring corrections: using market research in Vermont', *Corrections Management Quarterly*, 1 (3): 2–35.

Petersilia, J. (1999) 'Parole and prison reentry in the United States', in M. Tonry and J. Petersilia (eds) *Prisons.* Chicago, IL: University of Chicago Press.

Polk, K. (2001) 'Positive youth development, restorative justice, and the crisis of abandoned youth', in G. Bazemore and M. Schiff (eds) *Restorative and Community Justice: Repairing Harm and Transforming Communities.* Cincinnati, OH: Anderson.

Polk, K. and Kobrin, S. (1972) *Delinquency Prevention through Youth Development.* Washington, DC: Office of Youth Development.

Pranis, K. (1996) 'Communities and the justice system – turning the relationship upside down.' Paper presented to the Office of Justice Programs, US Department of Justice.

Pranis, K. (1997) 'From vision to action: church and society', *Presbyterian Church Journal of Just Thoughts*, 87 (4): 32–42.

Pranis, K. and Bazemore, G. (2001) 'Engaging community in the response to youth crime: a restorative justice approach.' Monograph prepared for the Office of Juvenile Justice and Delinquency Prevention, Balanced and Restorative Justice Project, US Department of Justice, Washington, DC.

Pranis, K., and Umbreit, M. (1992) *Public Opinion Research Challenges Perception of Wide Spread Public Demand for Harsher Punishment.* Minneapolis, MN: Minnesota Citizens' Council on Crime and Justice.

Presbyterian Church (1996) *Restoring Justice.* Louisville, KY: National Council of the Churches of Christ in the USA.

Putnam, R. (2000) *Bowling Alone: The Collapse and Revival of American Community.* New York, NY: Simon and Shuster.

Rose, D. and Clear, T. (1998) 'Incarceration, social capital and crime: implications for social disorganization theory', *Criminology*, 36 (3): 471–9.

Rosenbaum, D., Lurgio, A. and Davis, R. (1998) *The Prevention of Crime: Social and Situational Strategies. West/Wadsworth Contemporary Issues in Crime and Justice Series.* New York, NY: International Thomson.

Rutter, M. (1985) 'Resilience in the face of adversity: protective factors and resistance to psychiatric disorder', *British Journal of Psychiatry*, 147: 598–611.

Sampson, R. and Laub, J. (1993) *Crime in the Making: Pathways and Turning Points through Life.* Cambridge, MA: Harvard University Press.

Sampson, R., Rodenbush, S. and Earls, F. (1997) 'Neighborhoods and violent crime: a multi-level study of collective efficacy', *Science Magazine*, 277: 918–24.

Sampson, R. and Wilson, J. (1995) 'Toward a theory of race', in J. Hagan and R.D. Peterson (eds) *Crime and Urban Inequality.* Stanford, CA: Stanford University Press, 37–45.

Schneider, A. (1990) *Deterrence and Juvenile Crime: Results from a National Policy Experiment.* New York, NY: Springer-Verlag.

Schorr, L.B. with Schorr, D. (1989) *Within our Reach: Breaking the Cycle of Disadvantage.* New York, NY: Anchor Books, Doubleday

Schwartz, I.M. (1992) 'Public attitudes toward juvenile crime and juvenile justice: implications for public policy', in I. Schwartz (ed.) *Juvenile Justice Policy.* Lexington, MA: Lexington Books, 225–50.

Skogan, W. (1990) *Disorder and Decline: Crime and the Spiral of Decay in American Neighborhoods.* New York, NY: Free Press.

Sparrow, M., Moore, M. and Kennedy, D. (1990) *Beyond 911.* New York, NY: Basic Books.

Stuart, B. (1995) 'Sentencing circles – making "Real" differences.' Unpublished paper, Territorial Court of the Yukon.

Stuart, B. (1996) 'Circle sentencing – turning swords into ploughshares', in B. Galaway and J. Hudson (eds) *Restorative Justice: International Perspectives.* Monsey, NY: Criminal Justice Press, 193–206.

Sullivan, M. (1989) *Getting Paid: Youth, Crime and Work in the Inner City.* Ithaca, NY: Cornell University Press.

Travis, T. and Petersilia, J. (2001) 'Reentry reconsidered: a new look at an old question', *Crime and Delinquency*, 47 (3): 291–313.

Trice, H.M. and Roman, P.M. (1970) 'Delabeling, labeling, and Alcoholics Anonymous', *Social Problems*, 17: 538–46.

Umbreit, M. (1998) 'Restorative justice through victim offender mediation: a multi-site assessment', *Western Criminology Review*, 1 (1): 1–29.

Van Ness, D. (1993) 'New wine in old wineskins: four challenges of restorative justice', *Criminal Law Forum*, 4 (2): 251–76.

Van Ness, D. and Strong, K.H. (1997) *Restoring Justice.* Cincinnati OH: Anderson.

Werner, E. (1986) 'Resilient offspring of alcoholics: a longitudinal study from birth to 18', *Journal of Studies on Alcoholics*, 47: 34–40.

Wilkins, L.T. (1991) *Punishment, Crime and Market Forces.* Bookfield, VT: Dartmouth.

Young, M. (1995) 'Restorative community justice: a call to action.' Report for the National Organization for Victim Assistance, Washington, DC.

Zehr, H. (1990) *Changing Lenses: A New Focus for Crime and Justice.* Scottsdale, PA: Herald Press.

Chapter 3

Social capital and offender reintegration: making probation desistance focused

Stephen Farrall

Desistance and social capital

Introduction

In recent years increased attention has been given to the later stages of criminal careers and, in particular, to the reasons why people stop offending. From both initial and subsequent explorations a number of factors have emerged as related to the termination of offending careers. For serious persistent offenders, betrayal by co-offenders, experiencing traumatic events while offending and finding prison increasingly hard to cope with have been offered as reasons for desistance (Cusson and Pinsoneault 1986; Shover 1996; Hughes 1998). For those less committed to a 'criminal lifestyle', leaving home, family formation, entry into the labour market and disassociation from delinquent peers appear to be more frequently associated with desistance (see Sampson and Laub 1993; Warr 1998; Farrall and Bowling 1999; Farrall 2000). Many of the results of academic investigations into desistance are corroborated by autobiographies of desistance (e.g. Devlin and Turney 1999) and analyses of those autobiographies (e.g. Maruna 1997).

The purpose of this chapter is to explore the most salient of these findings in theoretical terms and, in particular, to explore desistance in relation to an emerging concept in criminology – social capital. While a conceptual link between social capital and desistance has been made in previous studies (Sampson and Laub 1993; and Laub *et al.* 1995), this contribution builds on this previous work by making the processes through which social capital encourages desistance and the role of non-custodial sentences in developing social capital the foci of the inquiry.

The socioeconomic correlates of desistance

While it is certainly true that a number of correlates of desistance have been established (see Farrall 2000, 2002; Laub and Sampson 2001 for reviews), gaining employment and family formation are two of the most commonly cited correlates. This is not to dismiss out of hand, of course, the arguments that 'internal' changes are also important in understanding desistance (Maruna 1999), nor is it to deny that serious felons make rational calculations about whether to offend or not (Shover and Thompson 1992; Tunnell 1992).

Employment

Several studies have charted the relationship between employment and desistance. Farrington *et al.* (1986: 351) noted that 'proportionally more crimes were committed by [members of the Cambridge cohort] during periods of unemployment than during periods of employment'. Mischkowitz reported that 'erratic work patterns were substituted by more stable and reliable behaviour' among his sample of desisters (1994: 313). Similar sentiments were expressed by Sampson and Laub (1993: 220–2) when they wrote that desisters were characterized as having 'good work habits and were frequently described as "hard workers"'. Similarly, Horney *et al.* found that starting work was related to reductions in offending, while ceasing to work was associated with the reinitiation of offending (1995: 665). Uggen (2000) found that those aged 27 and over were less likely to offend when provided with employment opportunities than those who were not offered such opportunities. (See also Cusson and Pinsoneault 1986; Ouimet and Le Blanc 1996.)

Family formation

Several studies have demonstrated that individuals cease to offend at about the same time that they start to form significant life partnerships (e.g. Irwin 1970; Parker 1976; Sampson and Laub 1993). Shover reported that 'The establishment of a mutually satisfying relationship with a woman was a common pattern [and] ... an important factor in the transformation of their career line' (1983: 213). More recently, Horney *et al.* (1995: 665) found that starting to cohabit with a partner (when compared to leaving one's partner) doubled the odds of desisting. Laub *et al.* (1998), provide evidence to suggest that 'good' marriages tend to grow stronger over time and in so doing are associated with reduced levels of criminality for males. Finally, as Meisenhelder (1977: 331) noted, families act as a means of certifying previous offenders as 'conventional people'.

Several studies have suggested that the experience of becoming a parent is also associated with desistance from offending (Irwin 1970: 203; Parker 1976: 41; Trasler 1979: 315; Caddle 1991: 37; Lebrich 1992: 59; Sampson and Laub 1993: 218), while other studies have also found a strong link between marriage, the formation of families and desistance (see, for example, Meisenhelder 1977, 1982; Cusson and Pinsoneault 1986; Ouimet and Le Blanc 1996; Adams 1997; Warr 1998). Summaries of these findings can be found in Ditchfield (1994), Farrall (2000, 2001) and Laub and Sampson (2001)[1].

Human and social capital

As Robison and Siles (1999: 47) note, there is now something of a debate over those social processes most appropriately associated with social capital. Some have suggested that social capital is best thought of as social connections between people (Bourdieu 1986) or that social capital is a resource which emerges from people's social ties (Coleman 1988), while others have more recently claimed that 'trust' (Fukuyama 1995) and engagement in civil society (Putnam 1995) are better ways of approaching the operationalization of social capital.[2]

Coleman (1990) refers to three types of capital – physical, human and social. Physical capital refers to the equipment which is required physically to produce something. Human capital refers to the skills and knowledge which an individual possesses. Social capital, on the other hand,

> is defined by its function. It is not a single entity but a variety of entities, with two elements in common: they all consist of some aspect of social structures, and they facilitate certain actions of actors – whether persons or corporate actors – within the structure. Like other forms of capital, social capital is productive, making possible the achievement of certain ends that in its absence would not be possible. (Coleman 1988: s.98)

The function of such a conceptualization is to identify the value of 'social capital' to social actors as resources which they can use to achieve their interests (1988: s. 101). Bourdieu's definition of social capital shares much in common with Coleman's. For Bourdieu (1986: 248–9) social capital is 'the aggregate of the actual or potential resources which are linked to [the] possession of a durable network of more or less insti-tutionalised relationships of mutual acquaintance and recognition … which provides each of its members with the backing of collectively owned capital'.

As such social capital

> originates in socially structured relations between individuals, in families and in aggregations of individuals in neighbourhoods, churches, schools and so on. These relations facilitate social action by generating a knowledge and sense of obligation, expectations, trustworthiness, information channels norms and sanctions. (Hagan and McCarthy 1997: 229)

Changes in some types of social capital alter the possibilities for various forms of social activity, and may serve to encourage the avoidance of delinquent acts in some people and the engagement in offending by others. Indeed a growing body of literature has started to link – at both conceptual and empirical levels – the relationship between social capital and the incidence of criminal events. For example, criminologists have started to chart the relationships between social capital and violent crime (see Rosenfeld *et al.*, n.d.; Hagan *et al.* 1995; Sampson *et al.* 1997; Kennedy *et al.* 1998; Moser and Lister 1999). Typically it has been found that those aggregations of individuals (e.g. communities) with lower levels of social capital experience a higher incidence of violent crime.

Because social capital is frequently conceptualized as 'socially structured relations between individuals, in families and in aggregations of individuals in neighbourhoods, churches, schools and so on' (Hagan and McCarthy 1997), it has often been operationalized in terms of family and kinship relations (Hagan *et al.* 1996; Sampson *et al.* 1999) and employment opportunities (Sampson and Laub 1993; Nagin and Paternoster 1994; Laub *et al.* 1995; Hagan 1997). Thus the current work on patterns of crime at the community level suggests a new theoretical avenue for interpreting and developing the relationships between employment, family formation and desistance observed at the individual level: *these social institutions encourage desistance by increasing an individual's stock of social capital.*[3] Consider, for example, the role of employment or, rather, for some people, the lack of it:

> Inadequate availability of employment is perhaps the biggest obstacle to successfully traversing the gap between a *troubled* adolescent and the entry into a *more stable* adulthood. (Hagan 1997: 299, emphasis added)

> Under [widespread youth unemployment], the peer group takes on a more important and more enduring dimension as the

principal (if not only) source of security, status, sense of belonging and identity. (Graham and Bowling 1995: 97)

It is contended here that employment, especially if it is in some way rewarding for the individual concerned, and family relationships which are in some way supportive, either emotionally or practically, can be understood as two of the most important ingredients of social capital for the individual in western societies (see also Sampson and Laub 1993: 18–19). This is not to say that we believe that society consists entirely of independent individuals – for the concept of social capital goes beyond mere individuals – but that it is important to understand how (and if) social capital works at an individual level and the ways in which this can be manipulated to encourage desistance. However, this begs the question whether employment and good familial relationships are the *outcomes* of social capital or the *precursors* of it?

The answer lies not in conceptualizing good family relationships and employment as *either* the precursors *or* the outcomes of social capital but, rather, as *both* the precursors and the outcomes, which echoes Coleman's dictum that 'social capital is defined by its function' (1988: s. 98). Similarly, Bourdieu (1986) writes: 'the profits which accrue from membership [of] a group are the basis of the solidarity which makes them possible.' To this end, social capital (namely, good family relationships and employment) is approached in the current analyses as both an *enabling* feature of an individual's life, and as a feature of that which *is enabled*.

The approach taken herein emphasizes the *relational* aspects of social capital. That is, those aspects of social capital which operate in social interactions between individuals and other groups and individuals. To this end this chapter touches on the extent to which social capital is 'active' or 'passive' (that is to say, pursued deliberately or created as a by-product of other social interactions); can be inherited from others (most commonly, one's parents); can become depleted or eradicated; requires investments before it can be fully utilized; and can be reactivated by others (in this case, probation officers). By focusing on the individual-level processes associated with social capital, we hope to understand more about how these processes operate in such a way that these can be manipulated in socially beneficial ways. In so doing we hope to bring the debates and issues surrounding the concept of social capital to bear on the theoretical and empirical interest in the termination of criminal careers.

'Tracking progress on probation': an innovative study

The data employed here come from a project which aimed to understand the processes that occurred during probation orders which were either conducive to desistance or which contributed to persistence. While it is true that the correlates of recidivism and desistance are well known, the mechanisms by which these correlates are produced – and in particular the role that criminal justice sanctions play in this – remain less well understood. In order better to understand the role of probation supervision in encouraging the processes associated with desistance, the project investigated the effects of probation supervision on the criminal careers and behaviour of two hundred probationers. A more thorough outline of the methodology, the rationale behind the study and its main findings can be found in Farrall (2002).[4] The general methodology builds on that developed by Burnett (see 1992, 1994, 2000, Chapter 7 this volume). Although the study was not designed to explore social capital, by investigating the role of social and personal changes as they related to desistance, the project provides the perfect basis for just such an exploration.

The existing research on the effectiveness of probation supervision had been identified as being deficient in a number of ways. Many studies were based entirely on the analysis of official records, such as probation case notes or officially recorded offending (see, *inter alia*, Radzinowicz 1958; Lloyd *et al*. 1994; May 1999), which severely limits the nature of the analyses undertaken. For example, it cannot be guaranteed that all information relevant to assessing the impact of the order will have been recorded. Did the probationer actually employ any new techniques for avoiding offending which were learnt during the order? Did the probationer really stop offending or just avoid detection?

Because so much of the probation literature ignores the social and personal circumstances which might influence an individual, it ignores the possibility that it may not have been probation supervision which aided desistance but the influence of other factor(s) – or a combination of probation and other factors.[5] There is a certain sense of irony haunting the literature with regards to this issue. Probation is a *community* penalty, but many have neglected to include the role of 'the community' in their investigations of probation supervision. This general neglect of social and personal factors is extraordinary in view of the well established fact that there is a strong link between some forms of offending and some social and personal circumstances (see, for example, the reviews of this literature in Johnson 1979; Tarling 1993; Adams 1997; Farrington 1997).

The solution to this was to understand probation interventions in the social and personal contexts in which probationers lived.

Additionally, very few research projects aimed at exploring probation outcomes have employed prospective longitudinal designs. Many researchers have therefore been unable to consider changes in variables *over time*. However, there is good reason to hypothesize that 'dynamic variables' relating to the probationer, such as changes in employment, marital status or drug dependency, may be related to probation outcomes (Andrews 1989). In recent years there has been an increasing interest in the role that dynamic variables can play in explaining successful probation outcomes. Only a longitudinal research design, which at each interview asks probationers about the sorts of problems they face, how these have changed from the time when previous interviews were conducted, how the probationer anticipates them to change in the future, and locates these in both the context of the probation order and the wider social context, can measure the effects of change in these variables and their impact on offending.

Operationalizing desistance

The operationalization of desistance employed in the current study has placed an emphasis on *gradual* changes in the rates and nature of the offences committed. Such an operationalization both better captures the true nature of desisting from offending – in which 'lulls' in offending, temporary resumption of offending and the such like are common – and provides a schema in which *reductions* in offence severity or the frequency with which offences were admitted to could be interpreted as indications of the emergence of desistance.

An important feature of this schema was that it allowed for changes in offending *trajectories* which indicated a shift in patterns of offending *towards desistance* to be charted. This entailed careful examinations of each probationer's reports of all their offending at each sweep of interviewing – the outline of the offence(s) committed, the amount of offences reported and the nature and severity of the offences. On this basis each probationer was classified into one of the five groups, as summarized in Table 3.1.[6]

Commonly observed increases in social capital

Theorizing employment and family relationships

Before considering the experiences reported by officers and pro-bationers, it is worth considering what employment and good family relationships 'do' to a person and how these might be considered

Table 3.1 Emerging desistance[7]

	Probationers' reports		Officers' reports	
	N	%	N	%
No offending	64	32	105	53
In the process of desisting	28	14	33	17
Continued offending (trivial)	20	10	15	8
Continued offending (non-trivial)	18	9	15	8
Continued offending (escalating)	27	14	30	15
Impossible to code (seen insufficiently)	42	21	1	–
Total	**199**	**100**	**199**	**100**

relevant to the issues surrounding social capital. Paid employment has the potential to achieve all the following: a reduction in 'unstructured' time and an increase in 'structured' time; an income, which enables 'home-leaving' and the establishment of 'significant' relationships; a 'legitimate' identity; an increase in self-esteem; use of an individual's energies; financial security; daily interaction with non-offenders; for men in particular, a reduction in the time spent in single-sex, peer-aged groups; the means by which an individual may meet his or her future partner; and ambition and goals, such as promotion at work.

Good family relationships share some of these features. An increase in 'structured' time and a decrease in 'unstructured' time are common features of marriage and family formation. Similarly such relationships can provide people with legitimate identities and increase self-esteem, contentment and emotional support. As Meisenhelder observed almost a quarter of a century ago:

> the family, as a major source of relational attachments, became a secure place for the respondents within the conventional community. These relational ties provided the respondents with both a resource for use when confronting exiting problems and a tie to conformity ... The social support of the family also seemed to regenerate the respondents' determination to abandon criminal behaviour. (1977: 327–8)

As well as representing something which could be jeopardized by further conviction, families help to structure time and activities.

Employment and familial support networks also represent two of the most frequently cited sources of social capital: 'Strong social relations ... represent social and psychological resources that individuals can draw on' (Laub *et al.* 1995: 93–4). As well as providing a wage, employment provides people with friendship networks and entry into other social entities such as work-based clubs or societies. Good familial relationships provide a further resource: advice on problems faced; loans of money or expensive items; contacts with parental friends; somewhere to live when other accommodation proves unsatisfactory; and so on. Social relationships forged at work and at home create a sense of obligation, reciprocal trust and provide individuals with information channels and knowledge. In short, they provide people with social capital.

Opening the 'black box' of social capital

Because the interviews were focused on changes in each probationer's circumstances, the factors which had led to these changes and the impact (especially in terms of offending) of these changes, the data set captured the processes by which social capital was activated in the lives of the probationers. In many instances, working parents either offered their sons and daughters work (if they were self-employed) or found opportunities for them via contacts they had through their own employment. For example, after Jerry [067] had got into trouble and was given a probation order, his father found him work with his delivery firm. By the end of his order, Jerry – who enjoyed working with his father – was in the process of desisting. Similarly, Jamie [115], who also showed signs of desisting, also found work via his father, albeit somewhat less smoothly:

> *How did you get this job then?*
> My old man was working with some bloke, he kept messing about ... so my old man got rid of him. I said I'd come and work [with my dad] I used to work with [him] all the time see, but [he] goes to me 'I ain't fucking having you work for me again, if you are going to keep messing about and going back in [prison]', so I says 'no, I ain't going back in there – give me a job'. So he gave me a job and I ain't been back [to prison].

Both these young men, having little of the sorts of social capital which would have found them work (such as previous or current employment experience), were reliant upon their respective fathers for formulating routes into employment for them. In this respect, each of them was able to 'inherit' their father's social capital. One of the probation officers interviewed about Jamie reported that his self-esteem had been increased as a result of his starting work:

> He seemed to be really motivated about these jobs … He had an identity with the job, he apparently enjoyed the job, he was working very late, getting rid of his energy that way. It appeared to me that the employment was where he got his identity and got a role for himself. (Jamie's probation officer, 3rd interview)

In other cases, probationers relied on their friends for employment opportunities. Jacob [057] was 21 years old when he started his probation order. He had received his first conviction when 15 years old and had in all ten convictions for a range of offences. When he was seen at the second interview he was asked to describe the 'biggest single change in his life' since the previous interview. He said 'getting a job', which he had been offered to him by a friend, and which he said had 'given me security, money, something to aim for. It's made me "come out of my shell". Made me behave myself because now I have more to lose'. He'd been working in a bakery as an assistant manager and at the third interview reported how the bakery was opening a new shop and in which he would be given a percentage of the profits. When asked again to describe the biggest change since the previous interview, Jacob said that he was 'developing, maturing in myself' and described himself as being 'more confident' (a fact which he attributed to having started work).

Feelings of confidence stemming from employment were common among the probationers in the current sample. Roger [150] reported that his work 'had given me confidence, meet people, get out there. Instead of before, I was stuck in doors, moping about'. Roger's employment not only improved his confidence but (and more importantly in terms of developing his own stocks of social capital) it also changed *others'* opinions of him. Roger's probation officer reported how, by starting work, his probationer's family no longer saw him as 'a druggie':

> because he is now working and providing for the household, all his pressures [with his family] have gone down. He was on the verge

of actually being thrown out, and [made] homeless, by them. And that has receded 'cause he is becoming – from their point of view – a productive and constructive member of the family, and therefore working *with* them instead of *against* them. Which is often the perception of families with drug addicts – 'no matter what they do, they still end up on drugs'.

Roger's case illuminates the role of social capital in desistance in two respects. First, Roger was able to consolidate his position in the family home and, as such, he remained in a stable environment (representing an increase in his social capital) which helped him to remain drug free. Secondly, it demonstrates how, in some cases, social capital (in this case family support) can be withdrawn from 'unco-operative' individuals. In addition to this, Roger also reported how having got one job, he felt that he could find other jobs in the future: 'I have got the confidence to go out and get another job. Whereas before, I didn't. I wouldn't bother.'

Clearly, then, families, by using their own connections to work, can help probationers enter (or re-enter) employment, suggesting that families represent a form of social capital. In some cases, gaining employment for young males appeared to be related to their father's employment and, as such, 'actively' developed.[8] As such it would appear that a family's social capital (where it exists) can be called upon in times of need. However, while this *gets* the probationer the job, *keeping* the job requires an investment of his or her own time and efforts. This is perhaps the key in understanding how social capital 'inherited' from one's parents can be transformed into part of the stocks of one's own social capital. Just as Laub *et al.* (1998) conceptualized marriage as akin to an investment process, so the creation of social capital requires its own investments. For example, one probationer [014] who started work during his order deliberately cut down on his alcohol intake so at not to jeopardize his new job. When seen for the last time, he had been promoted at work and said that he wished to avoid further trouble as he now had 'too much to lose' – a reference perhaps to his developing stock of social capital and the risks posed to this by further convictions? If this is the case, and it should be noted that many desisters report not wanting to offend again as they have 'too much to lose' (see Burnett 1992), then social capital represents not just a means for desisting but also a reason for continued 'reform'.

As well as helping their sons and daughters find employment, families provided a 'safe haven' which probationers could call upon in times of need. This was highlighted by the experiences of Sammy [153], who had almost died as a result of injecting into an artery in his arm. On leaving hospital, Sammy started living with his mother again after over ten years of living independently. Initially she had been reluctant to allow her son to come home to live with her on account of his drug use. However, after being contacted by Sammy's probation officer, she consented when she realized that Sammy would be homeless otherwise. When he was interviewed for the third time he was still living with his mother and reported that he had stopped offending as he had given up heroin.

There were several other examples of probation officers acting as a link between their probationers and their estranged families. In other words, as helping the probationer to 'activate' his or her social capital resources. Tracy [054], who had not got on well with her mother for several years and had lived apart from her family for several years, provided another instance of such work:

> She came here very, very distressed. It was a Friday, she had nothing, she felt completely isolated, no where to go, nothing to do all weekend, didn't know how she was going to cope. And I actually made phone calls to her mother and her sister and explained that I thought that she was trying, but did need some support, and the latest I've heard is – it's tentative, but I think communication … y'know sometimes people take notice if a probation officer rings them up and says 'I'm concerned about your sister – she does need a helping hand here', and I think that that is probably one thing that I have done. It is still very fragile of course.

At the third interview, Tracy herself recounted this story about how she had come to probation 'in a right state' and her officer had phoned her family to ask them for their support on her behalf: 'she rang round my family and helped me out with bus fares'.

Dominic [227], who eventually desisted, was in his mid-20s when he was given a six-month probation order for possession of heroin. His experiences illustrate how families of origin are often better equipped to help probationers desist than families of formation. Dominic had been an addict for about two years and was spending about £80 a day on heroin. He had managed to keep his addiction secret from his wife and their children (all of whom he lived with) and his wider family. Following his arrest, however, he was no longer able to conceal his heroin use, and his wife refused to let him stay in their house. His parents had initially 'disowned' him and, for a while, Dominic had lived with friends. By the time of the first interview, Dominic's parents were helping him to get off heroin, and his expenditure on heroin was down to £20 a day. At the time of the second interview his officer said that Dominic had 'made a big effort at getting off heroin', and from his own descriptions of his life at that time, it appeared that Dominic had successfully stopped using heroin. The motivation for this appeared to have been his desire to return to his family, and Dominic had indeed moved back with his wife and children. His parents, however, were sometimes still suspicious of him: 'If I look pale one day, they think I'm back on drugs again.'

At the third interview Dominic and his family were considering a move away from the area in which they had been living. This, it was hoped, would make it easier for Dominic to avoid other drug users and dealers in that area – although he had successfully avoided them so far. Dominic had until recently owed various dealers around £1,000 and, as such, had still not completely extricated himself from his involvement with 'deviant' others. However, his parents had started more readily to accept that he had stopped using heroin and had paid off the money which he owed to various dealers. Dominic reported that they were 'coming round for hours and being really nice' to him. Dominic said that he felt 'quite shocked' at this turn-around in their attitude, which he likened to being 'given another chance'. While Dominic appeared to have stopped using heroin and ceased his involvement in drug-related activities *before* his family paid off his debts to dealers, their continuing support and help in paying the dealers the money Dominic owed them encouraged him and helped to consolidate his desistance.

In some cases families either could not or would not help their offspring. Matthew [172] had started his probation order heroin-dependent and while still using heroin had burgled his parents' home. Shortly after this he started and successfully completed a residential de-tox and was, as a result, heroin-free. He was, however, then convicted for the earlier burglary of his parents' house and, as a result, expelled from his parents' home by them. This in turn led to the probationer living 'rough' on the streets and his eventual return to heroin use. He did not complete his probation order.

Summarizing the relationship between social capital and desistance

The vast majority of instances of the activation of social capital which were observed were related to the probationers' family and, in particular, their families of origin. That families of origin represent a form of social capital is, in itself, not a new finding (see Coleman 1988: s. 109–13). In the context sample under consideration, this is even less of a surprise. Because the sample consisted entirely of those aged 17–35 at the outset of their probationer orders, many of the sample were still dependent upon their families of origin to various degrees, and some had yet to form their own families. Thus families of origin represented the family group most commonly available to the probationers. Families of formation, even where they did exist for probationers, and while they provided the motivation to desist, did not often represent very much of a resource. Again this is hardly surprising: such families consisted of individuals who had little or no resources available to call upon – children (often very young at this point in many probationer's lives) or partners, who frequently were either in no better position than the probationers or who were absent.

The lack of evidence regarding employment as a form of social capital may be the result of the relatively short period of time during which data were collected. Many of the probation orders (and hence the fieldwork) were of two or less years' duration and, as such, the ties to work colleagues and wider forms of integration were perhaps less well established by the time the fieldwork had been completed. It must be remembered, of course, that families of origin have years during which the ties and obligations associated with social capital can be cultivated and as such they may be more amenable to exploitation in times of need. Thus the finding in the current sample that the activation of social capital was most frequently associated with the family of origin is a reflection of the 'span' of the fieldwork.

From the data analyses a number of tentative statements can be made about how social capital is related to desistance. While family/parental social capital can be 'inherited', there was some evidence to suggest that it required additional investments on the part of the probationer. It is not enough merely to obtain work – employers expect regular attendance and the probationer must obviously do so if he or she is to avoid dismissal. Similarly, because the family represented the main source of social capital for many of the probationers in the cohort followed, it was almost essential for probationers to comply with the wishes of their family. Failure to be seen as wishing to desist or being perceived as not being wholeheartedly behind efforts to desist could result in families withdrawing their support and, as such, access to their capital. However, and importantly, probation officers were well placed to be able to intervene in order to re-establish access to family social capital. The evidence available suggests that probation officers were sometimes better placed than probationers actively to call upon or activate this form of social capital, and that this was best achieved not through 'traditional' counselling techniques but via direct appeals to family members. Through these ways, officers reconnected probationers to their family's social capital.

Discussion and conclusion: adding investments in social capital to probation work

Policy suggestions for increasing individual probationer's social capital

Probation services already try to improve the human capital of the individuals they supervise by referring them to employment partnerships or by running short courses in 'thinking skills', safe drug use and so on. However, as Crow (2000: 121) has noted, studies of employment schemes have frequently been unable to demonstrate an impact on offending, a finding which he suggests is in part due to their being unable to address the wider problem of mass unemployment. In other words, such schemes were ultimately unable to act in such a way as to improve their participant's social capital as they ultimately had little direct control of or influence over wider meso and macro-level circumstances – in this case employment rates.

Human capital can be relatively easily gained. For example, group programmes can teach employment skills and partnerships can help to develop these but, ultimately, if local social and economic circumstances do not encourage employment then no assistance – regardless of intensity, design or commitment of staff – will be of any help. This perhaps suggests that the reason why 'traditional' one-to-one probation supervision and more recent innovations such as group programmes have experienced only limited success in helping probationers to desist is because, despite their good intentions, such interventions are unable to get at the heart of the problem facing many of those on probation: *low levels of social capital*. As such the strengthening of social capital should become one of the aims of social and criminal justice policy and accordingly the focus of much of the work undertaken by probation services.

How exactly should this proceed? Laub *et al.* (1995), building on Sampson and Laub (1993), point to two substantive areas in which they felt criminal justice policy could make potentially fruitful interventions: strengthening marriages and increasing attachments to the labour force. Laub *et al.* argue that counselling should be available so that offenders ... become better spouses and [to] help them through crises in their marriages by making appropriate counselling readily available. Helping offenders repair personal relationships, salvage marriages or improve interpersonal relationships so that permanent relationships are possible will all in the long run, contribute to law-abiding behaviour. (1995: 100–1)

These sorts of provisions already exist in England and Wales, although their use would not appear to be widespread on the basis of some of the findings from the current study. From analyses discussed in the main report of these findings (Farrall 2002: Ch. 6, Table 6.5, Ch. 9, Table 9.2) it would appear that officers did *not* readily address the family-related obstacles to desistance which they had reported their probationers as facing. In some respects this is understandable: probation work is currently obsessed with addressing 'offending related' factors. However, this is perhaps mistaken. Probation officers should not focus on 'offending related' factors but, rather, on '*desistance* related' factors. As Shover and Henderson have commented:

[current repressive crime control policies] ignore entirely the theoretically obvious: Offenders' behaviour can be changed not only by increasing threat but by also increasing *legitimate opportunities*. It is important to make this point if for no other reason than the fact that increased legitimate opportunities extend the choices to offenders. (1995: 243, emphasis in original)

If probation work became desistance focused rather than offending related, officers may feel that they had a clearer mandate to help probationers tackle their family problems. From the wider investigations into desistance, and from the analyses reported herein, the family has appeared to be a particularly strong resource for those attempting to desist to call upon. Families are (often) better resourced than individuals, have wider networks which penetrate other social circles to which the individual may not be able to gain access and, for some people, provide an avenue to escape from more harmful social contexts.[9] The call for a greater focus on probationers' families as a source of social capital which might aid desistance may in turn result in the greater involvement of officers in the attempts to tackle the 'family problems' and hence a greater success in actually resolving such problems.

Laub *et al.* (1995) also suggest that more should be done to increase the job prospects of probationers. They suggest that 'any probationer or parolee who is not working should be required, as a condition ..., to obtain work or appropriate job training'. This is, perhaps, rather draconian. No one should be forced into work if he or she does not wish to. However, the basic premise is still sound and, as such, begs the question: what can probation services do to alter significantly local economic contexts in such a way as to increase social capital and reduce offending?

One recent development in the UK does offer the hope that probation services will be able to alter local contexts. Surrey and Inner London Probation Services have both initiated schemes aimed at developing local employment opportunities which will meet the needs of their caseloads. Interestingly, the project in Surrey aimed to provide 'sheltered employment' in the form of a recycling scheme. Early indications (Sarno *et al.* 1999) are encouraging, but a final evaluation is still a long way off.

How might such schemes be developed in the future? It is not always easy to find work – and less easy still if one has few skills, a poor or non-existent employment record, a criminal conviction and knows few other people who work. Perhaps, then, probation services should – as well as referring some probationers to employment schemes – attempt to *create jobs locally* for their caseloads. In other words, probation services should provide sheltered employment in the form of schemes like the recycling scheme in Surrey. Probation services could find themselves being in a position to provide employment to suit a range of employment skills and needs. For example, a recycling scheme with its own chain of shops to sell reclaimed goods and goods made from recycled materials would provide the following types of posts: people to collect the goods for recycling; people to sort them for sale or recycling; people to make new goods from old materials or to refurbish partially damaged goods; people to work in the shops; clerical assistants to process payments (to employees) and supervise revenue from shops: and so on. Clearly, not all these skills could be met by probation caseloads, but a number of them could be. The aim of such a scheme would be to get people to the first rung of the employment ladder: a job. Employment provides a record of 'employability' in the form of people who can be approached to provide references and, as such, may well provide the basis of further jobs in other occupations. By offering work with a caring employer (the probation service) who understands the problems facing probationers, such as needing time off to attend court and probation appointments, and who is committed to a notion of social justice, schemes like those sketched above may be able to make a greater contribution to securing 'good' employment for probationers than has previously been the case.

Desistance focused not *offending related*

On the basis of the findings of this study such a research agenda should focus upon two main areas:

1. How probationers' social capital can be increased in such as way as to foster desistance.
2. What individual officers/the wider probation service can do about addressing not just offending-related factors but also *desistance*-related needs.

The second of these is perhaps the more straightforward of the two suggestions. Desistance, it is widely becoming accepted, is often the result of attachments to the labour force or to marriage partners or both (see, for example, Sampson and Laub 1993). The current research has found evidence to support these claims. The project also found that officers appeared to be reluctant to work with their probationers to address family and employment obstacles. Yet when officers *did* assist their probationers, their work appeared to supplement the efforts of the probationers and to be associated with greater rates of success (Farrall 2002: Ch. 9, Table 9.2b). More effort should be focused on how officers can support probationers address either their existing family problems or attempting to prepare them for events like parenthood. Similarly, more effort should be focused on getting probationers into employment (Bridges 1998). This might entail a shift in the orientation of probation work. One probationer [065], when asked what would prevent him from reoffending, replied:

Something to do with self progression. Something to show people what they are capable of doing. I thought that that was what [my officer] should be about. It's finding people's abilities and nourishing and making them work for those things. Not very consistent with going back on what they have done wrong and trying to work out why – 'cause it's all going around on what's *happened* – what you've already been punished for – why not go forward into something … For instance, you might be good at writing – push that forward, progress that, rather than saying 'well look, why did you kick that bloke's head in? Do you think we should go back into anger management courses?' when all you want to be is a writer. Does that make any sense to you at all? *Yeah,*

yeah. To sum it up, you're saying you should look forwards not back. Yeah. I know that you do have to look back to a certain extent to make sure that you don't end up like that [again]. The whole order seems to be about going back and back and back. There doesn't seem to be much 'forward'.

Increasing individuals' social capital will probably ultimately mean helping probationers address family problems providing them with legitimate employment, both of which will in turn help to foster the sorts of ties and social contacts which allow for the development of social capital. It is unclear exactly how well probation services will be able to influence local economic conditions or be able to reorientate their work towards desistance-focused matters. The suggestion made earlier, that probation services develop in some way employment schemes in which they are able to offer probationers work rather than referring them to other agencies, may be only one among a number of solutions.

Finally, these suggestions entail a further point. Namely, a step back from the *exclusive* focus on cognitive behavioural work which has dominated the probation work and What Works? agendas in recent years. As Rex (1999: 373; 2001) has correctly noted, even the original architects of such programmes saw them as *complementing* the social and economic problems faced by probationers. This is not to suggest that cognitive behavioural work is to be abandoned but, rather, that while it correctly focuses on increasing probationers' human capital, it is unable to address the wider social contexts in which these probationers live and as such is unable to address such social and economic needs.

Acknowledgements

The author would like to express his thanks to Roger Hood and the staff at the Probation Studies Unit, Centre for Criminological Research, Oxford University and to the staff of the probation services from which cases were selected for their support during the fieldwork on which this chapter is based. Versions of this chapter were greatly improved following comments from the editors and Susanne Karstedt. The final word of thanks must go to the 199 probationers who were kind enough to discuss their experiences of probation supervision and their criminal careers.

Notes

1   Despite the evidence to support the claims above, a number of reservations can be raised about the relationship of the factors mentioned and desistance. First of all, with regards to the 'employment–desistance' relationship, there is a wealth of studies describing the extent of crime at work (Ditton 1977; Henry 1978). More recently, Graham and Bowling found that employment is not associated with desistance for males aged 17–25 (1996: 56, Table 5.2). Similarly, numerous studies have failed to find an empirical connection between partnership and desistance (Knight *et al.* 1977; Rand 1987: 137; Mulvey and Aber 1988). Cusson and Pinsonneault (1986: 79–80) and Mischkowitz (1994: 319) followed West (1982: 101–4) in arguing that what is important (in terms of facilitating desistance) is not marriage *per se*, but, rather, the *quality* of the relationship. Finally, Mulvey and Aber (1988) and Rand (1987) were unable to find any firm link between parenthood and desistance.

At least some of these negative findings, however, can be reassessed following the findings of Uggen (2000) and Ouimet and Le Blanc (1996), which suggest that the impact of various life events upon an individual's offending is age graded. For example, Ouimet and Le Blanc (1996: 92) suggest that it is only from around the mid-20s that cohabitation with a woman was associated with desistance for the males in their sample. In a similar vein, Uggen (2000: 542) suggests that work appears to be a turning point in the criminal careers of those offenders aged over 27, while it has a marginal effect on the offending of younger offenders. Many of the earlier studies concerning the factors associated with desistance were unaware of this caveat and as such their findings that there was no impact of employment or partnership on desistance must be treated accordingly. For example, some of the earliest investigations of the relationship between employment and desistance relied upon relatively young populations. For example, Rand's (1987) sample was under 26 years of age, the members of Mulvey and La Rosa's (1986) sample were all between 15 and 20 years of age (average age 18) and, more recently, Graham and Bowling's (1995) sample were aged 17–25. Similarly, early investigations of the relationship between marriage and desistance were also based on relatively young populations: Mulvey and Arber's (1988) sample were aged between 16 and 19 years; Pezzin's (1995) were between 14 and 22; Rand's (1987) were under 26; Knight *et al.*'s (1977) sample were all under 21; and the later extension of Knight *et al.*'s analyses (Osborn and West 1979) followed these men until they were 22–23.

2   While trust and political participation are deserving of the attention of those interested in social capital, the conceptualization of social capital adopted for the purposes of the current analyses draws more directly from the earlier definitions of social capital. This is for two reasons. First, the work which has emphasized trust and civic engagement has been used at the meso and

macro levels of empirical investigation (e.g. Putnam 1995), while the current interest is with micro-level measures of social capital and its influence on the lives and offending careers of specific individuals. Secondly, while engagement in civic processes, etc., is readily accepted by the author to be *one* measure of social capital, it would appear that the emphasis placed on connections and social ties between people more easily fits with the current preoccupation (the processes of desistance from offending) and is in keeping with similar work in this vein (see Sampson and Laub 1993; Hagan 1994; Hagan *et al.* 1995).

3   In this respect, social capital, as Merton points out, represents a 'post-mature scientific discovery' (1995: 23, fn. 46). That is to say that it was technically achievable, understandable and its implications appreciable in some previous time.

4   Six probation services in England were recruited into the study, and in these a number of probation offices (in all 22) selected for fieldwork. All probationers aged 17–35 years and starting probation or combination orders of 6–24 months duration between the start of October 1997 and the end of March 1998 were eligible for inclusion in the study – regardless of offences committed, gender or race. The achieved sample was representative of English and Welsh probation caseloads when examined for age, gender, previous convictions and the offence for which the order was imposed. See Farrall (2002: ch. 3) for further details.

5   A point which few studying probation outcomes appear to have recognized (or been willing to admit to having recognized). Worrall (1997) is an exception. She writes: '[people] stop committing crimes for many reasons and the sentence they receive may be only one (and possibly the least significant) of several influential factors' (1997: 13).

6   The limitations of this approach are that estimations of desistance are made over a relatively short period of time (two years) and, as Farrington (1994: 528) has pointed out, periods of up to anything between seven and ten years without offending are no guarantee of desistance. To allow for this, it is intended to check cohort members' convictions at regular intervals.

7   A sufficient number of interviews to assess the probationer's offending trajectory had been completed with *both* the probationer and his or her supervising probation officers in 154 of the 199 cases. Of these 154, 109 (71 per cent) 'agreed' over the probationer's offending trajectory.

8   Without such routes into employment, these young men may have found gaining work harder. This suggests that criminal justice systems which are overly reliant on imprisonment may ultimately help to reinforce intergenerational patterns of offending (Farrington *et al.* 1998). Without working fathers who can provide a route into employment, many young males may find it harder to embark on one of the clearest pathways away from crime – a job.

9   This is not, however, to suggest that all families share these characteristics, or have them to the same degree. There are, of course, several scenarios

which one could imagine in which increased contact with one's family may be harmful for the individual concerned. In such cases other forms of social capital will require developing.

References

Adams, K. (1997) 'Developmental aspects of adult crime', in T. Thornberry (ed.) *Developmental Theories of Crime and Delinquency*. London: Transaction Press.

Andrews, D. (1989) 'Recidivism is predictable and can be influenced', *Focus on Correctional Research*, 1 (2): 11–18.

Bourdieu, P. (1986) 'The forms of social capital', in J.G. Richardson, (ed.) *Handbook of Theory and Research for the Sociology of Education*. New York, NY: Greenwood.

Bridges, A. (1998) *Increasing the Employability of Offenders*. Probation Studies Unit Report 5.

Burnett, R. (1992) *The Dynamics of Recidivism*. Oxford: Centre for Criminological Research, University of Oxford.

Burnett, R. (1994) 'The odds of going straight: offenders own predictions', in *Sentencing, Quality and Risk: Proceedings of the 10th Annual Conference on Research and Information in the Probation Service*, University of Loughborough, Midlands Probation Training Consortium, Birmingham.

Burnett, R. (2000) 'Understanding criminal careers through a series of in-depth interviews', *Offender Programs Report*, 4 (1).

Caddle, D. (1991) *Parenthood Training for Young Offenders: An Evaluation of Courses in Young Offender Institutions. Research and Planning Unit Paper 63*, London: Home Office.

Coleman, J.S. (1988) 'Social capital in the creation of human capital', *American Journal of Sociology* 94 (Suppl): s95–s120.

Coleman, J.S. (1990) *Foundations of Social Theory*. London: Belknap Press.

Crow, I. (2000) 'Evaluating initiatives in the community', in V. Jupp *et al.* (eds) *Doing Criminological Research*, London: Sage.

Cusson, M. and Pinsonneault, P. (1986) 'The decision to give up crime', in D.B. Cornish and R.V. Clarke (eds) *The Reasoning Criminal*. New York, NY: Springer-Verlag.

Devlin, A. and Turney, B. (eds) (1999) *Going Straight*. Winchester: Waterside Press.

Ditchfield, J. (1994) *Family Ties and Recidivism: The Main Findings of the Literature. Home Office Research Bulletin 36*. London: Home Office.

Ditton, J. (1977) *Part-time Crime: An Ethnography of Fiddling and Pilferage*. London: Macmillan.

Farrall, S. (2000) 'Introduction', in S. Farrall (ed.) *The Termination of Criminal Careers*. Aldershot: Ashgate.

Farrall, S. (2002) 'Rethinking what works with offenders: Probation, social context and desistance from crime', Cullompton: Willan.

Farrall, S. and Bowling, B. (1999) 'Structuration, human development and desistance from crime', *British Journal of Criminology*, 39 (2): 252–67.

Farrington, D.P. (1994) 'Human development and criminal careers', in M. Maguire *et al.* (eds) *The Oxford Handbook of Criminology* (1st edn). Oxford: Clarendon Press.

Farrington, D.P. (1997) 'Human development and criminal careers', in M. Maguire *et al.* (eds) *The Oxford Handbook of Criminology* (2nd edn). Oxford: Clarendon Press.

Farrington, D.P., Gallagher, B., Morley, L., St Ledger, R.J. and West, D.J. (1986) 'Unemployment, school leaving and crime', *British Journal of Criminology*, 26 (4): 335–56.

Farrington, D.P., Lambert, S. and West, D.J. (1998) 'Criminal careers of two generations of family members in the Cambridge Study in Delinquent Development', in *Studies on Crime and Crime Prevention*. Oslo: Scandinavian University Press.

Fukuyama, F. (1995) 'Social capital and the global ecomony', *Foreign Affairs*, 74 (5): 89–103.

Graham, J. and Bowling, B. (1995) *Young People and Crime. HORS* 145. London: HMSO.

Hagan, J. (1994) *Crime and Disrepute*. London: Pine Forge Press.

Hagan, J. (1997) 'Crime and capitalization: toward a developmental theory of street crime in America', in T. Thornberry (ed.) *Developmental Theories of Crime and Delinquency*. New Brunswick, NJ: Transaction Press.

Hagan, J., MacMillan, R. and Wheaton, B. (1996) 'New kid in town: social capital and the life course effects of family migration on children', *American Sociological Review*, 61: 368–85.

Hagan, J. and McCarthy, B. (1997) *Mean Streets*. Cambridge: Cambridge University Press.

Hagan, J., Merkens, H. and Boehnke, K. (1995) 'Delinquency and disdain: social capital and the control of right-wing extremism amongst East and West Berlin youth', *American Journal of Sociology*, 100 (4): 1028–52.

Henry, S. (1978) *The Hidden Economy: The Context and Control of Borderline Crime*. Oxford: Martin Robertson.

Horney, J., Osgood, D.W. and Haen Marshall, I. (1995) 'Criminal careers in the short term: intra-individual variability in crime and its relation to local life circumstances', *American Sociological Review*, 60: 655–73.

Hughes, M. (1998) 'Turning points in the lives of young inner-city men forgoing destructive criminal behaviours: a qualitative study', *Social Work Research*, 22: 143–51.

Irwin, J. (1970) *The Felon*. Englewood Cliffs, NJ: Prentice Hall.

Johnson, J.E. (1979) *Juvenile Delinquency and its Origins*. Cambridge: Cambridge University Press.

Kennedy, B. with others (1998) 'Social capital, income inequality, and firearm violent crime', *Social Science and Medicine*, 47 (1): 7–17.

Knight, B.J., Osborn, S.G. and West, D.J. (1977) 'Early marriage and criminal tendency in males', *British Journal of Criminology*, 17 (4): 348–60.

Laub, J., Nagin, D. and Sampson, R. (1998) 'Trajectories of change in criminal offending: good marriages and the desistance process', *American Sociological Review,* 63: 225–38.

Laub, J.H. and Sampson, R.J. (2001) 'Understanding desistance from crime', *Crime and Justice: An Annual Review of Research,* 28: 1–70.

Laub, J., Sampson, R., Corbett, R. and Smith, J. (1995) 'The public policy implications of a life-course perspective on crime', in H. Barlow (ed.) *Crime and Public Policy.* Oxford: Westview Press.

Leibrich, J. (1993) *Straight to the Point: Angles on Giving up Crime.* Otago, New Zealand: University of Otago Press.

Lloyd, C., Mair, G. and Hough, M. (1994) *Explaining Reconviction Rates: A Critical Analysis. Home Office Research and Planning Unit Report* 136. London: HMSO.

Maruna, S. (1997) 'Going straight: desistance from crime and life narratives of reform', *The Narrative Study of Lives,* 5: 59–93.

Maruna, S. (1999) 'Criminology, desistance, and the psychology of the stranger', in D. Canter, and L. Alison (eds) *The Social Psychology of Crime: Groups, Teams and Networks.* Aldershot: Ashgate.

May, C. (1999) *Explaining Reconviction Following a Community Sentence: The Role of Social Factors. Home Office Research Study* 192. London: HMSO.

Meisenhelder, T. (1977) 'An exploratory study of exiting from criminal careers', *Criminology,* 15 (3): 319–34.

Meisenhelder, T. (1982) 'Becoming normal: certification as a stage in exiting from crime', *Deviant Behaviour,* 3: 137–53.

Merton, R. (1995) 'Opportunity structure: the emergence, diffusion and differentiation of a sociological concept', in F. Adler and W. Laufer (eds) *The Legacy of Anomie Theory.* London: Transaction Books.

Mischkowitz, R. (1994) 'Desistance from a delinquent way of life?', in E.G.M. Weitekamp and H.J. Kerner (eds) *Cross-national Longitudinal Research on Human Development and Criminal Behaviour.* Kluwer Academic.

Moser, C. and Lister, S. (eds) (1999) *Violence and Social Capital. LCR Sustainable Development Working Paper* 5, Washington, DC: World Bank.

Mulvey, E.P. and Aber, M. (1988) 'Growing out of delinquency: development and desistance', in R.L. Jenkins and W.K. Brown (eds) *The Abandonment of Delinquent Behaviour: Promoting the Turnaround.* New York, NY: Praeger.

Mulvey, E.P. and LaRosa, J.F. (1986) 'Delinquency cessation and adolescent development: preliminary data', *American Journal of Orthopsychiatry,* 56 (2): 212–24.

Nagin, D. and Paternoster, P. (1994) 'Personal capital and social control: the deterrence implications of a theory of individual differences in criminal offending', *Criminology,* 32 (4): 581–606.

Osborn, S. and West, D. (1979) 'Marriage and delinquency: a postscript', *British Journal of Criminology,* 18 (3): 254–56.

Ouimet, M. and Le Blanc, M. (1996) 'The role of life experiences in the continuation of the adult criminal career', *Criminal Behaviour and Mental Health,* 6: 73–97.

Parker, H. (1976) 'Boys will be men: brief adolescence in a down-town neighbourhood', in G. Mungham and G. Pearson (eds) *Working Class Youth Culture*. London: Routledge.

Pezzin, L.E. (1995) 'Earning prospects, matching effects and the decision to terminate a criminal career', *Journal of Quantitative Criminology*, 11 (1): 29–50.

Putnam, R. (1995) 'Bowling alone: America's declining social capital', *Journal of Democracy*, 6: 65–78.

Radzinowicz, L. (ed.) (1958) *The Results of Probation*, London: Macmillan.

Rand, A. (1987) 'Transitional life events and desistance from delinquency and crime', in M.E. Wolfgang *et al.* (eds) *From Boy to Man, from Delinquency to Crime*. Chicago, IL: University of Chicago Press.

Rex, S. (1999) 'Desistance from offending: experiences of probation', *Howard Journal of Criminal Justice*, 38 (4): 366–83.

Rex, S. (2001) 'Beyond cognitive behaviouralism? Reflections on the effectiveness literature', in A. Bottoms, *et al.* (eds) *Community Penalties: Change and Challenges*. Cullompton: Willan Publishing.

Robison, L.J. and Siles, M.E. (1999) 'Social capital and household income distributions in the US: 1980–1990', *Journal of Socio-economics*, 28: 43–93.

Rosenfeld, R., Messner, S. and Baumer, E. (n.d.) 'Social capital and homicide.' Unpublished monograph.

Sampson, R.J. and Laub, J.H. (1993) *Crime in the Making: Pathways and Turning Points through Life*. London: Harvard University Press.

Sampson, R., Morenoff, J. and Earls, F. (1999) 'Beyond social capital: spatial dynamics of collective efficacy for children', *American Sociological Review*, 64: 633–60.

Sampson, R., Raudenbush, S. and Earls, F. (1997) 'Neighbourhoods and violent crime: a multi-level study of collective efficacy', *Science*, 277: 918–24.

Sarno, C., Hough, M., Nee, C. and Herrington, V. (1999) *Probation Employment Schemes in Inner London and Surrey – an Evaluation*, Home Office Research Findings 89. London: Home Office.

Shover, N. (1983) 'The later stages of ordinary property offender careers', *Social Problems*, 31(2): 208–18.

Shover, N. (1996) *Great Pretenders: Pursuits and Careers of Persistent Thieves*. Oxford: Westview Press.

Shover, N. and Henderson, B. (1995) 'Repressive crime control and male persistent thieves', in H. Barlow (ed.) *Crime and Public Policy*. Oxford: Westview Press.

Shover, N. and Thompson, C. (1992) 'Age, differential expectations and crime desistance', *Criminology*, 30 (1): 89–104.

Tarling, R. (1993) *Analysing Offending*. London: HMSO.

Trasler, G. (1979) 'Delinquency, recidivism and desistance', *British Journal of Criminology*, 19: (4): 314–322.

Tunnell, K.D. (1992) *Choosing Crime*. Chicago, IL: Nelson-Hall.

Uggen, C. (2000) 'Work as a turning point in the life course of criminals: a duration model of age, employment and recidivism', *American Sociological Review*, 67: 529–46.

Warr, M. (1998) 'Life-course transitions and desistance from crime', *Criminology*, 36 (2): 183–215.

West, D.J. (1982) *Delinquency: Its Roots, Careers and Prospects*. London: Heinemann.

Worrall, A. (1997) *Punishment in the Community*. London: Longman.

Part II
Methodological Considerations

Chapter 4

Connecting desistance and recidivism: measuring changes in criminality over the lifespan

Shawn D. Bushway, Robert Brame and Raymond Paternoster

Introduction

Desistance and recidivism are obviously related, both conceptually and empirically. Desistance signals the end of a criminal career, and recidivism is the renewal of the offending career after some 'intervention', usually contact with the criminal justice system (arrest or incarceration, for example). Clearly, people who recidivate and 'relapse' into offending have not desisted from crime. Somewhat surprisingly given the unambiguous linkage between desistance and recidivism, research in one area is rarely reflective of research in the other. This is partly a function of the focus of each research agenda. On one hand, desistance research is grounded in the criminal career paradigm.[1] Empirical desistance research tends to use representative samples of the population over a number of years to explore the causes of desistance among the subgroup who offends.[2] On the other hand, recidivism research is more policy focused and is often concerned about the effect of a given criminal justice intervention on a targeted population of (usually serious) offenders in a relatively short period of time, usually one to three years.

Not withstanding these differences, we agree with the premise of this book that much can be learnt by the interplay between the two research literatures. In this chapter, we focus on similarities in the measurement of desistance and recidivism. In the process we develop an empirical and conceptual approach that explicitly embeds the concept of recidivism into a developmental understanding of offending over the life course.

Measuring desistance and recidivism

Recidivism research

In traditional recidivism research, the focus is on determining whether or not someone who has offended in the past and as a result of which comes into contact with the criminal justice system (an 'intervention') subsequently becomes involved in crime again over some relative short-term follow-up period (usually from one to five years). The primary motivation behind recidivism studies, then, is to identify those who suffer a 'relapse' into crime. Those who relapsed were termed recidivists, while those who did not were termed non-recidivists or desisters. However, starting in the 1970s, a group of methodologists observed that this definition of recidivism is very static, and suggested that it misses *variation over time* in failure or relapse rates that might be substantively interesting (for a review, see Maltz 1984 or Schmidt and Witte 1988). One solution to this problem is survival time models, which focus on time until failure, or the probability of failure in time t, given that the individual has not yet failed by time t (the hazard rate). The main advantage of this approach, illustrated most recently by Land *et al.* (1994), is that the method can identify short-term changes in the probability of failure that would otherwise be missed by a one-time-only failure analysis.

One could argue, however, that this emphasis on variation in hazard rates is not very useful for the study of desistance, at least in part because in the traditional treatment of hazard rates, all individuals are assumed to be recidivists and absolute desistance (the cessation of offending) is, therefore, strictly speaking, impossible. Indeed, as Maltz (1984) and Schmidt and Witte (1988) have pointed out, under this framework all individuals will eventually recidivate if we simply watch them for a sufficiently long period of time. Because this is unrealistic if some prior offenders really do desist from committing crimes, it is desirable to specify a mathematical model that allows for a framework like the one described above which (1) applies to individuals who will eventually recidivate; and (2) allows for absolute cessation of offending among those who have actually desisted. Such survival time models, commonly called 'split population' models, specify an incomplete cumulative distribution function (CDF) for the relationship between the passage of time and the probability that an individual recidivates (Maltz 1984; Schmidt and Witte 1988). Under the standard survival time model, the probability that an individual recidivates approaches 1.0 as the passage of time approaches infinity. With the split-population survival time model, this limiting probability is allowed to be less than 1.0 and we can use the information in the data to estimate its value.[3] Estimation of split-population models has suggested two important conclusions: (1) the risk of recidivism is not constant over time but instead tends to be at its peak at the beginning of a follow-up period and declines thereafter; and (2) in most empirical applications the limiting failure time CDF will be significantly less than 1.0. This latter finding implies the presence of a group of individuals who truly desist from crime (Chung *et al*. 1991).[4]

Once the hazard rate has been estimated, researchers attempt to identify factors which can account for changes that are observed over time. The inferential difficulty in this empirical task is distinguishing genuine behavioural changes from stable individual differences that produce a spurious relationship between some event and reoffending. The problem is that stability in offending behaviour in the population can be the result of static individual differences or dynamic causal processes (see, e.g., Hagan and Palloni 1988: 96–7; Nagin and Paternoster 1991). In addition, changes in offending activity can be consistent with a variety of processes ranging from stable individual differences in combination with uniform changes in the population, to measurement error, to true shifts in the propensity to offend caused by exogenous forces (Greenberg 1991: 37–9). For example, as noted above, recidivism studies have often identified a decline in the risk of offending (i.e. the hazard rate) throughout the follow-up period. A decline of this kind could be viewed as evidence of a decrease in individual criminality. But such a decline is also consistent with a process where the most crime-prone individuals most quickly leaving a pool of individuals who reoffend less quickly (Maltz 1996: 32).

Controls for stable individual differences in survival models can be included only through the use of observed covariates. We would note that observed covariates are good if they effectively capture all population heterogeneity. If important covariates are omitted from the model, unobserved heterogeneity continues to exist. The problem for making accurate causal inferences is that any unobserved heterogeneity will be captured in the hazard rate, and could be inadvertently accounted for by time-varying factors which are correlated with time-stable factors. In addition, because hazard rates are estimated for the entire sample at one time, the effect of any intervention must affect all individuals in the same proportional way, regardless of the developmental context. Or, to put it another way, everyone is assumed to follow the same process after the intervention. This is a highly restrictive assumption in the sense that it forces the researcher to assume rather than test that Gottfredson and Hirschi are correct in positing that everyone follows the same process of change. Yet it is clearly possible that the process differs in systematic ways across people.

For example, suppose that the process of recidivism varies systematically as people age. The typical survival model controls for age as a covariate but does not consider the possibility that the very shape of the hazard rate will be different for offenders of different ages. This example highlights the fact that the applications of the typical survival model have focused on the time until the next event without placing these spells into the larger developmental context of a person's life. As a result of this event-specific focus, there is reason to doubt that recidivism studies of individual events can effectively identify the dynamic causal factors that lead to short-term or long-term changes in offending propensity over the life course.

Desistance research

Desistance research is much less well developed than the study of recidivism. In fact, a recent review by Laub and Sampson (2001) concluded that there is considerable conceptual discord with respect to the very measurement of desistance. Desistance has traditionally been measured as not having offended for a certain number of years (from 1 to 12 years) after some arbitrary cut-off age (for example, age 18; e.g. Farrington and Hawkins 1990). This is very similar to the classic definition of a non-recidivist, with the only difference being the trigger point in recidivism is usually some type of intervention rather than a particular cut-off age. One potentially troubling aspect of this framework is the problem of 'false desistance' (Barnett *et al.* 1986; Greenberg 1991: 18–19). This is fundamentally an error of misclassification whereby one who has not yet truly desisted from criminal activity is classified as a desister simply because we have not yet observed any new criminal activity. It is also useful to view this source of uncertainty as a missing data problem. If we could simply observe individuals long enough, then we would be able to determine whether they have truly recidivated. In the course of a typical desistance study, however, we do not always have the opportunity to observe individuals for a sufficiently long period of time for them to 'display their true colors' (Greenberg 1991: 22).

Beyond the fact that it is difficult to identify when an individual has definitely desisted apart from at his or her death (Elliot *et al.* 1989), researchers have also questioned what we learn by focusing on the state of absolute desistance rather than the process of desistance (see, e.g., Laub, Nagin, and Sampson 1998; Bushway *et al.* 2001; Laub and Sampson 2001; Maruna 2001). These researchers suggest, describing the process by which offending has changed over time to a level that approximates zero. This is usually done by estimating the time path or trajectory of criminality (defined as the propensity to offend) over the lifespan, paying particular attention to people who have experienced substantial changes in their offending rates over time and are now experiencing near zero offending rates. Once this process has been described, researchers can identify events, experiences or important life transitions that might have precipitated this process.

This shift in focus to understanding how rates of offending change over time has brought the study of desistance back to the criminal career paradigm that first suggested focusing on desistance. Criminal career research from the beginning focused on the estimation of lambda, the rate of offending. This was assumed to be an estimate of an individual's criminality or propensity to offend. While initially estimated as time stable over the criminal career in the criminal career framework, in recent years researchers have made considerable effort to develop ways to trace a time path of criminality within individuals' lifespans. We will refer to this avenue of research as 'lifespan' research to distinguish it from the earlier criminal career research.

A key analytical contribution in this area has been the development of semi-parametric finite mixture models (so-called trajectory models) (Nagin and Land 1993; Land and Nagin 1996; Laub *et al.* 1998; Nagin 1999) which allow researchers to estimate distinct longitudinal trajectories of criminal offending activity (as measured by counts of criminal acts at different points in time) that at least approximately characterize three of the four long-term criminal career dimensions discussed by Blumstein *et al.* (1988): (1) onset or initiation; (2) frequency or rate of offending activity while one is active; and (3) the approximate duration of the criminal career.[5] In recent years, lifespan researchers have been able to make considerable progress both in their efforts to reach a better understanding of how crime changes with age throughout various populations and in their efforts to reach a better understanding of the factors that might produce such changes.

As in the study of recidivism, a central inferential task in the use of trajectory models for lifespan analysis is to distinguish between individual stability and 'meaningful' (non-spurious) change. These models undertake this task by allowing the data to identify the existence of distinct groups of individuals who each have their own pattern or distribution of offending over the lifespan. In other words, the entire population is not forced to follow the same basic pattern of change, as in the typical survival model. Instead, the model groups individuals according to which grouping best fits the model and allows each group to have their own trajectory with its own unique shape. Ideally, we would be able to estimate a separate trajectory for each individual, but since we only observe offending and not the underlying offending propensity we have to rely on estimates based on groupings of 'similar' individuals.

This procedure has great descriptive value because it allows researchers to determine the amount of variation that exists in both levels of offending and changes in offending over the lifespan, including changes that appear to lead to desistance. For example, Laub *et al.* (1998) followed a group of adolescent offenders up to the age of 30. They identified two distinct trajectories approaching a state of approximate desistance (one by the age of 20, the other by the age of 30). The analysis showed that marriage had a substantial impact on the behaviour of individuals in the group that desisted by the age of 30 but no impact on those who desisted by the age of 20 – those individuals in the latter group had already changed their behaviour prior to marriage. In this sense, lifespan analyses using semi-parametric finite mixture models avoid some of the rigidity associated with survival time models commonly used in recidivism studies. To date, applications of this approach to lifespan data have revealed considerable variety in the shape of age–crime trajectories throughout different populations, some of which include a discernible transition from a state of active offending to one of virtual desistance. Recent reviews of this literature can be found in Nagin (1999) and Bushway *et al.* (2001).

Within this approach, one unresolved issue involves the issue of intermittency (see Chapter 5 this volume). Intermittency involves short-term changes in criminality and suggests that individuals do not initiate and subsequently cease offending but move between repeated periods of activity and inactivity in criminal offending. Trajectory models focus on estimating rates of offending over time and assume that individuals are always active at a rate that changes over time. This approach follows a quadratic or cubic form – thereby placing a premium on long-term change at the cost of inaccurately describing important short-term change. Moreover, these trajectory models rely on the Poisson functional form, which assume that each event is independent of the next event. This assumption is violated if crime occurs in 'sprees' which is one way that offending can be intermittent.

Given these concerns, Nagin and Land (1993) allowed for an intermittency parameter to be estimated over the estimated timespan in the trajectory model. This intermittency parameter, which is literally the probability of being active in a given period, is close to one at the peak of offending, suggesting that offenders are always active during the peak periods of activity (the age of 20 in Nagin and Land 1993: Table 5). The intermittency probability declines as individuals age pass the age of 20, which suggests that declines in offending rates could be masking a tendency to become more sporadic, and it sends a potential warning that declines in offending rates to zero (or close to zero) may not be permanent or absolute desistance.

Unfortunately, having estimated rates and intermittency parameters separately for groups, it becomes increasingly difficult to understand how jointly to interpret rates and intermittency parameters. Both capture something about changes in the propensity to offend over time but, because of the many non-linear parameters involved, the interpretation of these patterns is quite complicated.

Common ground in the measurement of recidivism and desistance

Thirty years ago, recidivism and desistance were complementary measures. Those who failed after a certain period were recidivists, and those who did not were desisters. But as we reviewed above, this static approach to thinking about recidivism and desistance has been effectively rejected. Now, cutting-edge recidivism studies focus on hazard rates of offending over time and cutting-edge desistance studies focus on measuring trajectories of offending rates over time. So where is the new common ground?

Right under our feet, as it turns out. It is a well-known fact in statistics and quantitative criminology that these two models are actually measuring the same concept, with hazard rate models focusing on *short-term* change in the propensity to offend and the trajectory models focusing on *long-term* change in the propensity to offend. For example, having noted that the hazard rate focuses on the hazard of involvement in a given criminal event,[6] Hagan and Palloni (1988: 97) observe that:

> [T]he expected number of criminal events during the age interval being examined is a unique function of these hazards. This expected number of criminal events is what Blumstein *et al.* are estimating when they calculate lambda (offending rate). So, lambda is a summary of the combined hazards of criminal events of various orders over a period time.

As a result, the use of trajectories of rates to study desistance has brought the study of desistance conceptually very close to the study of recidivism. In their article, Hagan and Palloni (1988) present arguments for focusing on the causal nature of the events, rather than on the rate of offending. At the time they made their argument, however, empirical methods only allowed for the estimation of time-stable rates for individuals. The ability to capture time variation in offending rates while controlling for individual heterogeneity, combined with the new emphasis on the *process* of desistance, provides a persuasive counter-argument for a focus on the more long-term perspective. The focus of survival models on the timing of events may help to resolve the problem of intermittency found in current trajectory analysis. In the remainder of this chapter we propose an approach which recognizes this link and combines the strength of both approaches to study desistance.

Analytic strategy

The above discussion raises the possibility that we might be able productively to combine some of the features of survival time models commonly employed in recidivism research with semi-parametric finite mixture models commonly employed in lifespan analyses. A useful model would be one which builds directly on both traditions. In this section we briefly discuss some of the technical aspects of each approach and then describe a relatively simple statistical model that links them together. We should also point out that these proposals are neither new nor particularly innovative (see, for example, the development of a discrete-time approximation to a semi-parametric hazard rate model discussed in Land and Nagin 1996: 177–80). Our main goal here is simply to call attention to them and to advocate that we begin to apply them to the study of desistance and recidivism where the data are sufficiently detailed.

Before we provide the technical details we will simply describe the idea intuitively. Suppose we have arrest data over the lifespan and we know the exact date of the arrest. The conventional approach in lifespan or trajectory analysis would be to count the number of events (arrests) in a given timespan and use that to estimate rates of offending over time. Yet this approach is open to concerns about intermittency, concerns that could be ameliorated if we took advantage of the information we actually possess regarding the time between arrests. In other words, simply calculating events in a time period misses information that can be used to model propensity to offend over the lifespan.

For example, suppose that we know that three events occurred in a year. Without other information, the best we could conclude is that they occurred on average four months apart. But they could have all happened in the first three months, which would provide a different picture of activity than if they were evenly spaced throughout the year. The ideal model would allow us to estimate the hazard rate model of time until the next event in the context of an age-based trajectory of offending rate. The following description lays out a way to do that based on what is a very simple and straightforward relationship between two probability distributions found in any introductory probability text – the Poisson probability distribution and the exponential probability distribution.

A very simple form of the survival time model is one which assumes that the time to the next event is a random variable drawn from an exponential probability distribution. Under an exponential model, we assume that the hazard rate (i.e. the conditional probability of offending at a particular moment in time, conditional on not offending prior to that time) is constant throughout the population and over time. While this is restrictive, it is worth pointing out that most applications of semi-parametric finite mixture models have assumed that event count outcomes are drawn from a Poisson distribution which, in turn, is based on the assumption that events arrive according to an exponential process. In other words, when we calculate the sum of the events that arrive by an exponential process, we have a Poisson random variable (see, e.g., Lehoczky 1986: 384–5).[7] These event count models have become powerful tools for studying population variation in offending rates and for investigating how those rates change throughout the lifespan, despite the relatively simple form of the distribution.[8]

We proceed by providing a brief technical description of the trajectory model. For those interested in more details, we refer them to Nagin and Land (1993) or Nagin (1999). The usual form of the finite mixture model for Poisson distributed event counts places analytic focus on the rates at which events occur. We begin by assuming that the population comprises K distinct, but unobserved, groups of individuals each of which can be characterized by its own offending trajectory. The likelihood function for this type of model is given by:

$$L(\lambda, \pi \mid y) = \prod_{i=1}^{N} \left[\sum_{j=1}^{K} \pi_j \left(\prod_{t=1}^{T} \frac{\exp(-\lambda_{jt}) \lambda_{jt}^{y_{it}}}{y_{it}!} \right) \right]$$

where y_{it} is a frequency count of the number of events experienced by individual i at time t and λ_{jt} is the rate at which events arrive for individuals in group j of the population at time t. Each of the $i = 1, 2, \ldots$ N individuals has unconditional probability, π_j, of being a member of group j. The model, described in full by Nagin (1999), does require that the distribution of π_j be discrete, but an important advantage of this framework is that it places no restrictions on the shape of the distribution of π_j. A key feature of this model is that it allows us to trace the time path of the offence rate, λ, for each of the $j = 1, 2, \ldots K$ groups in the population, thereby providing us with a window through which to view important shifts in offending activity over the lifespan.

From the well established literature (see, e.g., Schmidt and Witte 1988: 37, 53) on the use of survival time models to study criminal recidivism, it is also useful to provide a brief technical description of the simple exponential survival model. The likelihood function for a censored exponential version of the survival time model is given by:

$$L(\lambda \mid d) = \prod_{i=1}^{N} \left[\lambda \times \exp(-\lambda d_i) \right]^{c_i} \times \left[1 - \exp(-\lambda d_i) \right]^{(1-c_i)}$$

where d denotes the amount of waiting time or duration from the beginning of a 'spell' until the event of interest (i.e. involvement in a criminal offence) occurs for those who are observed to experience the event ($c_i = 1$) and it denotes the amount of waiting time or the duration from the beginning of the spell until the end of the observation period for those who are not observed to experience the event. We say that the latter group of individuals are 'censored' (i.e. $c_i = 0$) because we do not know whether they eventually would experience the event; all we can see is that they have not experienced the event by the end of the observation period. For those individuals who are censored, the contribution to the likelihood function is the complement of the exponential cumulative distribution function of the probability of experiencing an event with increasing waiting time. For those individuals who are not censored, the contribution to the likelihood function is the exponential probability density of the waiting time to the point where the event occurs. This differential contribution to the likelihood function depending on whether one is 'censored' or not is the primary means by which survival time models deal with the uncertainty that is created by our inability to observe whether or not one has truly desisted.

Note that in this survival time likelihood function, we assume that we only observe individuals for one spell. In this context a spell is considered to be a period of time that lasts between the beginning of an observation period whose length is fixed for all individuals and the end of the observation period (for those who have not experienced an event prior to the end of the period) or the time that the event is experienced.

From this definition it is clear that if a spell begins at the beginning of period t, there must be at least 1 spell within that period but there will always be one more spell than the number of events that are observed to occur during that period (i.e. $y_{it} = S_{it} - 1$ where S_{it} is the number of spells occurring during period t).

Now, a critical point is that T (lambda), which is the rate at which events occur, has the same mathematical definition in both these likelihood functions. This implies that if we have access to the times at which events occur, we can combine important features of the finite mixture Poisson likelihood function with the survival time likelihood function to yield the following result:

$$L(\lambda, \pi \mid d) = \prod_{i=1}^{N} \left(\sum_{j=1}^{K} \pi_j \times \left[\prod_{t=1}^{T} \prod_{s=1}^{S} \left[\lambda_{jts} \times \exp\left(-\lambda_{jts} d_{its}\right) \right]^{c_{its}} \times \left[1 - \exp\left(-\lambda_{jts} d_{its}\right) \right]^{(1-c_{its})} \right] \right)$$

where each individual's contribution to the likelihood function comprises the waiting times to each event (i.e. each of the $s = 1, 2, \ldots S$ spells) within each age period such that the event count variable is $y_{it} = S_{it} - 1$. The kernel of this likelihood function has the same structure as the exponential survival time model described above except we now allow for multiple ages and multiple spells within each age and we furthermore allow for unobserved population heterogeneity through the use of a finite mixing distribution. When exact times of events are available, which is usually true in studies of official records, we expect that this estimator will prove to be a valuable tool for developing inferences about the time path of population variation in criminal offending rates.

Despite the somewhat imposing form of this likelihood function, this model might be as easy to implement as the readily available zero inflated Poisson (rate plus intermittency) trajectory model, and would be easier to interpret, since the measured rate would reflect both the short and long-term timing of the events across each of the trajectory groups. Given a more accurate description of the process by which offending propensities change over time, we might then expect more readily to find the answers to what causes the process of desistance.

Conclusion

Recent research on desistance has begun to focus on changes in the rate of offending as individuals age over the life course, primarily through the use of trajectory methods. This approach is very good at describing long-term change in behaviour that we feel is central to the study of desistance, in particular because it does an excellent job of separating dynamic individual change from static individual differences. Trajectory methods, however, have struggled with an adequate description of the arrival of offending events, as in the case of intermittent offending. Recidivism research, on the other hand, uses survival models to describe the timing of events – precisely the weakness of trajectory methods. Survival models, however, are fairly weak at differentiating between stable individual differences and dynamic individual change and fail to place the issue of recidivism into the large developmental span context.

In this chapter we note that not only are survival models and trajectory models both measuring the same thing – changes in the propensity to offend – but that also, *under certain assumptions, both approaches are estimating the same statistical parameter, lambda (the rate of offending).* Building on this insight, we refer to the work of other researchers in the larger criminal career/lifespan literature to propose a statistical model that combines the best features of both the trajectory model and the survival model. We believe that this model, or models like it, showcase the best current approach adequately to describe the process(es) of change in offending propensity over the life course.

Of course, researchers will not always be able to estimate this model due to lack of information. But is there a way to apply the insight from this chapter to a standard study of recidivism? Our main arguments were that desistance trajectories do a better job than typical survival models of controlling for heterogeneity and of placing any given event into the context of the life span. In the standard recidivism model, researchers include observed measures of individual differences as a proxy for time-stable differences in criminal propensity or population heterogeneity. For example, Visher *et al.* (1991) control for criminal history, information on the current commitment, substance abuse, school problems and family background. The variable with the most explanatory power is usually criminal history (Visher *et al.* 1991). This makes sense, since criminal history, such as the number of prior arrests, is related to the offending rate. Given our observation that the offending rate and the hazard rate are measuring the same concept. the offending rate *should* be able to predict the hazard rate. It is analogous (but not identical) to the inclusion of a lagged dependent variable (prior behaviour) in more conventional regression analyses of criminal offending. As such it is also an excellent approach to controlling for population heterogeneity – in fact, one could make the argument that the pre-existing rate of offending at the time of incarceration would be the perfect control for individual heterogeneity.[9] In the presence of such a measure, any change after the period of incarceration should be due to dynamic or contemporaneous factors, rather than individual differences.

Of course, controlling for the rate is easier said than done. Present research typically includes the number of arrests and the age of the offender, and sometimes even the length of time between first and incident arrests. A rudimentary measure of the offending rate would be the number of arrests divided by the career length. But this approach assumes that there has been no change in the offending rate over the course of the offender's career, a dubious assumption at best given the evidence from trajectory modelling. We think that a more fruitful approach would be to group offenders using the trajectory method and to use the rate of offending at the time of incarceration as a proxy for the offending rate of the individual.[10]

Because trajectories are based on offending over age, this approach would be reasonably straightforward to estimate in samples of roughly the same age, such as the CYA cohort used by Visher *et al.* (1991), but much more difficult in samples with a range of ages such as that used by Escarela *et al.* (2000). This latter type of sample asked the researcher to compare hazard rates of people who are from a developmental perspective on different paths. If age matters, in a psychological, sociological and/or biological sense, we do not expect to see the same changes in criminality among 20-year-olds and 40-year-olds. This point remains even if age is included in the model as a time-stable constant, since developmental theories such as interactional theory (Thornberry 1987) and social control theory (Sampson and Laub 1993) make clear statements about how change varies with age.[11]

The analysis by Escarela *et al.* (2000) allows for a simple demonstration of this point. They model hazard rates for sex offenders convicted in 1973 in England over 15 years. They have information on arrests in the previous 10 years, a limitation with a benefit, since the control for criminal history is now actually a rudimentary measure of offending rate over the last 10 years. They find, as in Visher *et al.* (1991), that criminal history is an excellent predictor of rearrest. They also find that age at entry matters, suggesting that people who are older are more likely to desist, even holding constant the previous rate of offending. This result is consistent with the idea that criminality declines as people age. It is also consistent with the idea that recidivism studies are enhanced if we place them in the developmental context of the life course.

One way to do this without implementing our full model would be separately to examine the impact of an intervention on people who have observably different developmental histories of offending, in much the same way that researchers have begun to identify and then study different patterns of desistance. Or, to put it another way, we might want to consider the interaction of the impact of the intervention on an individual's developmental history. For example, the researcher could estimate the developmental trajectories of all individuals prior to the incident arrest and then allow the impact of a given intervention to vary by group. This approach might have the practical benefit of identifying individuals who are developmentally amenable to change. Theoretically, this approach also has the benefit of embedding the concept of recidivism explicitly into a developmental understanding of offending over the life course. We are then again led to the observation that initiated this chapter – that studies of recidivism and desistance from crime can profitably learn from each other.

Notes

1   The National Research Council's report on criminal careers (Blumstein *et al.* 1986) concluded that a comprehensive understanding of how criminal careers evolve can only be reached when researchers attend to the four distinct dimensions of a criminal career: (1) participation or onset of involvement in crime among those who initiate involvement in criminal activity; (2) the frequency of offending activity (the number of offences that an individual actually commits); (3) the seriousness and mix of crimes committed; and (4) the duration of the criminal career (the amount of time that elapses between the initiation and termination of a criminal career). Desistance, which marks the end of a criminal career, is intimately related to duration, frequency and the mix and seriousness of offences committed and therefore has important theoretical significance within the criminal career paradigm (Blumstein *et al.* 1986: 27).

2   See Laub and Sampson (2001) for a review. There are of course exceptions; see in particular the research by Laub *et al.* (1998) and Uggen (2000), both of which use a group of ex-offenders to study desistance.

3   It is worth pointing out that this model is technically a finite mixture model in the same sense that many models used in contemporary 'lifespan' research are finite mixture models. To be specific, each approach assumes that the probability distribution of what is observed depends on which

'group' an individual belongs to where the group is actually unobserved.

4   Unfortunately, this approach does not allow researchers to identify this group of desisters and, as a result, it cannot be used to study desistance *per se*.

5   Although some effort has been expended to examine how longitudinal trajectories of offending may vary across different types of crime and levels of crime seriousness among the same individuals, this work is less well developed (Nagin and Tremblay 1999).

6   People who have no offences are at hazard for a first criminal event; those who offend once are at a hazard for a second criminal event, etc.

7   Under the assumption that the process generating the event count data is Poisson and the rate at which events occur is denoted by λ, then the average waiting time to the next event is drawn from an exponential distribution with mean $1/\lambda$.

8   There is an interesting trade-off here. By relying on a relatively simple parametric form, trajectory models are able to deal effectively with issues of population heterogeneity to identify real change. On the other hand, recidivism studies using survival models have explored a number of very sophisticated parametric forms but have not been able to deal effectively with issues of population heterogeneity.

9   It also provides an interesting opportunity to quantify expectations about survival rates. Often studies will report the total failure rate at the end of the survey period. For example, Visher *et al.* (1991) report that 88 per cent of the sample had failed after approximately 3 years. It is hard to evaluate this result but, with information about the rate of offending, we can say something very basic about what we might have expected based on previous behaviour. The average previous arrests is highly skewed, so instead we use the fact that 80 per cent of the sample had at least 4 arrests over 4.14 years to generate a rate of 1 arrest per year. Using the exponential distribution, we would expect that 95 per cent of the offenders would fail if nothing changed, a back-of-the-envelope estimate that is very close to what is observed. A similar analysis using survival rates provide by Escarela *et al.* (2000) dramatically overestimates failure over 16 years, a result consistent with the idea that criminality declines as people age. The average age at release is 30 years for Escarela *et al.* (2000) and roughly 18 for Visher *et al.* (1991).

10 Other approaches are also possible – the key is somehow to group offenders according to offending rate prior to the incident event.

11 This is less of an issue in the type of very flexible hazard models such as that used by Visher *et al.* (1991) since the covariates are allowed to have an impact on the hazard rate that changes over time.

References

Blumstein, A., Cohen, J. and Farrington, D.P. (1988) 'Criminal career research: its value for criminology', *Criminology*, 26: 1–35.

Bryk, A.S. and Raudenbush, S.W. (1992) *Hierarchical Linear Models for Social and Behavioral Research: Application and Data Analysis Methods*. Newbury Park, CA: Sage.

Bushway, S.D., Piquero, A.R., Broidy, L.M., Cauffman, E. and Mazerolle, P. (2001) 'An empirical framework for studying desistance as a process', *Criminology*, 39: 491–513.

Chung, C.P., Schmidt, P. and Witte, A.D. (1991) 'Survival analysis: a survey', *Journal of Quantitative Criminology*, 7: 59–98.

Escarela, G., Francis, B. and Soothill, K. (2000) 'Competing risks, persistence, and desistance in analyzing recidivism', *Journal of Quantitative Criminology*, 16: 385–414.

Farrington, D.P. and Hawkins, J.D. (1991) 'Predicting participation, early onset, and later persistence in officially recorded offending', *Criminal Behaviour and Mental Health*, 1: 1–33.

Hagan, J. and Palloni, A. (1988) 'Crimes as social events in the life course: reconceiving a criminological controversy', *Criminology*, 26: 87–100.

Land, K.C., McCall, P.L. and Parker, K.F. (1994) 'Logistic versus hazards regression analyses in evaluation research: an exposition and application to the North Carolina court counselors' Intensive Protective Supervision project', *Evaluation Review*, 18: 411–37.

Lattimore, P.K., Visher, C.A. and Linster, R.L. (1995) 'Predicting rearrest for violence among serious youthful offenders', *Journal of Research in Crime and Delinquency*, 32: 54–83.

Laub, J.H., Nagin, D.S. and Sampson, R.J. (1998) 'Good marriages and trajectories of change in criminal offending', *American Sociological Review*, 63: 225–38.

Laub, J.H. and Sampson, R.J. (2001) 'Understanding desistance from crime', *Crime and Justice: A Review of Research*, 28: 1–69.

Maltz, M.D. (1984) *Recidivism*. New York, NY: Academic Press.

Nagin, D.S. (1999) 'Analyzing developmental trajectories: a semiparametric, group-based approach', *Psychological Methods*, 4: 139–57.

Nagin, D., Farrington, D. and Moffitt, T. (1995) 'Life course trajectories of different types of offenders', *Criminology*, 33: 111–39.

Nagin, D.S. and Land, K. (1993) 'Age, criminal careers, and population heterogeneity: specification and estimation of a nonparametric, mixed Poisson model', *Criminology*, 31: 327–62.

Nagin, D.S. and Paternoster, R. (1991) 'On the relationship of past and future participation in delinquency', *Criminology*, 29: 163–90.

Rowe, D.C., Osgood, D.W. and Nicewander, A.W. (1990) 'A latent trait approach to unifying criminal careers', *Criminology*, 28: 237–70.

Sampson, R.J. and Laub, J.H. (1993) *Crime in the Making: Pathways and Turning Points through Life*. Cambridge, MA: Harvard University Press.

Schmidt, P. and Witte, A.D. (1988) *Predicting Recidivism Using Survival Models*. New York: Springer-Verlag.

Thornberry, T. (1987) 'Toward an interactional theory of delinquency', *Criminology*, 25: 863–91.

Uggen, C. (2000) 'Work as a turning point in the life course of criminals: a duration model of age, employment, and recidivism', *American Sociological Review*, 65: 529–46.

Visher, C.A., Lattimore, P.K. and Linster, R.L. (1991) 'Predicting the recidivism of serious youthful offenders using survival models', *Criminology*, 29: 329–66.

Chapter 5

Somewhere between persistence and desistance: the intermittency of criminal careers

Alex R. Piquero

Introduction

One of the best documented facts of criminal behaviour is its strong correlation with age. First identified over one hundred years ago (Quetelet 1831), researchers have observed that, with age, criminal behaviour tends to decline. Thus it should come as no surprise to many that questions about the patterning of criminal careers and why they change over the life course are at the core of contemporary criminology (Shover 1996: 121).

Towards this end, researchers have explored patterns of criminal behaviour over the life course. Theoretical and empirical papers have dealt with topics related to the debate between general and developmental theories (Moffitt 1993; Hirschi and Gottfredson 1995; Sampson and Laub 1995; Bartusch *et al.* 1997; Paternoster *et al.* 1997), as well as the criminal career dimensions of onset (Simons *et al.* 1994; Paternoster and Brame 1997), frequency (Smith *et al.* 1991; Piquero 2000), specialization (Blumstein *et al.* 1988; Piquero *et al.* 1999) and persistence (Dean *et al.* 1996). Moreover, recent work has begun to explore within-individual variability in offending over time (Horney *et al.* 1995; Laub *et al.* 1998; Piquero *et al.* 2002).

Within the criminal career paradigm (Piquero, Farrington and Blumstein 2003), one of the neglected areas of study has been the desistance from criminal behaviour (for important exceptions, see Shover and Thompson 1992; Laub *et al.* 1998). Although researchers note that, by their early to mid-20s, most criminals begin to cease their criminal activity, desistance, or the 'voluntary termination of serious criminal participation' (see Shover 1996: 121), has been difficult to study, largely because of the fact that, until death, individuals can still offend (Blumstein *et al.* 1982; Spelman 1994; Bushway *et al.* 2001).

The fact that desistance may be difficult to observe directly raises the following questions: (1) do criminal careers stop and restart throughout one's criminal career; and (2) if so, then what causes these consecutive stop and starts? The task at hand is to uncover information about the concept of intermittency, or the observation of temporary suspensions from criminal activity. Although the concept of intermittency has only recently been recognized (Barnett *et al.* 1989; Nagin and Land 1993; Horney *et al.* 1995), the idea that offenders are not constantly offending has been accepted for quite some time (Glaser 1964; Matza 1964; Frazier 1976; Miesenhelder 1977; Luckenbill and Best 1981). Still, the concept has not been extensively studied in such a way as to offer theoretical guidance as to its occurrence.

In this chapter, I discuss the concept of intermittency, its use in empirical research and its current lack of theoretical explanation. Then I apply several criminological theories to the observed pattern of intermittency in criminal careers. The chapter concludes by highlighting a number of theoretical and empirical research possibilities for the study of intermittency in criminal careers.

Desistance

It has been acknowledged that crime has a temporal dimension (Cusson and Pinsonneault 1986) and, as a result, researchers have spent a great deal of energy trying to chart the trajectory of criminal behaviour over the life course (see Blumstein *et al.* 1986). This has been so much the case that a new subfield of criminology, life-course criminology, has emerged (see Piquero and Mazerolle 2001). One of the key facets of this research area is desistance.

By the time they reach the age of 28, most offenders seem to stop offending (Blumstein and Cohen 1987). Accounting for why this is the case has long been of interest to criminologists. This is no surprise since questions (and answers) regarding termination from criminal activity bear import for matters of both theory and policy.

Although the idea of studying desistance has captured the imagination of many criminologists, theoretical and methodological problems have plagued sustained research attention. For example, the criminal career literature traditionally imagines desistance as an event – an abrupt cessation of criminal behaviour. For example, Baskin et al.

(1994: 127) define desistance as 'the cessation of a pattern of criminal behavior' while Farrall and Bowling (1999) describe desistance as the 'moment that a criminal career ends.' Empirical researchers have translated these and other definitions into empirical operationalizations that have desistance varying from a one-year crime-free period (Loeber *et al.* 1991), to a two-year crime free period (Maruna 2001), to a ten-year crime-free period (Farrington and Hawkins 1991). But are these operationalizations really capturing the notion of desistance? Several researchers such as Farrington (1986: 201) have warned that 'even a five-year or ten year crime-free period is no guarantee that offending has terminated'.

The problem with operationalizing desistance, then, is one of permanence. As Frazier (1976: 175) pointed out, 'how do we ... know when a change is permanent?' The problem can perhaps be best summarized by Maruna's (2001) recent work in this area:

> suppose we know conclusively that the purse-snatcher ... never committed another crime for the rest of his long life. When did his desistance start? Is not the voluntary termination point or concluding moment the very instant when the person completes (or terminates) the act of theft? If so, in the same moment that a person becomes an offender, he also becomes a desistor. That cannot be right.

Maruna's (2001: 26) 'fix' to the definitional problem is to define desistance as 'the long-term abstinence from crime among individuals who had previously engaged in persistent patterns of criminal offending'. As a result, Maruna places the focus on the maintenance of crime-free behaviour rather than the decision to refrain from further crime. Still, even this definition worries some researchers who have regarded desistance as the 'process of reduction in the rate of offending ... from a nonzero level to a stable rate empirically indistinguishable from zero' (Bushway *et al.* 2001: 500).

Although I do not take the position that desistance cannot (nor should not) receive continued theoretical and empirical work, at the same time I believe that an equally interesting but neglected aspect of criminal careers is the extent to which offenders experience zig zags in and out of criminal activity throughout their careers in crime. After all, 'a career in crime [is] a variable and varying process' (Meisenhelder 1977: 320). Although the observation of lulls and relapses in the drug addiction and abuse literature is common (Bromwell *et al.* 1986), similar lulls in criminal careers have received less attention. As Glaser (1964: 318; see also Meisenhelder 1977; Luckenbill and Best 1981: 200) has argued:

> The view of criminality as a zig-zag path suggests that it may be more fruitful for rehabilitation objectives to shift the focus of criminological theories from the search for the processes that make for persistence in crime. What we need is the development and test of a theory on the conditions that promote change from crime to noncrime and back again.

The notion that offenders experience brief lapses and sporadic episodes of crime occurring at sometimes unpredictable intervals is considered in the following section.

Intermittency

As a result of the observation that desistance is difficult to study because many offenders stop and restart their offending activity, several researchers have shifted their focus to the concept of 'temporary desistance' (see Tunnell 1992: 94–5). For example, several studies showed that desistance 'is not necessarily permanent and may simply be part of a continuing process of lulls in the offending of persistent criminals' (Clarke and Cornish 1985: 173). Thus many offenders cyclically or temporarily desist from crime (Petersilia *et al.* 1978; Petersilia 1980; Rowe *et al.* 1990). As one of the Rand studies indicated: 'The adult offense rate exceeded one crime per month of street time for 94 percent of the intensive offenders but for only 21 percent of the intermittent offenders. Most striking, over his full career the average intensive offender committed about ten times as many crimes as the intermittent offender' (Petersilia *et al.* 1978: xi). Thus many serious offenders may be more realistically viewed as individuals who alternate from criminal to non-criminal means of pursuing economic and other objectives rather than as persons who are persistently criminal (Glaser 1964: 317). Perhaps the most conclusive evidence to date on this issue was carried out by Barnett and his colleagues.

Using a sample of London males, Barnett *et al.* (1989) examined how empirical models that partialled the offending population into distinct classes of offenders (i.e. frequents and occassionals) adequately predicted the criminal careers of sample members between their 25th and 30th birthdays. Left curious by the fact that some of the 'frequents' had a longer time to reconviction after the age of 25 than expected, and the fact that the 'low risk' offender typology contained more recidivists than expected, Barnett *et al.* further explored their data. An interesting finding emerged. Sixteen offenders labelled 'frequents' had extremely low probabilities of recidivism; however, five of them actually did recidivate. After studying the criminal careers of these five men, Barnett and colleagues found that all five men started offending relatively late (around the age of 16), had almost six convictions in a short period and then ceased their criminal careers around the age of 19. At least, that is what it seemed like initially. Further investigation into these careers yielded another interesting finding. After seven years without any convictions, all the men were reconvicted at an average age of 27, and three of them had another conviction around the age of 29 (Barnett *et al.* 1989: 384). From this the authors concluded that 'more elaborate models might incorporate the concept of intermittency, whereby offenders go into remission for several years and then resume their criminal careers' (1989: 384).

The research by Barnett *et al.* (1989) led to several other efforts designed further to explore intermittency. One of these efforts, led by Nagin and Land (1993), extended the Barnett *et al.* intermittency finding by directly incorporating an intermittency parameter into an advanced statistical model. Specifically, Nagin and Land examined whether the aggregate-level pattern typical of the age–crime curve held at the individual level, and thus asked if there were distinctive age–crime trajectories within the population of offenders. The importance of the Nagin and Land approach is its specification of a semi-parametric model of criminal careers that contains a number of nuances that separate it from other empirical models. Two parts of their model bear import for the matter at hand.

Following previous research documenting the importance of controlling for unmeasured time-stable individual differences in the analysis of longitudinal data, the first unique characteristic of the Nagin and Land model is its allowance for offending heterogeneity that does not take on a parametric form. They accomplished this task by adapting a semi-parametric estimation procedure that approximates any un-specified continuous distribution of unobserved heterogeneity with a combination of discrete distributions. The relevance of this feature is that it does not force the researcher to apply some particular probability distribution to the unmeasured individual differences; as a result, the model is flexible enough to be applied to any type of underlying probability distribution.[1] Secondly, they included an intermittency parameter which accounted for discrete changes in individual patterns of offending. For example, their statistical model recognizes that some individuals may go through periods of active offending (where lambda > 0) but these periods may be interspersed with periods of dormancy (where lambda = 0). Thus the intermittency parameter is expected to capture discontinuous jumps from a 'state of zero criminal potential to positive criminal potential' (Nagin and Land 1993: 334).[2] Using the London data, they found that models incorporating an intermittency parameter that allowed for periods of both activity and inactivity performed better than models without such a parameter, a finding that was replicated with the second Philadelphia birth cohort study (Land *et al.* 1996: 420–1). Also, the intermittency parameter displayed a single-peaked age trajectory and varied across individuals as a function of observable characteristics and prior offending, but with parameter estimates distinct from those of offence frequency. Although they recognized the importance of intermittency, they also cautioned that 'the concept of intermittency is problematic because a promising theoretical explanation for why it should occur has yet to be offered'. Enter the work of Horney and her colleagues.

Using a sample of incarcerated felons, Horney *et al.* (1995) sought to provide one plausible explanation for intermittency. Guided by the work of Sampson and Laub, Horney *et al.* argued that intermittency occurred, in part, because of changes in social control variables such as employment, marriage and so forth.

Their study provided a unique approach towards understanding criminal careers – namely, the use of retrospective data with event calendars. Horney *et al.* employed hierarchical linear models to study month-to-month variations in offending as related to changes in local life circumstances by asking offenders to consider a reference period based on the date of the arrest that led to the current incarceration. Using an event calendar, the inmates were then asked to identify those street months during which they had been on probation, on parole, going to school, working, living with a girlfriend, living with a wife, drinking heavily or using drugs. A check was then placed in the months when these things occurred. The crime calendar was created in a similar fashion; that is, offenders were asked to determine the months during which they committed any burglaries, personal robberies, business robberies, assaults, thefts, auto thefts, frauds, forgeries or drug deals. Their results revealed general support for the hypothesis that local life circumstances influenced short-term change in involvement in criminal behaviour. For example, in terms of predicting any criminal behaviour, going to school and living with a wife incurred negative, inhibitory effects, while living with a girlfriend and illegal drug use incurred positive, exacerbating effects. In sum, their analysis revealed evidence for month-to-month changes in criminal offending as a function of changes in involvement in local life circumstances.

Two others explored the stops and starts associated with criminal activity. Using data on over 500 Boston men, Laub *et al.* explored how 'good marriages' were related to the desistance process. Their results showed that, after controlling for periods of intermittency, good marriages were related to desistance from crime, and that the influence of quality marital bonds was gradual and cumulative over time. Piquero and his colleagues (2002) studied the relation between changes in local life circumstances and changes in the joint covariation of violent and non-violent crime for a sample of 524 parolees from the California Youth Authority who were followed for seven years post-parole. These authors found that, after controlling for street time and persistent individual differences, a measure of stakes in conformity was negatively related to non-violent crime while, at the same time, non-whites were significantly more likely to accumulate violent arrests.

As can be seen, extant research has shown that criminal activity incurs stops and starts within offending careers, and that several social variables are related to changes in criminal activity. Still, researchers have been slow to develop a consistent, working definition and operationalization of intermittency that may help unify related research efforts.

Since it seems that some sort of 'termination takes place all the time' (Maruna 2001), and is not long-lasting, it can and should be recognized as a temporary suspension in criminal activity that is in need of both documentation and empirical scrutiny. With this in mind, I follow the work of Elliott *et al.* (1989) by avoiding the variable 'termination' and defining intermittency as *a temporary abstinence from criminal activity during a particular period of time only to be followed by a resumption of criminal activity after a particular period of time*. Empirically, intermittency can be operationalized as the time between successive criminal events, controlling of course for exposure time (i.e. time for which individuals are free on the street to commit crime). This distance of time, then, becomes the variable to be explained. Why these temporary suspensions begin and end is the focus of the next section.

Theoretical accounts of intermittency

Several years ago, Glaser (1964: 54) commented that 'Those who lived in both the criminal and the conventional social worlds may walk a zigzag path between the two'. At first glance, this observation appears consistent with several criminological theories, and in this section some of these theories are assessed for their correspondence with intermittency.[3] We begin with one theory that seems to have been written expressly for the purpose of detailing intermittency, Matza's (1964) theory of delinquent drift.

Matza's theory of delinquent drift

Unlike many other criminological theories of the time, Matza's theory of delinquent drift was not aimed at viewing criminality as a permanent property of individuals. Instead, Matza chose to conceive of deviance as something that individuals sporadically drifted in and out of during certain periods of the life course. As delinquents were committed neither to a life of criminal activity nor a life of conventional activity, their lives were characterized by a flirtation, now and again, with criminal and deviant behaviour.

In relation to intermittency, Matza's theory seems to afford delinquents with a constant set of choices as to their involvement in both conventional and unconventional activities. Offenders, especially during their juvenile years, are expected to evidence frequent intermittent offending spells and are always at the ready for either delinquent or conventional actions. As Matza (1964: 28) notes:

> The delinquent is casually, intermittently, and transiently immersed in a pattern of illegal action ... The delinquent transiently exists in a limbo between convention and crime, responding in turn to the demands of each, flirting now with one, now the other, but postponing commitment, evading decision. Thus, he drifts between criminal and conventional action.

For Matza (1964: 55), the drifting delinquent approximates the substantial majority of juvenile delinquents who do not become adult criminals compared to the minority who do. The drifter begins to cease his or her involvement in unconventional behaviour by the time adulthood approaches because adulthood is marked by the addition of new affiliations, such as work and marriage, which 'cannot be slandered as kid stuff and thus dismissed'. This point is also recognized by Arnett

(2000) whose recent work on 'emerging adulthood' presents a similar characterization of entrance into the adult period of the life course. Some delinquents, however, go on to adult criminal careers, which are likely, at least according to Matza, not to be characterized by intermittent offending patterns. These individuals, Matza (1964: 56) claims, are in fact committed to their misdeeds and an unconventional lifestyle: 'They *decide* to be criminals.'

Matza's theory can be seen as providing the impetus for continued elaboration of the influences of social control mechanisms over the life course. One exemplar of this continued 'fleshing out' can be seen in the work of Sampson and Laub.

Sampson and Laub's age-graded informal social control theory

Sampson and Laub's theory builds on the work of classic social control theories in that it takes as it its central causal explanation an individual's involvement and investment in informal social control mechanisms over the life course. The primary mechanisms at work in their conceptualization involve education, employment and conventional relationships such as marriage. The social relations between individuals and these institutions of social control are characterized as a form of social investment, or social capital. In theory, one's investment in institutions of informal social control conveys the sense that the more one is invested, the more one has to lose by engaging in criminal activity.

Unlike its earlier control theory predecessors, however, Sampson and Laub's theory recognizes that individual offending patterns evidence both continuity and change over the life course. For example, relevant research indicates that involvement in anti-social behaviour extends throughout the life course. That is, childhood and adolescent anti-social behaviour are very strong predictors of juvenile delinquency, which is also a strong predictor of crime, alcohol and drug abuse in adulthood. Thus the continuity portion of their theory states that adult offenders are likely also to have been juvenile offenders who were likely also to have evidenced childhood anti-social behaviours.

At the same time, Sampson and Laub recognize that not all problem children and juvenile delinquents go on to become adult offenders. Thus criminal careers evidence significant patterns of change that must be accounted for. Salient life events and the development of social bonds in adulthood and beyond, especially those related to work and to a spouse, can counteract early involvement in anti-social behaviour. However, for Sampson and Laub it is not the mere presence of a spouse or a job that leads to changed ways; instead, it is the investment in the relations between the individual and his or her job and spouse that creates the social capital that is necessary to move offenders away from an unconventional lifestyle towards a more conventional one. Broken ties, moreover, can lead to a resumption of criminal activity. Although Sampson and Laub have not devoted a significant amount of attention to the concept of intermittency, their theory can clearly account for changes, either upward or downward, in the trajectory of criminal activity during short periods of time.

Moffitt's developmental taxonomy

Unlike traditional explanations of criminal behaviour, Moffitt's developmental taxonomy attempts to account for the variation in offending patterns that underlie the aggregate age–crime curve. Specifically, Moffitt's theory builds on Robins' (1966) paradox which suggests that, while adult criminal behaviour virtually requires juvenile delinquency, not all juvenile delinquents go on to become adult offenders.

In order to accomplish this task, Moffitt outlines a theory that includes two groups of offenders, each of whom possesses a unique aetiology towards criminal behaviour as well as a unique criminal repertoire. The first group of offenders, life-course persistent, engage in problematic behaviour throughout the life course as a result of an interaction between neuropsychological deficits and disadvantaged environments. These individuals begin offending early in the life course, engage in a wide range of anti-social and criminal acts, including violence, and desist much later (if at all) in the life course. For these offenders, continuity is the norm, while change is unlikely. The second group of offenders, adolescence limited, engage in delinquent activities that are confined, for the most part, to the juvenile period of the life course as a result of the perceived maturity gap. That is, when individuals reach adolescence they begin to covet adult-like behaviours and goods and, when they realize that such things are beyond their reach, they seek the aid and comfort of similar-aged peers who are going through the same issues. The dynamic interplay between the maturity gap and the peer social context of adolescence sets the stage for involvement in adult-like behaviours such as staying out late, alcohol and drug use, vandalism and premarital sexual intercourse. Adolescence-limited offenders do not, however, cross the line into the violence domain. Aside from a small number of adolescents who are ensnared into adult crime as a result of a drug habit or incarceration experience, the majority of adolescents begin to desist from their flirtation with delinquency as they enter early adulthood. Since these individuals do not have any sort of neuropsychological deficit, their verbal proficiencies and social skills make them adept at meeting the demands and expectations of adult life.

Moffitt is pretty clear about the probability of desistance for each of her two offender classifications. For example, she argues that individuals' reactions to life transition events (job, marriage, etc.) will vary depending on the personal anti-social histories of offenders. Among life-course persistent offenders, their injurious childhoods make them more likely to select jobs and spouses that support their anti-social lifestyles. On the other hand, since adolescence-limited offenders do not suffer from the same set of injurious childhoods, they are better able to find the kinds of spouses and jobs that support and maintain desistance.

Moffitt is silent with regard to the intermittent nature of criminal careers; however, her theory appears promising for developing cogent explanations of intermittency. For example, it may be the case that, like Matza's drifters, adolescence-limited offenders may experience significant intermittency patterns during the teenage years, when adolescence-limited and life-course persistors are difficult to disentangle (Moffitt 1993). Then, as they enter adulthood, the intermittency periods should begin to grow larger and larger among adolescence-limiteds because of their decline in criminal activity, whereas it should not for life-course persistors.

Agnew's general strain theory

In an effort to build upon the limitations identified with macro-level versions of strain theory, Agnew's (1992) general strain theory (GST) focuses on negative relationships with others. Expanding on the concept of strain, Agnew identified three sources of strain, including: (1) removal of positively valued stimuli; (2) presentation of noxious stimuli; and (3) failure to achieve positively valued goals. While classic strain theories stop at the strain portion of the strain–crime relationship, Agnew recognizes that people respond differently to strainful experiences. Thus he allows for an intervening variable of negative emotion to mediate the relationship between strain and crime. Individuals can experience a wide range of negative emotions, including fear, distress, depression and, most importantly, anger. Agnew's GST continues the causal process by hypothesizing that there are a variety of ways individuals cope with negative emotions and strainful life experiences, including emotional and/or religious coping.

Agnew (1997) has recently laid out how GST can account for patterns of stability and change over the life course that draws, in part, from Moffitt's two-fold typology. GST explains the stability of criminal behaviour primarily through its introduction of traits that increase the likelihood that an individual will (1) experience negative relationships; (2) interpret these relationships as aversive; and (3) react to this adversity with criminal behaviour. These traits can include but are not necessarily limited to irritability, minimal tolerance for frustration, hyperactivity, attention deficits, impulsivity, insensitivity to others and deficient problem-solving. Regarding change, GST accounts for the peak (and falling) of crime during adolescence by changes in (1) the extent of negative relations with others; (2) the tendency to interpret such relations as aversive; and (3) the tendency to cope with adversity through delinquency. Specifically, the peak in crime during adolescence is due to an increase in negative relations at this time and an increased tendency to interpret such relations as aversive and to then react with criminal behaviour. Individuals with the traits described earlier are likely to experience negative treatment from others at all ages, to interpret this negative treatment as aversive and to react by engaging in criminal or anti-social behaviours (Agnew 1997: 113). However, the large majority of adolescents do experience significant changes in the factors that cause change. Specifically, as most adolescents become adults, their social world begins to narrow and they have more control over the nature of this world (Agnew 1997: 114; see also Tittle 1995). The reduction in crime evidenced during early adolescence, then, is accounted for by GST in part to the narrowing of one's social world and the greater choice over one's associates that results. In essence, there are fewer people to treat the adult in a negative manner and these people are less likely to engage in negative behaviour (Agnew 1997: 115).

Although Agnew's application of GST to issues related to continuity and change is novel, it remains virtually silent on desistance, and even more so on intermittency. However, just like Moffitt's typology, GST can accommodate a focus on intermittent offending patterns. For example, an interesting aspect of GST is its expectation that strainful events come and go, at a fairly rapid pace so long as they are not enduring strainful events. Thus a bad break-up or a bad semester at college, while certainly strain producing, are also somewhat time-bounded events in the sense that they are temporary strains. When these strainful events are present, one could expect a higher probability of criminal activity (and thus a smaller intermittency incubation), while when such strains disappear or are removed, then the intermittency period should grow longer.

Deterrence explanations

Although there is no single deterrence theory, the main elements of the deterrence doctrine are common to most variations. For example, most accounts of deterrence offer that criminal activity is least likely when the certainty, celerity and severity associated with sanction threats are high. The most important property of deterrence, however, concerns the certainty associated with sanction threats; if individuals perceive great risk from the imposition of sanctions, they will be unlikely to engage in criminal behaviour.

Gibbs (1975) was one of the first scholars to highlight the need for studying different sorts of deterrence, and two of these bear import for present purposes: absolute and restrictive deterrence. The former deals with the situation in which individuals never engage in a criminal act because they are either deterred as a result of the fear of sanction threats or are morally deterred (i.e. they cannot even consider engaging in the act because they are morally opposed to it). The latter, restrictive deterrence, has to do with the situation in which offending frequency is curtailed, by some level, due to sanction imposition. Restrictive deterrence can take the form of changes in offence type as well as offence frequency. At its core, however, restrictive deterrence holds that individuals alter their offending patterns due to sanction threats, and limit their offending because of continued fear of sanction imposition.

Thus intermittent patterns in offenders' careers could be a function of sanction imposition and/or continued fear of sanction imposition. In fact, several accounts of desistance suggest that the repeated imposition of formal sanctions has the effect of bearing down on offenders so much so that they often report that they expect to go straight because they just cannot tolerate additional time in jail (see, generally, Tunnell 1992; Shover 1996).

As can be seen, several criminological theories bear fruit for the explanation of intermittent offending patterns. In the next section I raise a number of intermittency-related research questions to be addressed in future research, some of which are related to the theories identified, other which are more general in nature.

Questions to be addressed and research directions to get us there

Thus far I have provided evidence to suggest that, for some individuals, their involvement in criminal activity can be characterized as more or less intermittent. Still, there is a dearth of knowledge on offending patterns over the life course in general, and about intermittency in particular. In this section I outline several potentially important, yet untapped research questions that may uncover evidence that could help researchers better understand the stops and starts evidenced by many offenders throughout their careers in crime.

First, it may be the case that intermittent patterns may be more common for some offences rather than others (Clarke and Cornish 1985: 170). For example, among those crimes for which there is ample opportunity for most offenders to engage in the act, say minor theft or drug use, intermittent patterns may be less frequent than, say, for other crimes for which there is a lack of opportunity for most offenders including securities fraud, homicide, running a prostitution ring, etc.[4] Thus, among many offenders, common criminal acts, such as drug sales, should evidence small time periods between successive crimes because such acts occur frequently (see English and Mande 1992; Jacobs 1999), whereas relatively uncommon criminal acts, such as homicide, should evidence longer time periods between successive crimes.

In a related fashion, within-individual differences in intermittency would also make for a new, and interesting, aspect of studying offence and offender specialization. For example, since the commission of violent acts throughout one's individual career appears to be a function of offence frequency as opposed to some sort of specialized offence pattern (see Farrington 1989; Piquero 2000; Piquero and Buka 2002), it seems that intermittency periods for non-violent offences are likely to be shorter as opposed to the intermittency periods for violent offences which seem likely to be longer. A related issue that may be interesting concerns that of displacement of particular crimes to some other target (commercial premises rather than houses) or to another form of crime. Since desistance is not necessarily permanent and may simply be part of a continuing process of lulls in the offending of persistent criminals (Clarke and Cornish 1985: 173), it can be seen that studying desistance from one type of crime may likely begin the study of onset or persistence in another form of crime. Thus simply studying the change in offence frequency over time, while certainly interesting and of substantive import, does not fully capture the within-individual mix of several persistence/desistance careers that may vary across type of crime. Given that some research shows an increased tendency to specialize with advancing age (Piquero et al. 1999), charting the stops and starts across crime types within individual's careers would make for an interesting study, and Maltz and Mullay's (2000) methodological approach would be useful on this front.

Secondly, are the predictors of intermittency across offence types similar or different? For example, if a strong and successful marriage increases the length of time between violent criminal acts, does it also lengthen the time between non-violent criminal acts, or could it generate other forms of criminal activity? In essence, research is needed on the extent to which the factors associated with intermittency for one crime type are the same as the factors associated with intermittency for another crime type.

Thirdly, how is intermittency within individuals exhibited over the life course (i.e. across age)? For example, during the adolescent time period, are intermittency periods rather short as adolescents move in and out of various situations and acts, both illegal and legal, quickly? As these same adolescents make their way into 'emerging adulthood', do they begin to 'find their way' and move away from criminal activity as Matza and others would predict? Is it the case that with age, intermittency periods grow longer such that offenders begin to slow down, or burn out, with time? Is there an age by offence type interaction when it comes to studying intermittency patterns within offenders? For example, with property crime peaking in late adolescence, does this mean that intermittency patterns for property crime grow over time? And since violent crimes tend to peak a bit later in the life course, does it mean that there are larger violence intermittency patterns prior to late adolescence, smaller ones during the 'emerging adulthood' time period, and then larger ones later? Is there even more variation within larger categories of violent and non-violent crime? For example, tax evasion peaks later in the life course largely due to opportunity.

Fourthly, how does alcohol and drug use and abuse influence patterns of intermittency? For example, among heroin addicts, research consistently shows evidence of repeated cycles of remission and resumption of use often occurring over extended periods (Hser *et al.* 2001). Several studies have shown that relapse after some clean period is still possible, and is more likely among those addicted to heroin than those addicted to alcohol. Thus, are intermittency periods between successive robberies, for example, a function of an offender's level of drug use and abuse? For example, several ethnographic, qualitative and quantitative studies have shown that during periods of alcohol and drug use, offenders are more likely to engage in criminal acts compared to periods when they are not using alcohol and drugs (e.g. Anglin and Hser 1990; Decker and Wright 1994, 1997).

Fifthly, are there different intermittent periods among different groups of offenders defined by race and/or sex? Little research has explored gender and/or race differences in desistance in general (see

Uggen and Kruttschnitt 1998), and even fewer studies have explored differences in desistance and intermittency across race (see Piquero *et al.* 2002b). Is it possible that females, as a result of their lower level of criminal involvement especially in violent crimes, evidence much larger intermittent patterns? Save for a few qualitative and quantitative studies (see Warren and Rosenbaum 1986; Maher and Daly 1996; Baskin and Sommers 1998), researchers have not given significant attention to the longitudinal study of female careers in crime. Similar issues relate to the relationship between race and intermittency. Given that non-whites evidence more extensive involvement in certain types of violent crime (Blumstein *et al.* 1986), is it the case that whites evidence longer intermittent periods for violent crimes? The study of intermittency across race and gender becomes even more interesting because of several documented differences in the factors related to persistence and desistance across race and gender. If race and gender differences in the correlates associated with continued (or discontinued) crime exist, is it also the case that such differences manifest in a study of intermittency?

Table 5.1 presents a brief overview of the research needs in the area of intermittency. Still, some cautions should be noted.

Table 5.1 Research issues related to the study of intermittency

Areas	Questions to be answered
Natural history	1 Does intermittency increase or decrease with time?
	2 Do local life circumstances (i.e. wife, school, job) relate to intermittency patterns?
	3 Are intermittency periods longer for violent crimes as opposed to non-violent crimes?
	4 Is there within-individual variability in how intermittent periods vary across types of crime?
	5 Do different types of offenders evidence different intermittency patterns?
	6 Are intermittency patterns influenced by alcohol and/or drug use and abuse?
	7 Do groups defined by race and sex evidence different intermittency patterns?
	8 How do correctional and policy responses influence subsequent intermittency patterns?
	9 Do various treatments and interventions influence subsequent intermittency patterns?

Cautions when studying intermittency

Although the study of intermittency is likely to provide useful insight into patterns of within-individual offending that will relate to matters of both theory and policy, several issues arise that may provide temporary road-blocks for research efforts. Below I provide a partial list of these road-blocks that I hope are helpful to researchers as they continue efforts in studying intermittency.

First, researchers interested in studying intermittency are in need of a data structure that makes it feasible to study the time between successive criminal acts. For example, central to the intermittency enterprise is a data structure that contains dates of criminal events. Dates are necessary because they allow researchers to calculate the intermittent periods of study which, of course, is what is ultimately being explained. In most efforts devoted to the study of criminal careers, researchers have employed official records, largely because they contain dates of events. This is not to suggest that self-report records cannot be useful; in fact, just the opposite is true especially since official records only tap the criminal acts that come to the attention of the formal authorities. Although the debate between official and self-report data has long been of interest to criminologists, studying patterns of intermittency with both official and self-report data will make for an important contribution.

Secondly, and related to the issue of data sources, is the kind of self-report data-collection technique employed in studying intermittency. One promising approach is the life-calender method that was exemplified in Horney *et al.* (1995). Recall that those researchers asked Nebraska inmates to make notations during months in which they were active or inactive in both criminal behaviour as well as several local life circumstances thought to be related to involvement in criminal behaviour. This approach has the advantage that it creates the time-ordered structure needed to study patterns of intermittency; however, it treats the units as months. It may be the case that the data need to be broken down further into weeks rather than months because there could be inter-month variation especially in the disorganized lives of many chronic offenders (e.g. Horney *et al.* 1995: 670). Data from the life-calender method then, could be used alongside official records to provide a more complete account of intermittency patterns.

Thirdly, studying patterns of intermittency among drug sellers is likely to be complicated. For example, drug sellers engage in several sales per day (see English and Mande 1992). Thus the time distance between crime events may be difficult to model, and that which is modelled may not provide any intuitive information regarding intermittency. Such a problem may be the case among other types of offenders such as prostitutes who engage in several offences within any given day or evening. Thus researchers must deal with the fact that some offenders engage in multiple crimes per day, while others spread their criminal involvement across multiple time periods. Although it is likely that the latter group of offenders will be the ones who are most susceptible for studying intermittency, it does not necessarily mean that the intermittency periods of drug sellers is not worth empirical scrutiny.

Fourthly, researchers need to be careful not to confuse incarceration stints for intermittency. For example, Piquero and his colleagues (2001) recently documented the importance of controlling for street time when studying longitudinal trajectories of criminal activity. Using data for several hundred parolees from the California Youth Authority, they found that without controlling for street time, about 90 per cent of their sample was observed to have desisted. However, with controls for street time, they found that only about 70 per cent of their sample was observed to have desisted. The reason for this finding was related to incarceration stints. Some of the offenders were locked up during the post-parole period and thus were unable to engage in criminal acts. As can be seen, without controls for street time, researchers studying intermittency may inadvertently confuse incarceration stints for intermittency periods. Although street time data are difficult to collect, the life-calender method provides one useful mechanism for controlling for street time because it queries offenders on their street and incarceration time.[5]

Fifthly, researchers should also bear in mind that high-rate criminal offenders are also likely to experience an earlier death as a result of their criminally active lifestyles (Lattimore *et al.* 1997). Thus a false desister may actually be a dead offender. Collection of death certificates and related information should help ward off this potential problem.

Conclusion

The purpose of this chapter has been to document the importance of studying intermittency in offending patterns. Towards this end, several criminological theories were explored for their ability to explain intermittency. In addition, I offered one method by which intermittency can be defined and operationalized, as well as several interesting hypotheses that could be explored as researchers further study intermittency in offending patterns. Finally, I briefly highlighted several cautions that should be explored when studying intermittency. Although a focus on the study of intermittency initially raises questions about whether 'true desistance' should be a policy goal of correctional programming, it does not necessarily advocate the abandonment of desistance research. Instead it creates a complementary focus towards how criminal justice programmes could devote their attention and resources towards more incremental improvements in the lives of offenders, an approach which has been met with some success in the drug abuse area (Hser *et al.* 2001: 508).[6]

Given the constant zig-zaging between conventional and un-conventional lifestyles, as well as the difficulty surrounding the study of 'true desistance', it may be fruitful to devote complimentary attention to the study of how and why offenders go back and forth from offending to non-offending and back again. Research into the patterning of intermittency within and across criminal careers generally, as well as the factors that influence intermittency more specifically, also bears import for current criminological debates. For example, scholars advocating developmentally oriented theories of crime argue that the factors leading to one criminal typology are not necessarily the same as the factors that lead to membership in another criminal typology. It seems important to determine the extent to which offender trajectories evidence (or fail to evidence) distinct intermittent patterns, as well as the extent to which the factors associated with intermittency for one typology are the same as those for another typology. Such research has the potential to contribute further to the knowledge base regarding the patterning of criminal careers.

In the end, this chapter will have achieved its goal if it helps criminologists recognize that there lies something between persistence and desistance that is worthy of study, and that a sustained research agenda follows. Criminal careers are variable and, although knowledge on the length of criminal careers is certainly important for matters related to both theory and policy (Blumstein *et al.* 1982; Spelman 1994), at the same time many offenders spend long periods of time in which they refrain from criminal activity (Chaiken and Rolph 1987), and examining the factors associated with these lulls may provide important clues as to improving policy responses that may speed along the desistance process.

In sum, it does not necessarily follow that just because people abandon crime for a period of time, the desistance process has been accomplished (Shover 1996: 122). As Meisenhelder (1982: 152) noted, 'Any social reality is bounded by horizons of more or less open possibility … Thus, criminal behavior remains, as it does for us all, a possibility'. In fact many offenders reduce their frequency, switch offence types or 'lull out' for a while: for months or even years. But the possibility of a return to crime lingers. As one of Cusson and Pinsonneault's (1986: 78) offenders commented: 'I couldn't say that I would never start again. It could still happen.'

Notes

1 For example, if the underlying distribution of individual differences conformed to a gamma distribution then an application of some other parametric distribution to the data would be somewhat suspect. However, since the Nagin and Land approach models individual differences in a semi-parametric form, it models whatever type of probability distribution is present in the data. This flexibility is an added and important facet of their approach.

2 One of the main assumptions in the Nagin and Land model is that individuals commit crimes according to a Poisson process which requires the assumption that criminal events be independent. However, if criminal events tend to cluster because individuals tend to go on crime sprees, the independence assumption fails (Nagin and Land 1993: 357). Thus, crime sprees may complicate the study of intermittency. This temporal clustering of crimes might be contributing to the apparent explanatory power of intermittency.

3 Unfortunately, space precludes a review of these theories in great detail as well as a survey of several other theories which could account for the intermittency process. This presents a promising opportunity for future research.

4 Some readers might claim that intermittent patterns exist due to specialization and the knowledge required to engage in such actions. Yet, Benson and Moore (1992) not withstanding, evidence for specialization among most crime types is rather limited (see Gottfredson and Hirschi 1990; Paternoster et al. 1998; Piquero et al. 1999).

5 Of course, researchers need to keep in mind that, during lock-up, individuals can still engage in criminal acts.

6 For example, the concept of 'relapse' has been at the forefront of the drug abuse literature and, given what is known about intermittent offending patterns, perhaps the term relapse could be useful within criminal career circles as well.

References

Agnew, R. (1992) 'Foundation for a general strain theory of crime and delinquency', *Criminology*, 30: 47–87.

Agnew, R. (1997) 'Stability and change in crime over the life course: a strain theory explanation', in T. Thornberry (ed.) *Developmental Theories of Crime and Delinquency: Advances in Criminological Theory*. New Brunswick, NJ: Transaction Publishers.

Anglin, M.D. and Hser, Y.I. (1990) 'Treatment of drug abuse', in M. Tonry (ed.) *Drugs and Crime: Crime and Justice: An Annual Review of Research*. Chicago, IL: University of Chicago Press.

Arnett, J.J. (2000) 'Emerging adulthood: a theory of development from the late teens through the twenties', *American Psychologist*, 55: 469–80.

Barnett, A., Blumstein, A. and Farrington, D.P. (1989) 'A prospective test of a criminal career model', *Criminology*, 27: 373–85.

Bartusch, D., Lynam, D., Moffitt, T.E. and Silva, P.A. (1997) 'Is age important? Testing a general versus a developmental theory of antisocial behavior', *Criminology*, 35: 13–48.

Baskin, D. and Sommers, I. (1998) *Casualties of Community Disorder: Women's Careers in Violent Crimes*. Boulder, CO: Westview Press.

Baskin, D., Sommers, I. and Fagan, J. (1994) 'Getting out of the life: crime desistance by female street offenders', *Deviant Behavior*, 15: 125–49.

Benson, M.L. and Moore, E. (1992) 'Are white-collar and common offenders the same? An empirical and theoretical critique of a recently proposed general theory of crime', *Journal of Research in Crime and Delinquency*, 29: 251–72.

Blumstein, A. and Cohen, J. (1987) 'Characterizing criminal careers', *Science*, 237: 985–91.

Blumstein, A., Cohen, J., Das, S. and Moitra, S.D. (1988) 'Specialization and seriousness during adult criminal careers', *Journal of Quantitative Criminology*, 4: 303–45.

Blumstein, A., Cohen, J. and Hsieh, P. (1982) 'The duration of adult criminal careers', *Final Report Submitted to the National Institute of Justice*. Washington, DC.

Blumstein, A., Cohen, J., Roth, J. and Visher, C. (1986) *Criminal Careers and 'Career Criminals'*. Washington, DC: National Academy Press.

Bromwell, K.D., Marlatt, G.A., Lichtenstein, E. and Wilson, G.T. (1986) 'Understanding and preventing relapse', *American Psychologist*, 41: 765–82.

Bushway, S., Piquero, A.R., Mazerolle, P., Broidy, L. and Cauffman, E. (2001) 'A developmental framework for empirical research on desistance', *Criminology*, 39: 491–515.

Chaiken, J.M. and Rolph, J.E. (1987) *Identifying High-rate Serious Criminal Offenders*. Santa Monica, CA: Rand.

Clarke, R.V. and Cornish, D.B. (1985) 'Modeling offenders' decisions: a framework for research and policy', in M. Tonry (ed.) *Crime and Justice: An Annual Review of Research*. Chicago, IL: University of Chicago Press.

Cusson, M. and Pinsonneault, P. (1986) 'The decision to give up crime', in D.B. Cornish and R.V. Clarke (eds) *The Reasoning Criminal*. New York, NY: Springer-Verlag.

Dean, C.W., Brame, R. and Piquero, A. (1996) 'Criminal propensities, discrete groups of offenders, and persistence in crime', *Criminology*, 34: 547–74.

Decker, S.H. and Wright, R. (1994) *Burglars on the Job*. Boston, MA: Northeastern University Press.

Decker, S.H. and Wright, R. (1997) *Armed Robbers in Action*. Boston, MA: Northeastern University Press.

Elliott, D.S., Huizinga, D. and Morse, B. (1989) *Multiple Problem Youth: Delinquency, Substance Use, and Mental Health Problems*. New York, NY: Springer-Verlag.

English, K. and Mande, M. (1992) *Measuring Crime Rates of Prisoners*. Denver, CO: Colorado Department of Public Safety, Division of Criminal Justice, Office of Research and Statistics.

Farrall, S. and Bowling, B. (1999) 'Structuration, human development and desistance from crime', *British Journal of Criminology*, 39: 253–68.

Farrington, D.P. (1986) 'Age and crime', in M. Tonry (ed.) *Crime and Justice: An Annual Review of Research*. Chicago, IL: University of Chicago Press.

Farrington, D.P. (1989) 'Self-reported and official offending from adolescence to adulthood', in M. Klein (ed.) *Cross-national Research in Self-reported Crime and Delinquency*. Dordrecht: Kluwer.

Farrington, D.P. and Hawkins, J.D. (1991) 'Predicting participation, early onset, and later persistence in officially recorded offending', *Criminal Behaviour and Mental Health*, 1: 1–33.

Frazier, C.F. (1976) *Theoretical Approaches to Deviance: An Evaluation*. Columbus, OH: Merrill.

Gibbs, J.P. (1975) *Crime, Punishment, and Deterrence*. New York, NY: Elsevier.

Glaser, D. (1964) *The Effectiveness of a Prison and Parole System*. Indianapolis, IN: Bobbs-Merrill.

Gottfredson, M.R. and Hirschi, T. (1990) *A General Theory of Crime*. Stanford, CA: Stanford University Press.

Hirschi, T. and Gottfredson, M.R. (1995) 'Control theory and the life-course perspective', *Studies on Crime and Crime Prevention*, 4: 131–42.

Horney, J., Osgood, D.W. and Marshall, I. (1995) 'Criminal careers in the short-term: intra-individual variability in crime and its relation to local life circumstances', *American Sociological Review*, 60: 655–73.

Hser, Y., Hoffman, V., Grella, C.E. and Anglin, M.D. (2001) 'A 33-year follow-up of narcotics addicts', *Archives of General Psychiatry*, 58: 503–08.

Jacobs, B. (1999) *Dealing Crack: The Social World of Streetcorner Selling*. Boston, MA: Northeastern University Press.

Land, K.C., McCall, P.L. and Nagin, D.S. (1996) 'A comparison of Poisson, negative binomial, and semiparametric mixed Poisson regression models, with empirical applications to criminal careers data', *Sociological Methods and Research*, 24: 387-442.

Lattimore, P.K., Linster, R.L. and MacDonald, J.M. (1997) 'Risk of death among serious young offenders', *Journal of Research in Crime and Delinquency*, 34: 187–209.

Laub, J.H., Nagin, D.S. and Sampson, R.J. (1998) 'Trajectories of change in criminal offending: good marriages and the desistance process', *American Sociological Review*, 63: 225–38.

Loeber, R., Stouthamer-Loeber, M., Van Kammen, W. and Farrington, D.P. (1991) 'Initiation, escalation, and desistance in juvenile offending and their correlates', *Journal of Criminal Law and Criminology*, 82: 36–82.

Luckenbill, D.F. and Best, J. (1981) 'Careers in deviance and respectability: the analogy's limitations', *Social Problems*, 29: 197–206.

Maher, L. and Daly, K. (1996) 'Women in the street-level drug economic: continuity or change?', *Criminology*, 34: 465–91.

Maltz, M.D. and Mullay, J.M. (2000) 'Visualizing lives: new pathways for analyzing life course trajectories', *Journal of Quantitative Criminology*, 16: 255–81.

Maruna, S. (2001) *Making Good: How Ex-Offenders Reform and Reclaim their Lives*. Washington, DC: American Psychological Association Books.

Matza, D. (1964) *Delinquency and Drift*. New York, NY: Wiley.

Meisenhelder, T. (1977) 'An exploratory study of exiting from criminal careers', *Criminology*, 15: 319–34.

Meisenhelder, T. (1982) 'Becoming normal: certification as a stage in exiting from crime', *Deviant Behavior*, 3: 137–53.

Moffitt, T. (1993) 'Adolescence-limited and life-course persistent antisocial behavior: a developmental taxonomy', *Psychological Review*, 100: 674–701.

Nagin, D.S. and Land, K.C. (1993) 'Age, criminal careers, and population heterogeneity: specification and estimation of a nonparametric, mixed Poisson model', *Criminology*, 31: 327–62.

Paternoster, R. and Brame, R. (1997) 'Multiple routes to delinquency? A test of developmental and general theories of crime', *Criminology*, 35: 49–84.

Paternoster, R., Brame, R., Piquero, A., Mazerolle, P. and Dean, C.W. (1998) 'The forward specialization coefficient: distributional properties and subgroup differences', *Journal of Quantitative Criminology*, 14: 133–54.

Paternoster, R., Dean, C.W., Piquero, A., Mazerolle, P. and Brame, R. (1997) 'Generality, continuity and change in offending', *Journal of Quantitative Criminology*, 13: 231–66.

Petersilia, J. (1980) 'Criminal career research: a review of recent evidence', in N. Morris and M. Tonry (eds) *Crime and Justice: An Annual Review of Research. Volume 2*. Chicago, IL: University of Chicago Press.

Petersilia, J., Greenwood, P.W. and Lavin, M. (1978) *Criminal Careers of Habitual Offenders*. Washington, DC: US Department of Justice.

Piquero, A.R., Farrington, D.P. and Blumstein, A. (2003) 'The criminal career paradigm', in M. Tonry (ed.) *Crime and Justice: A Review of Research. Volume 30*. Chicago: University of Chicago Press.

Piquero, A.R. (2000) 'Frequency, violence and specialization in offending careers', *Journal of Research in Crime and Delinquency*, 37: 392–418.

Piquero, A.R., Blumstein, A., Brame, R., Haapanen, R., Mulvey, E.P. and Nagin, D.S. (2001) 'Assessing the impact of exposure time and incapacitation on longitudinal trajectories of criminal offending', *Journal of Adolescent Research*, 16: 54–74.

Piquero, A.R., Brame, R., Mazerolle, P. and Haapanen, R. (2002) 'Crime in emerging adulthood', *Criminology*, 40: 137–69.

Piquero, A.R. and Buka, S.L. (2002) 'Investigating race and gender differences in specialization in violence', in R.A. Silverman, T.P. Thornberry, B. Cohen and B. Krisberg (eds) *Criminology at the Millennium*. Boston, MA: Kluwer.

Piquero, A.R., MacDonald, J. and Parker, K.F. (2002b) 'Race, local life circumstances, and criminal activity'. *Social Science Quarterly*, 83: 654–70.

Piquero, A.R. and Mazerolle, P. (2001) *Life-course Criminology*. Belmont, CA: Wadsworth.

Piquero, A.R., Paternoster, R., Mazerolle, P., Brame, R. and Dean, C.W. (1999) 'Onset age and offense specialization', *Journal of Research in Crime and Delinquency*, 36: 275–99.

Quetelet, A. (1831) *Research on the Propensity for Crime at Different Ages*. Cincinnati, OH: Anderson.

Robins, L. (1966) *Deviant Children Grown Up*. Baltimore, MD: Williams & Wilkins.

Rowe, D.C., Osgood, D.W. and Nicewander, W.A. (1990) 'A latent trait approach to unifying criminal careers', *Criminology*, 28: 237–70.

Sampson, R.J. and Laub, J.H. (1995) 'Understanding variability in lives through time: contributions of life-course criminology', *Studies on Crime and Crime Prevention*, 4: 143–58.

Shover, N. (1996) *Great Pretenders*. Boulder, CO: Westview Press.

Shover, N. and Thompson, C.Y. (1992) 'Age, differential expectations, and crime desistance', *Criminology*, 30: 89–104.

Simons, R., Wu, C.I., Conger, R. and Lorenz, F. (1994) 'Two routes to delinquency: differences between early and late starters in the impact of parenting and deviant peers', *Criminology*, 32: 247–75.

Smith, D., Visher, C. and Jarjoura, R. (1991) 'Dimensions of delinquency: exploring the correlates of participation, frequency, and persistence of delinquent behavior', *Journal of Research in Crime and Delinquency*, 28: 6–32.

Spelman, W. (1994) *Criminal Incapacitation*. New York, NY: Plenum.

Tittle, C.R. (1995) *Control Balance*. Boulder, CO: Westview Press.

Tunnell, K.D. (1992) *Choosing Crime: The Criminal Calculus of Property Offenders*. Chicago, IL: Nelson-Hall.

Uggen, C. and Kruttschnitt, C. (1998) 'Crime in the breaking: gender differences in desistance', *Law and Society Review*, 32: 339–66.

Warren, M.Q. and Rosenbaum, J.L. (1986) 'Criminal careers of female offenders', *Criminal Justice and Behavior*, 13: 393–418.

Part III
Applied Research on Desistance

Chapter 6

Jail or the army: does military service facilitate desistance from crime?

Leana Allen Bouffard and John H. Laub

Introduction

Historically, military service and military-style training have been viewed as an effective correctional tool. The military has traditionally been viewed as a maturing experience – an environment and experience that will make 'men' out of boys (Arkin and Dobrofsky 1978). Because of this belief it has been a widely accepted practice for parents to send troublesome and delinquent boys to a military academy, boarding school or even boot camp to emulate a military way of life (Bryant 1979; Osler 1991; MacKenzie and Parent 1992). Criminal justice officials, especially judges, have also supported this notion by ordering some offenders to join the military as an alternative to trial or prison (Shattuck 1945; Mattick 1954). Additionally, correctional philosophy has focused on the use of military-style training and discipline to punish and reform offenders (Morash and Rucker 1990; MacKenzie and Parent 1992). The discipline of a military atmosphere was expected to deter offenders by instilling obedience and respect for authority and by teaching individuals how to live a structured, disciplined lifestyle (Morash and Rucker 1990).

Despite these beliefs, little is known about the relationship between military experience and criminal behaviour. Few studies have examined the influence of military service on behaviour, and most of this research has not looked at crime. Of those authors who have tried to determine the influence of military service on criminal or violent behaviour, many do not attempt to distinguish behaviour that appears to be due to a predisposition to criminality from behaviour resulting from military experience. The best studies, in terms of distinguishing predisposition from causation, have looked at military service in a life-course context. While these studies tend to find a beneficial effect of military experience, other research produces contradictory results. For example, studies examining the relationship between combat experience in Vietnam and later violence suggest a potentially criminogenic effect of some types of military service (see, for example, Boulanger 1986; Shaw *et al.* 1987). This study explores the relationship between military service and later criminal behaviour across different periods of time with the goal of determining whether military service facilitates desistance from crime.

Military service and the desistance process

The belief that military service can facilitate desistance stems from two ideas: (1) that the military environment removes the opportunity to commit crime; and/or (2) that military training teaches responsibility and discipline, thereby deterring future crime. One potentially corrective influence is the drastic change in lifestyle required when entering the military. Recruits must leave civilian society behind, removing themselves from the potentially criminogenic influence of their peers or environment. Elder and Hareven (1993) describe the military as a setting for dramatic life change because it draws large numbers of individuals from diverse communities, separating them from the civilian community and from the influence of family and friends. For some individuals, the military may offer the opportunity to escape from disadvantaged environments by providing job training and educational opportunities (see Browning *et al.* 1973; Elder 1987; Sampson and Laub 1996).

The military also actively seeks to instil structure and discipline with the initial basic training experience and with continued rigorous training throughout the military career. It is commonly thought that this disciplined environment will encourage a responsible lifestyle and discourage criminal behaviour (Bryant 1979). Sampson and Laub (1993) view the military as a positive turning point in the lives of delinquents because it is an environment that provides them with an attachment to conventional society and informal social norms.

In actuality, many factors may be responsible for transitions in the life course that may be engendered by military service. Hollingshead (1946) contends that recruits enter military service with a civilian reference and a set of values incompatible with military objectives. For this reason, entry into the military involves a re-education or socialization process in which individuals learn military norms and the military lifestyle. Elder (1999) describes three possible reasons that the military may have a beneficial influence in life: the military encourages social independence, provides time away from the pressures of the transition to adulthood and allows for a broader range of perspectives and experience. Browning and colleagues (1973) also suggest that the military may provide a beneficial environment, especially for disadvantaged groups like women and minorities. They contend that the military provides job training and other educational benefits that may not be as readily accessible to these groups in civilian society.

In a recent review of the literature on desistance from crime, Laub and Sampson (2001) note that, while there are multiple pathways to desistance, there are some general processes or mechanisms at work. What appears to be important about the desistance process is that it entails to varying degrees the following items: a 'knifing-off' of the past from the present; new situations that provide both supervision and monitoring as well as new opportunities of social support and growth; and new situations that provide opportunity for transforming one's identity. The experience of 'knifing-off' of individuals from their immediate environment and offering them a new script for the future is consistent with what the military strives to accomplish. Thus there is good reason to believe that serving in the military should facilitate desistance from crime. Indeed, Laub and Sampson (2001) found that serving in the military, along with marriage and work, were the significant factors in understanding desistance from crime.

Of course, it is possible that military service may have a detrimental influence in the life course. Some characteristics of the military lifestyle or of service may interfere with any impact it has on desistance. Possible reasons for this negative effect include the military interrupting existing social roles (Sampson and Laub 1996), teaching individuals to solve conflict aggressively and to use weapons (Hakeem 1946) and introducing unique stresses, such as separation from family (Bohannon *et al.* 1995). Some men must also serve in combat situations, which could result in later problems like post-traumatic stress disorder (Shaw *et al.* 1987). Some authors suggest that individuals in the military who are trained in the use of weapons and in hand-to-hand combat may respond aggressively or violently to conflict or provocation outside the military environment (Hakeem 1946; Bryant 1979; Dubanoski and McIntosh 1984).

Military service and criminal behaviour

Little research has looked at the relationship between military service and criminal behaviour in the context of a person's life. In general, studies using samples of men who served during the Second World War or Korea concluded that the amount of crime in the military during this time was much less than that in civilian society (MacCormick and Evjen 1946). During this period, some men with criminal records were allowed to serve in the military, and Shattuck (1945) found that these men performed just as well as soldiers without a criminal background. More specifically, a follow-up of men released from Illinois penitentiaries to serve during the war showed that they experienced generally satisfactory adjustment to the military lifestyle (Mattick 1954). In fact, one study found that the recidivism rate for men paroled into the army during this time was less than the rate for those paroled into civilian life (Bryant 1979).

Only a few studies have examined military service and criminal behaviour from a life-course perspective (Rand 1987; Sampson and Laub 1993, 1996). Sampson and Laub (1993) examined military experience among boys who were sampled in the Gluecks' *Unraveling Juvenile Delinquency* study (1950). Sheldon and Eleanor Glueck collected longitudinal data on a matched sample of delinquents and non-delinquents born between 1924 and 1932. These boys reached adulthood between 1942 and 1950, and a majority of the men in this sample served in the military during the late stages of the Second World War or the Korean War (Glueck and Glueck 1968). In a reanalysis of these data, Laub and Sampson (1995) found a great deal of continuity in offending from childhood to adulthood, including offences during military service. More of those defined as delinquent in childhood were charged while in the military compared to non-delinquents. Delinquents were also much more likely to commit serious and frequent offences and to receive a dishonourable discharge (Sampson and Laub 1993). In addition to the striking continuity of behaviour through military service, there were also cases in which the military was described as a beneficial turning point in life. Laub and Sampson (1995) conclude that, for some men in the Glueck sample, the military had a positive impact, helping them to overcome childhood disadvantage (for specific examples, see Laub and Sampson 1993; Sampson and Laub 1996).

Rand (1987) also looked at the influence of military service on officially recorded recidivism in the 1945 Philadelphia birth cohort. Boys in this sample reached adulthood (age 18) in 1963, during the early stages of the Vietnam War. This study included longitudinal data on all boys who were born in Philadelphia in 1945 and who were still living there between their 10th and 17th birthdays. In her study, Rand (1987) included only those boys who had committed index or serious offences. In terms of desistance, white men with military experience stopped offending (in terms of official records) two years earlier than white men with no military experience, but there was no significant difference in the age at last offence for non-whites. In general, this study appears to indicate a small influence of military service on later criminal behaviour.

In a study of men who served in the military during the Vietnam War, Robins (1994, 1993) and her colleagues (1975, 1974) found a much different relationship between military service and later offending. The authors interviewed a sample of enlisted men one year after their return from Vietnam. At later follow-ups, the men were matched to a group of men who were eligible for the draft but had not served in the military. These studies generally found that while there was more drug use among servicemen during the Vietnam War than expected, very few men continued their use when they returned to the USA. Both military factors and pre-service behaviour predicted continued drug use after service during Vietnam. However, the relationship between drug use before and after military service and later arrests was contingent upon the continued use of drugs after service. This series of studies suggests a complicated picture of the relationship between military service and criminal behaviour. Whereas most servicemen discontinue their problem behaviour after service, those who continue also experience later problems including increased arrests.

Bachman and colleagues (1999) also examined the relationship between military service and drug use from a life-course perspective. These authors used longitudinal data derived from the 'Monitoring the Future' survey over two decades (cohorts of 1976–95) to look at changes in drug use after entering the military and across historical periods. For a number of different high-school graduating classes, this study found that the prevalence of drug use decreased after entering the military, and there was more of a decline for individuals who entered the military compared to those who started a full-time job or who entered college. This pattern indicates a greater likelihood of desistance from drug use for those individuals who entered military service.

Studies that have looked at the influence of military service in a life-course framework have generally found that military experience affects later life outcomes, including marital relationships (see Pavalko and Elder 1990), education (see Elder and Caspi 1990), employment (see Cohen et al. 1995; Sampson and Laub 1996) and criminal behaviour. In particular, studies examining the relationship between military service and criminal behaviour or drug use have typically found a beneficial effect in terms of desistance. Research has generally indicated that military service is associated with both continuity in offending and the reduction of criminal behaviour. As Sampson and Laub (1993) found, some individuals with criminal records may continue their criminal behaviour during military service. For other individuals, military service may encourage desistance.

Research strategy

To investigate whether military service is associated with desistance from crime, we analysed longitudinal data from multiple cohorts of individuals. To be selected for this study, the data must have included information about both criminal behaviour and military service and must have provided information on the timing of events, denoted either by the year, age or range of ages at which an event occurred. We found four cohorts that met these criteria. Each data set is longitudinal, containing at least two waves of information and providing measures of childhood and adolescent delinquent behaviour, adult offending, military experience and a variety of other factors. Additionally, the information provided is specific with regard to the timing of events, especially concerning military service. Finally, these cohorts span several decades in an effort to determine whether the influence of military service changes with the historical context of service. The four cohorts used in this study are Lyle Shannon's (1942, 1949) Racine, Wisconsin, birth cohorts (see Shannon 1994), the 1945 Philadelphia birth cohort (Wolfgang *et al.* 1994), and the National Longitudinal Survey of Youth (Center for Human Resource Research 1995).

Importantly, the four cohorts selected for this study cover the period of time from just prior to the Vietnam War to the early part of the all-volunteer force. The oldest cohort (those born in 1942) reached the age of 18 in 1960, and the youngest group of subjects (born in 1963) reached the age of 18 in 1981. The two cohorts in Lyle Shannon's study of delinquency in Racine, Wisconsin, served immediately before and during the Vietnam War (see Shannon 1994). The males selected into the 1945 Philadelphia birth cohort follow-up also served during the Vietnam War (see Wolfgang *et al.* 1994). Finally, the sample of men and women in the National Longitudinal Survey of Youth were eligible to serve in the military after the end of the draft and during the transition to an all-volunteer force (see Cohen *et al.* 1995).

Hypotheses

Previous research suggests that military service is associated with either the continuation of or a decline in criminal behaviour. Since our analyses are particularly interested in desistance and desistance is a process that is only relevant for individuals who have begun offending, we will focus on those cohort members with a record of juvenile delinquency. In particular, we hypothesize that delinquents who serve in the military are more likely to desist than those with no military experience. First, desistance will be examined in terms of the lack of a police contact in adulthood. We expect that delinquents who enter the military will be less likely to have an adult police contact. Secondly, desistance may be measured by the age of a person's last offence or police contact. We predict that delinquents who serve in the military will desist earlier (i.e. they will be younger at their last recorded police contact).

It is possible that military service may have the greatest effect on the most serious offenders. These are the individuals most in need of 'knifing-off' or a drastic change in their environment and life circumstances. Military service provides such a dramatic change. We predict that, among the more serious juvenile offenders, those who serve in the military will be more likely to show a pattern of desistance in terms of both the lack of an adult police contact and the age at last contact.

Data elements

In 1977, Lyle Shannon began collecting data from three birth cohorts in Racine, Wisconsin (see Shannon 1994). Both juvenile and adult police contact data were collected for the members of each cohort in 1977 when the 1942 cohort was 35, the 1949 cohort was 28 and the 1955 cohort was 22 years old. Additionally, a subset of individuals from the 1942 and 1949 cohorts were interviewed, and researchers collected information about a wide variety of sociodemographic characteristics, including military service, marriage and employment. Data from these interviews were used for our analyses. A total of 332 individuals were interviewed from the 1942 cohort, and 554 were interviewed from the 1949 cohort. Since individuals in these two cohorts experienced different historical events at different periods in their lives, each cohort will be analysed separately.

Subjects in Shannon's 1942 cohort were very young children during the Second World War and the Korean War and reached adulthood (the age of 18) in 1960, before the beginning of the Vietnam War. Thus they grew up during the 1950s, a period of relative economic prosperity and stability. Those who entered the military served immediately prior to and during the Vietnam conflict. Among the 155 men in this cohort, about 40 per cent had active-duty military experience, and most of those (nearly 80 per cent) entered military service before the start of the Vietnam War in 1964.[1] Subjects in the 1949 cohort were born at the beginning of the Korean War, and they turned 18 in 1967, after the Vietnam War had begun. These individuals experienced the 1950s during their early childhood and went through adolescence during the more tumultuous period of the 1960s. Nearly 40 per cent of the 243 men in this cohort had active-duty military experience, and more than 80 per cent of those who served entered the military between 1967 and 1969. This period of time corresponds to the dramatic build-up of forces in southeast Asia around the time of the Tet Offensive in 1968.

The third cohort used in this study is the 1945 Philadelphia birth cohort (Wolfgang *et al.* 1987). The researchers selected boys into this cohort based on the criteria that the boys must have been born in Philadelphia in 1945 and that they must have been residents of Philadelphia between their tenth and seventeenth birthdays (see Wolfgang *et al.* 1972 for details). The data collected for boys in the original cohort consisted solely of official records, but a smaller sample was later interviewed and followed until their thirtieth birthday (see Wolfgang *et al.* 1987 for details). Men in this cohort were born in 1945 and reached adulthood (their eighteenth birthday) in 1963, at the early stages of the Vietnam War. They grew up during the 1950s and reached late adolescence and early adulthood during the 1960s. Of the 565 follow-up interviews conducted, about 48 per cent served on active duty in the military, and more than 90 per cent of those began their service before 1966.

The final cohort is the National Longitudinal Survey of Youth (NLSY). The National Longitudinal Survey of Youth is a panel survey that has been conducted annually since 1979 (Cohen *et al.* 1995). Two samples were originally selected. The first was designed to be representative of non-institutionalized, civilian youths who were born between 1957 and 1964 and lived in the USA in 1979 (Center for Human Resources Research 1995). The second sample was drawn from Department of Defense rosters and was designed to represent individuals who were born between 1957 and 1961 and who were serving in the military in September of 1978 (Center for Human Resources Research 1995). The first interviews were conducted with both samples in 1979 when subjects were between 14 and 22 years old, and subjects were interviewed yearly until 1994. The men in this sample were born between 1957 and 1963 and grew up during the period of the Vietnam War. These subjects reached adulthood between 1975 and 1981, after the end of the Vietnam War. Thus the men were eligible to enter the armed forces (18 years old) after the end of the draft and during the early period of the all-volunteer force. Overall, the National Longitudinal Survey of Youth sample included 515 men with active-duty military service and 4,055 men with no military experience.

Measurement issues

There has been extensive debate in the literature about how to define and measure desistance from crime (see Laub and Sampson 2001 for a review). In this study, desistance was examined in two different ways. First, we look at whether the men had a police contact as an adult. Adulthood was defined as the period of time from the age of 18 until the end of the follow-up period.[2] The three birth cohorts collected detailed information on official police contacts and followed individuals until their late 20s. The National Longitudinal Survey of Youth used self-reports of offending, including self-reported police contacts for non-traffic offences.[3] Desistance may also be measured by the age of an individual's last offence. This variable is only relevant for the three birth cohorts, so the National Longitudinal Survey of Youth will be excluded from analyses of age at last arrest.

In terms of military service, these analyses focused on men who indicated that they had served on active duty in the military.[4] For all four cohorts, military service was measured as a dichotomous variable with 0 representing no service and 1 representing service on active duty. Additional variables were used in the multivariate analyses. These included race (white coded as 0 and non-white coded as 1), education (a continuous variable reflecting the highest grade completed), socio-economic status and number of juvenile police contacts. Socioeconomic status was measured differently across the cohorts. In the Racine cohorts, this variable reflects an aggregate measure of the socioeconomic status of the neighbourhood where each subject was raised. In the Philadelphia cohort, this variable measures the family's yearly income when the subject was an adolescent. In the National Longitudinal Survey of Youth, Socioeconomic Status (SES) measures yearly income in 1979.

Results

As displayed in Table 6.1, across three of the four cohorts, delinquents who entered the military were much less likely to have an adult police contact. In the 1942 Racine birth cohort, about 47 per cent of delinquents who did not enter the military but only 36 per cent of delinquents who

137

Table 6.1 Percentage of delinquents with adult police contact by military service

Cohort	Military (%)	Non-military (%)
Racine 1942[1]	35.5	47.1
	$\chi^2 = 0.90$	
Philadelphia 1945[2]	35.2	46.3
	$\chi^2 = 2.24$	
Racine 1949[3]	50.0	49.3
	$\chi^2 = 0.01$	
National Longitudinal Survey of Youth[4]	31.2	64.4
	$\chi^2 = 34.05$**	

Notes:
Chi-square values have one degree of freedom.
1   $n = 31$ military and 34 non-military for Racine 1942.
2   $n = 91$ military and 82 non-military for Philadelphia 1945.
3   $n = 58$ military and 67 non-military for Racine 1949.
4   $n = 80$ military and 844 non-military for National Longitudinal Survey of Youth.
*$p < .05$; **$p < .01$.

did enter the military had an adult police contact ($\chi^2 = 0.90$; $p = .34$). Similarly, 46 per cent of delinquents in the Philadelphia cohort had an adult police contact, but only 35 per cent of delinquents who entered the military had an adult contact ($\chi^2 = 2.24$; $p = .14$). The same pattern appeared in the National Longitudinal Survey of Youth. About 64 per cent of delinquents who did not enter the military and only 31 per cent of delinquents who entered the military had an adult contact ($\chi^2 = 34.05$; $p < .01$). While these results were not consistently significant, this pattern suggests that juvenile delinquents who served in the military were more likely to desist from crime than delinquents with no military experience. In two of the birth cohorts, there was an absolute difference of over ten percentage points. Even though this difference was not significant, it is large enough to suggest that there is some impact of military service.

The only cohort in which this pattern did not occur was the Racine 1949 cohort. In this cohort, about half of each group had an adult contact ($\chi^2 = 0.01$; $p = .93$). Most men in this cohort served in the Vietnam War between 1967 and 1969 during which there was a dramatic build-up of forces around the time of the Tet Offensive in 1968. During this period, selection processes were drawing a different group of people (Segal

1989; Gimbel and Booth 1996), which may have included more serious delinquents or individuals more inclined to continue their offending.

Table 6.2 presents results from multivariate analyses predicting adult offending and including race, education, socioeconomic status, age (for the National Longitudinal Survey of Youth) and number of juvenile offences as control variables. Controlling for these factors, military service is consistently related to the reduced likelihood of an adult

Table 6.2 Logistic regression models predicting adult police contacts among delinquents

Variables	Racine 1942[1]			Philadelphia 1945[2]		
	b	Exp(b)	Wald	b	Exp(b)	Wald
Constant	−0.91	0.40	0.16	0.94	2.55	0.57
Military service	−0.39	0.68	0.50	−0.56	0.57	2.70
Non-white	8.57	5263.50	0.10	0.66	1.92	1.93
Education	0.04	1.04	0.05	−0.16	0.85	3.34
SES	−0.05	0.96	0.72	0.05	1.05	0.09
Age	—	—	—	—	—	—
Number of juvenile contacts	0.12	1.13	1.55	0.20	1.22	6.23*

Variables	Racine 1949[3]			National Longitudinal Survey of Youth[4]		
	b	Exp(b)	Wald	b	Exp(b)	Wald
Constant	4.27	71.37	5.15*	6.89	983.92	88.70***
Military service	−0.55	0.58	1.47	−0.54	0.58	3.75
Non-white	0.23	1.26	0.17	−0.39	0.68	6.40*
Education	−0.38	0.68	8.02**	0.01	1.01	0.05
SES	−0.01	1.00	0.02	0.00	1.00	1.70
Age	—	—	—	−0.34	0.71	41.28***
Number of juvenile contacts	0.29	1.33	10.97**	—	—	—

Notes:
1   $n = 65$ for Racine 1942.
2   $n = 173$ for Philadelphia 1945.
3   $n = 125$ for Racine 1949.
4   $n = 924$ for National Longitudinal Survey of Youth.
*$p < .05$; **$p < .01$; ***$p < .001$.

contact in all four cohorts. However, this effect is not statistically significant. Despite the lack of significant findings in these analyses, there is a consistent pattern in the relationship between military service and having an adult police contact, suggesting that desistance may occur more frequently for those with military experience.

Age at last arrest

Another way of measuring desistance is by the age at which a person had his or her last recorded police contact. In Table 6.3, we present bivariate analyses of age at last contact by military service.[5] Across all three birth cohorts, there was no significant difference in age at last contact for men who served in the military versus those with no military experience. The largest difference in age at last contact occurred in the Philadelphia cohort where there was a difference of more than a year (18.2 for the military group and 19.4 for the non-military group). However, this difference was still not statistically significant.

Table 6.4 presents results from multivariate regression models predicting age at last police contact and controlling for race, education, socioeconomic status and number of juvenile contacts. In all three cohorts, there appears to be no significant relationship between military

Table 6.3 Average age of last contact by military service

Cohort	Military		Non-military
Racine 1942[1]	20.68		21.00
	(6.35)		(5.44)
		$t = 0.22$	
Philadelphia 1945[2]	18.15		19.43
	(4.69)		(5.28)
		$t = 1.68$	
Racine 1949[3]	18.78		18.28
	(3.51)		(4.50)
		$t = -0.69$	

Notes:
These values represent the mean age of last contact with standard deviations in parentheses.
1   $n = 31$ military and 34 non-military for Racine 1949.
2   $n = 91$ military and 82 non-military for Philadelphia 1945.
3   $n = 58$ military and 67 non-military for Racine 1949.
$*p < .05; **p < .01; ***p < .001.$

Table 6.4 Regression models predicting age of last police contact

Variables	Racine 1942[1]			Philadelphia 1945[2]			Racine 1949[3]		
	b	SE b	t-ratio	b	SE b	t-ratio	b	SE b	t-ratio
Constant	22.04	5.94	3.71***	18.70	2.35	7.95***	23.58	2.68	8.79***
Military service	-0.03	1.42	-0.02	-1.25	0.67	-1.87	-0.01	0.65	-0.01
Non-white	6.33	2.80	2.26*	2.41	0.96	2.53*	1.40	0.82	1.70
Education	-0.15	0.44	-0.33	-0.22	0.16	-1.37	-0.47	0.19	-2.46*
SES	-0.08	0.14	-0.54	0.29	0.33	0.86	-0.04	0.05	-0.79
Number of juvenile contacts	0.27	0.26	1.05	0.64	0.13	4.84***	0.28	0.07	4.14***

Notes:
1 $n = 65$ for Racine 1942.
2 $n = 173$ for Philadelphia 1945.
3 $n = 125$ for Racine 1949.
*$p < .05$; **$p < .01$; ***$p < .001$.

service and age at last contact when control variables were included. Though military service does not appear to influence age of desistance in these analyses, it is important to note that for the military group, the average age of last police contact occurred at an age when the men were serving in the military. It appears that most men who entered military service desisted during or shortly after their service. Across the three cohorts, between 65 and 75 per cent of men who entered the military desisted by the age of 21.

Serious delinquency and military service

The third hypothesis in this study suggested that the military may be most effective for serious delinquents. We defined serious delinquents as those having at least three police contacts as a juvenile or having a violent offence as a juvenile.[6] Table 6.5 presents bivariate analyses comparing serious delinquents who entered the military and those who did not serve in the military in terms of both having an adult police contact and age at last contact. In the 1942 Racine cohort and the Philadelphia birth cohort, serious delinquents who entered military service were much less likely to have an adult police contact. In the 1942 cohort, 25 per cent of serious delinquents who entered the military and 60 per cent of those who did not serve in the military had an adult police contact. Similarly, in the Philadelphia cohort, about 47 per cent of serious delinquents who entered the military and more than 65 per cent of those who did not enter the military had an adult contact. Although these results were not statistically significant, it is likely due to the small sample sizes. Thus there is a good indication that military service is related to an increased likelihood of desistance for serious delinquents. On the other hand, results from the 1949 Racine cohort were similar to previous analyses in finding no significant difference between the military and non-military groups in terms of the per cent with a later police contact.

In Table 6.6, we present results from multivariate analyses predicting desistance in adulthood and controlling for race, education, socio-economic status and the number of juvenile contacts. In all three cohorts, the effect of military service was negative, suggesting a reduced likelihood of having an adult contact. However, this coefficient was only significant in the 1942 Racine cohort. Controlling for race, education, socioeconomic status and the number of juvenile contacts, serious delinquents who entered the military were significantly less likely to have an adult police contact ($b = -3.77$; Wald = 4.07). These results

Table 6.5 Percentage of serious delinquents with adult police contact and average age of last contact by military service

Cohort	Percentage with adult contact[1]		Age of last contact[2]	
	Military	Non-military	Military	Non-military
Racine 1942[3]	25.0	60.0	19.92	22.07
			(6.14)	(5.24)
	$\chi^2 = 3.31$		$t = 0.98$	
Philadelphia 1945[4]	46.9	65.5	20.13	21.83
			(4.68)	(5.60)
	$\chi^2 = 2.14$		$t = 1.29$	
Racine 1949[5]	67.7	65.4	20.48	20.65
			(3.03)	(4.04)
	$\chi^2 = 0.04$		$t = 0.18$	

Notes:
1   Chi-square values have one degree of freedom.
2   Mean values with standard deviations in parentheses.
3   $n = 12$ military and 15 non-military for Racine 1942.
4   $n = 32$ military and 29 non-military for Philadelphia 1945.
5   $n = 31$ military and 26 non-military for Racine 1949.
*$p < .05$; **$p < .01$; ***$p < .001$.

suggest that serious delinquents who served in the military during this period were more likely to desist from crime compared with those with no military experience.

We also examined age at last contact for serious delinquents. Bivariate analyses found little difference in age at last police contact between those who served in the military and those who did not serve (see Table 6.5). Multivariate analyses were also estimated to predict age at last police contact for those men identified as serious delinquents (see Table 6.7). In these analyses, the direction of the effect of military service was consistently negative, suggesting that serious delinquents who entered the military desisted earlier than those who did not serve in the military. However, the coefficients were not statistically significant for any of the models.

Table 6.6 Logistic regression models predicting adult police contacts among serious juvenile delinquents

Variables	Racine 1942[1]			Philadelphia 1945[2]			Racine 1949[3]		
	b	Exp(b)	Wald	b	Exp(b)	Wald	b	Exp(b)	Wald
Constant	10.41	33,238.42	1.87	3.11	22.33	1.19	0.77	2.16	0.08
Military service	-3.77	0.02	4.07*	-0.68	0.51	1.26	-0.20	0.82	0.07
Non-white	7.19	1,325.68	0.01	0.10	2.70	1.64	0.30	1.35	0.09
Education	-0.50	0.61	1.21	-0.41	0.67	2.74	-0.15	0.86	0.66
SES	-0.62	0.54	4.17*	0.17	1.18	0.34	-0.02	0.98	0.06
Number of juvenile contacts	0.20	1.22	0.94	0.20	1.22	2.80	0.35	1.42	5.39*

Notes:

1 $n = 27$ for Racine 1942.
2 $n = 61$ for Philadelphia 1945.
3 $n = 57$ for Racine 1949.

$*p < .05; **p < .01; ***p < .001.$

Table 6.7 Regression models predicting age at last police contact among serious juvenile delinquents

Variables	Racine 1942[1]			Philadelphia 1945[2]			Racine 1949[3]		
	b	SE b	t-ratio	b	SE b	t-ratio	b	SE b	t-ratio
Constant	30.97	9.00	3.44**	20.66	4.67	4.42***	23.48	3.52	6.67***
Military service	−2.64	1.97	−1.34	−1.13	1.18	−0.96	−0.02	0.91	−0.02
Non-white	6.94	5.44	1.27	3.43	1.46	2.35*	1.35	1.11	1.22
Education	−0.44	0.62	−0.71	−0.43	0.37	−1.16	−0.31	0.25	−1.23
SES	−0.58	0.22	−2.68*	0.40	0.54	0.75	−0.05	0.08	−0.68
Number of juvenile contacts	0.15	0.36	0.42	0.53	0.18	2.92**	0.14	0.08	1.76

Notes:
1 $n = 27$ for Racine 1942.
2 $n = 61$ for Philadelphia 1945.
3 $n = 57$ for Racine 1949.
$*p < .05; **p < .01; ***p < .001.$

Conclusions and implications

The relationship between military service and criminal behaviour is a topic that has not received much research attention, particularly in regard to desistance from crime. Drawing on data from three longitudinal birth cohorts and the National Longitudinal Survey of Youth, we found a consistent pattern of results indicating a possible beneficial impact of military service on desistance. Specifically, desistance may be more likely for delinquents who enter the military. However, few of our results were statistically significant, which precludes us from making any definitive conclusions. Interestingly, there were significant results when it came to considering the impact of military service for serious delinquents. In the 1942 cohort of men who served at the beginning of the Vietnam War, military service significantly reduced the likelihood of a later offence among serious juvenile delinquents. There also appeared to be a relationship between military service and desistance for serious delinquents in the Philadelphia birth cohort. These results support our suggestion that the impact of military service may be most relevant for the most serious offenders, although this finding did not hold up for the 1949 cohort from Racine.

The three birth cohorts (birth years of 1942, 1945 and 1949) consisted of men who were eligible for military service during different periods of the Vietnam War. Men in the National Longitudinal Survey of Youth were eligible for service at the beginning of the all-volunteer force. Using these different cohorts allowed us to see whether the relationship between military service and desistance varied over time and by the conditions of service. Much to our surprise, we found that our results do not necessarily appear to be conditioned upon historical period.

There is much to consider when assessing the role of military service in the desistance process and in many ways our data are quite limited. Specific characteristics of military service, including combat, training, benefits, rank and assignment, may provide the determining factors in the desistance process. For example, some research suggests that combat experience is related to later violence. Boulanger (1986) found that even 10–16 years after military service, combat veterans were more violent than non-combat veterans. Additionally, combat veterans have a greater frequency of arrest, particularly for violent offences, compared to non-combat and non-veterans (Laufer *et al*. 1981). It may be that those men who served during the later stages of the Vietnam War were also more likely to see combat, thus negating any generally beneficial impact of military service.

It is also possible that the benefits associated with military service are important factors in facilitating desistance from crime. The original GI Bill, introduced during the Second World War, provided large numbers of servicemen with job counselling and placement, job training, loans and education (Segal 1989). These benefits may be responsible for the beneficial outcomes associated with military service during this period, including reduced criminal behaviour. Research has demonstrated that higher levels of education and stable employment are related to reduced offending (see National Research Council 1993; Sampson and Laub 1993). Thus providing service members with these opportunities through military service should also be related to reduced offending, especially for individuals who would not otherwise have these opportunities.

Unfortunately, the data available do not allow us to explore the mechanisms that may account for the relationship between military service and desistance. There is little information available about the specific characteristics of military service and the post-military experience. These may be important in determining who is likely to continue their offending and who desists and should be part of future research on military service and desistance from crime.

Another important issue for consideration in future research is selection. Research is able to address who enters the military, and some data are available to determine whether military service is linked to later criminal behaviour. However, there are few data sets that combine information regarding selection into the military with later life outcomes. The demographic makeup of individuals entering the military changed dramatically during the years covered in this study (Segal *et al.* 1998), so it would be important to consider those factors in more detail. Selection may be especially relevant for the volunteer force where service is a choice for all members.

Though our study is primarily exploratory and much more needs to be done, some important evidence has emerged. In considering the characteristics that influence whether events promote desistance, military service has the potential to provide a dramatic change in life circumstances, roles and responsibilities while promoting discipline and structure. Results from this study suggest that the military may produce desistance from crime, especially for the most serious offenders. While these results might appear to suggest specific criminal justice policies (i.e. military-style boot camps for offenders), it is too soon to make specific recommendations. Available research has not yet determined the mechanism(s) that may be responsible for desistance.[7] Before these findings can be useful for sentencing and criminal justice policy, we must determine how military service and desistance are related. The next step is to assess exactly what it is about the military experience that facilitates desistance from crime and to see whether those experiences can be replicated in parallel settings such as national service (see Uggen and Janikula 1999).

Notes

1 Between the 1942 and 1949 cohorts, only a very few women had military service. Because this number is inadequate for statistical analysis and because the Philadelphia cohort does not include females, women were excluded from our analyses.

2 Police contacts for men with military service were examined individually to ensure proper temporal order. For these men, adult police contacts were defined as those contacts that occurred after the age of 18 and after entry into the military. This only affected the offending breakdown for a very small number of men.

3 We recognize that one problem with desistance research thus far is an arbitrary follow-up period with no clear indication that offending has necessarily ceased (Laub and Sampson 2001). However, since individuals in the birth cohorts were followed until their late 20s, the lack of a police contact over more than a decade should provide a reasonably accurate representation of desistance.

4 Some men were identified as having served in the National Guard or reserves. The nature of this type of service is different from active-duty military service in terms of both the type and consistency of training as well as the lifestyle surrounding service. For this reason, service in the National Guard or reserves was not treated as active-duty military service.

5 Since the procedure for measuring criminal behaviour in the National Longitudinal Survey of Youth was different from the birth cohorts, no measure of age at last contact was available. For this reason, the National Longitudinal Survey of Youth was excluded from these analyses.

6 Variables were not available in the National Longitudinal Survey of Youth to determine which men were serious juvenile delinquents, so the National Longitudinal Survey of Youth was excluded from these analyses.

7 In fact, studies examining the effectiveness of boot camps have generally found that military-style structure and discipline alone do not reduce recidivism (MacKenzie and Souryal 1995).

References

Arkin, W. and Dobrofsky, L.R. (1978) 'Military socialization and masculinity', *Journal of Social Issues*, 34 (151): 154–5.

Bachman, J.G., Freedman-Doan, P., O'Malley, P.M., Johnston, L.D. and Segal, D.R. (1999) 'Changing patterns of drug use among US military recruits before and after enlistment', *American Journal of Public Health*, 89: 672–7.

Bohannon, J.R., Drosser, Jr, D.A. and Lindley, S.E. (1995) 'Using couple data to determine domestic violence rates: an attempt to replicate previous work', *Violence and Victims*, 10: 133–41.

Boulanger, G. (1986) 'Violence and Vietnam veterans', in G. Boulanger and C. Kadushin (eds) *The Vietnam Veteran Redefined: Fact and Fiction*. Hillsdale, NJ: Lawrence Erlbaum Associates, 79–90.

Browning, H.L., Lopreato, S.C. and Poston, Jr, D.L. (1973) 'Income and veterans status: variations among Mexican Americans, blacks, and Anglos', *American Sociological Review*, 38: 74–85.

Bryant, C.D. (1979) *Khaki-collar Crime: Deviant Behavior in the Military Context*. New York, NY: The Free Press.

Center for Human Resource Research (1995) *NLS Users' Guide*. Columbus, OH: Ohio State University.

Cohen, J., Warner, R.L. and Segal, D.R. (1995) 'Military service and educational attainment in the all-volunteer force', *Social Science Quarterly*, 73: 397–409.

Dubanoski, R.A. and McIntosh, S.R. (1984) 'Child abuse and neglect in military and civilian families', *Child Abuse and Neglect*, 8: 55–67.

Elder, Jr, G.H. (1987) 'War mobilization and the life course: a cohort of World War II veterans', *Sociological Forum*, 2: 449–73.

Elder, Jr, G.H. (1999) *Children of the Great Depression: Social Change in Life Experience (25th anniversary edition)*. Boulder, CO: Westview Press.

Elder, Jr, G.H. and Caspi, A. (1990) 'Studying lives in a changing society: Sociological and personological explorations', in A.I. Rabin *et al*. (eds) *Studying Persons and Lives*. New York, NY: Springer, 201–47.

Elder, Jr, G.L. and Hareven, T.K. (1993) 'Rising above life's disadvantage: from the Great Depression to war', in G.H. Elder *et al*. (eds) *Children in Time and Place: Development and Historical Insights*. Cambridge: Cambridge University Press, 3–21.

Gimbel, C. and Booth, A. (1996) 'Who fought in Vietnam?', *Social Forces*, 74: 1137–57.

Glueck, S. and Glueck, E. (1950) *Unraveling Juvenile Delinquency*. New York, NY: Commonwealth Fund.

Glueck, S. and Glueck, E. (1968) *Delinquents and Nondelinquents in Perspective*. Cambridge, MA: Harvard University Press.

Hakeem, M. (1946) 'Service in the armed forces and criminality', *Journal of Criminal Law and Criminology*, 37: 120–37.

Hollingshead, A.R. (1946) 'Adjustment to military life', *The American Journal of Sociology*, 51: 439–47.

Laub, J.H. and Sampson, R.J. (1993) 'Turning points in the life course: why change matters to the study of crime', *Criminology*, 31: 301–25.

Laub, J.H. and Sampson, R.J. (1995) 'Crime and context in the lives of 1,000 Boston men, circa 1925–1955', in Z.S. Blau and J. Hagan (eds) *Current*

Perspectives on Aging and the Life Cycle. Vol. 4. Delinquency and Disrepute in the Life Course. Greenwich, CT: JAI Press, 119–39.

Laub, J.H. and Sampson, R.J. (2001) 'Understanding desistance from crime', in M. Tonry (ed.) *Crime and Justice.* Chicago, IL: University of Chicago Press.

Laufer, R.S., Yager, T., Frey-Wouters, E. and Donnellan, J. (1981) 'Post-war trauma: social and psychological problems of Vietnam veterans in the aftermath of the Vietnam War', in A. Engendorf *et al.* (eds) *Legacies of Vietnam: Comparative Adjustment of Veterans and their Peers.* New York, NY: Center for Policy Research, 318–473.

MacCormick, A.H. and Evjen, V.H. (1946) 'Statistical study of 24,000 military prisoners', *Federal Probation*, 10: 6–11.

MacKenzie, D.L. and Parent, D. (1992) 'Boot camp prisons for young offenders', in J.M. Byrne *et al.* (eds) *Smart Sentencing: The Emergence of Intermediate Sanctions.* Newbury Park, CA: Sage.

MacKenzie, D.L. and Souryal, C. (1995) 'Inmates' attitude change during incarceration: a comparison of boot camp with traditional prison', *Justice Quarterly*, 12: 325–54.

Mattick, H. (1954) 'Parolees in the army during World War II', *Federal Probation*, 24: 49–55.

Morash, M. and Rucker, L. (1990) 'A critical look at the idea of boot camp as a correctional reform', *Crime and Delinquency*, 36: 204–22.

National Research Council (1993) *Losing Generations: Adolescents in High Risk Settings.* Washington, DC: National Academy Press.

Osler, M.W. (1991) 'Shock incarceration: hard realities and real possibilities', *Federal Probation*, 55: 34–43.

Pavalko, E.K. and Elder, Jr, G.H. (1990) 'World War II and divorce: a life-course perspective', *American Journal of Sociology*, 95: 1213–34.

Rand, A. (1987) 'Transitional life events and desistance from delinquency and crime', in M.E. Wolfgang *et al.* (eds) *From Boy to Man, from Delinquency to Crime.* Chicago, IL: University of Chicago Press, 134–62.

Robins, L.N. (1993) 'Vietnam veterans' rapid recovery from heroin addiction: a fluke or normal expectation?', *Addiction*, 88: 1041–54.

Robins, L.N. (1994) 'Lessons from the Vietnam heroin experience', *Harvard Mental Health Letter*, 5: 5–6.

Robins, L.N., Davis, D.H. and Goodwin, D.W. (1974) 'Drug use by US Army enlisted men in Vietnam: a follow-up on their return home', *American Journal of Epidemiology*, 99: 235–49.

Robins, L.N., Helzer, J.E. and Davis, D.H. (1975) 'Narcotic use in Southeast Asia and afterward: an interview study of 898 Vietnam returnees', *Archives of General Psychiatry*, 32: 955–61.

Sampson, R.J. and Laub, J.H. (1993) *Crime in the Making: Pathways and Turning Points through Life.* Cambridge, MA: Harvard University Press.

Sampson, R.J. and Laub, J.H. (1996) 'Socioeconomic achievement in the life course of disadvantaged men: military service as a turning point, circa 1940–1965', *American Sociological Review*, 61: 347–67.

Segal, D.R. (1989) *Recruiting for Uncle Sam: Citizenship and Military Manpower*. Lawrence, KS: University Press of Kansas.

Segal, D.R., Burns, T.J., Falk, W.W., Silver, M.P. and Sharda, B.D. (1998) 'The all-volunteer force in the 1970s', *Social Science Quarterly*, 79: 390–411.

Shannon, L.W. (1994). *Juvenile Delinquency and Adult Crime, 1948–1977 [Racine, Wisconsin]: Three birth cohorts* (computer file). Conducted by University of Iowa, Iowa Urban Community Research Center; 2nd ICPSR edn Ann Arbor, MI: Inter-university Consortium for Political and Social Research.

Shattuck, E.S. (1945) 'Military service for men with criminal records', *Federal Probation*, 9: 12–14.

Shaw, D.M., Churchill, C.M., Noyes, Jr, R. and Loeffelholz, P.L. (1987) 'Criminal behavior and post-traumatic stress disorder in Vietnam veterans', *Comprehensive Psychiatry*, 28: 403–11.

Uggen, C. and Janikula, J. (1999) 'Volunteerism and arrest in the transition to adulthood', *Social Forces*, 78: 331–62.

Wolfgang, M.E., Figlio, R.M. and Sellin, T. (1972) *Delinquency in a Birth Cohort*. Chicago, IL: University of Chicago Press.

Wolfgang, M.E., Figlio, R.M. and Sellin, T. (1994) *Delinquency in a Birth Cohort in Philadelphia, Pennsylvania, 1945–1963* (computer file). Conducted by University of Pennsylvania, Wharton School; 3rd ICPSR edn Ann Arbor, MI: Inter-university Consortium for Political and Social Research.

Wolfgang, M.E., Thornberry, T.P. and Figlio, R.M. (1987) *From Boy to Man, from Delinquency to Crime*. Chicago, IL: University of Chicago Press.

Chapter 7

To reoffend or not to reoffend? The ambivalence of convicted property offenders

Ros Burnett

Introduction

Practitioners in the criminal justice system routinely deal with the paradox of offenders who say they will desist from further offending but who, shortly afterwards, reoffend.[1] Those working with these offenders are then faced with questions about whether the initial declaration had been genuine, whether the wish to go straight was not aligned with intention, or whether the individual had been unable to fulfil a resolution to desist because of pressures and misfortune. Similarly, research has found that 'straight expectations fail to make a difference in post release desistance' (Shover and Thompson 1992: 99; see also Piliavin *et al.* 1986). Again, questions are raised, this time for the researcher: is the motivation for desistance distinct from expectation and choice? What are the situational influences which constrain the choice to desist? Are long-term goals abandoned in favour of immediate desires and demands? Some individuals do indeed succeed in keeping to their resolve: what makes the difference?

To answer these questions – unless their mental states are to be regarded as epiphenomenal to the causes of their recidivism – we need to understand the hearts and minds of the people whose behaviour is being studied. What is required is an exploration of the subjective domain,[2] including decision-making processes (Cornish and Clarke 1986), their motivations and interpretations of their situation (Katz 1991; Jacob and Wright 1999) and their constructs, implicit understanding and meaning systems (e.g. Kelly 1955; Harré *et al.* 1985; Dweck 2000) – no less than the whole person, drawing on key dimensions of personality such as personal strategies and self-narratives (McAdams 1994; Maruna 1999).

Criminology has not always offered the most hospitable climate for the study of what goes on in people's heads. In recent years, a substantial proportion of criminological work conveys a model of soft determinism, wherein offenders, like everyone else, 'are neither wholly free nor completely constrained, but fall somewhere between' (Matza 1964: 27). However, the methodology and research enterprises have emphasized correlates of crime and background risk factors, and the result can be an image of the offending person as one who is 'a relatively passive figure' (Clarke and Cornish 1985: 148). Some contributors to the discipline contend that empirical research is dominated by the deterministic model (Agnew 1995) and that criminology still has a 'positivistic bent' whereby internal states are not explicitly addressed (Jacobs and Wright 1999: 164). Farrington has recently acknowledged the powerful influence in criminology of the 'risk factor prevention paradigm' (2000: 1); this, in turn, has been reflected in policy and practice (Kemshall 1998; Robinson 2002).

It would be erroneous to imply, though, that criminology has embargoed exploration of the offender's perspective. The discipline has also been host to areas of investigation which place a premium on the subjective dimension. For example, a principle of the Chicago School which emerged as long ago as the 1920s but which has 'never died' (Short 1997: 5) was that the voice of the individuals being studied should be heard. This was followed by David Matza's influential call for criminologists to adopt a method of 'appreciation' in which the 'aim is to comprehend and to illuminate the subject's view and to interpret the world as it appears to him' (1969: 25). Cornish and Clarke's (1986) initiative in the 1980s ushered in a number of studies of offenders' decision-making processes (e.g. Cromwell *et al.* 1991; Tunnell 1992; Shover 1996). During the 1990s there was a resurgent interest in the phenomenological context of crime wherein the individual's motivations, interpretations and subjective responses to the situation are all-important (e.g. Katz 1988; Hagan and McCarthy 1997; Jacobs and Wright 1999).

At the crux of many of these subjective-level studies is the issue of how much reasoning, choice and forward-thinking underlies criminal activity. Rational choice theories of crime treat the offender as a decision-maker who employs a criminal calculus, weighing risks and benefits before making the choice to commit an offence. However, studies in this vein, far from showing the criminal to be a systematic and logical thinker, as the label might imply, uncover other influences and motivations and reveal that decision-making associated with crime is subject to 'cognitive limitation, short-cut decision-making and processing heuristics' (Lattimore and Witte 1986: 133). Tunnell (1992) concludes that the notion of the criminal calculus is not strictly applicable because the burglars he studied did not consider the risks, only the benefits. At the time of doing burglaries they did not think about getting caught; indeed, they saw themselves as immune from arrest. Drugs and drink are used to deaden fearful apprehension before making the, by then, clouded decision to commit the risky act of burglary (Cromwell *et al*. 1991; Tunnell 1992). Further, as pointed out by Tunnell, those who are involved in crime on a regular basis do not make a decision at all because crime is something they do as a routine. A recurrent research observation is that persistent offenders do not usually engage in forward-planning, either with respect to crime or their future in general, but tend to live for the moment (Katz 1991; Shover 1996; Jacobs and Wright 1999).

The timing and timescale of studies exploring offenders' decision-making and motivation are critical. In a recent address to the American Psychological Association, Farrington highlighted a residual gap in explanations of crime: 'Existing research tells us more about the development of criminal potential than about how that potential becomes the actuality of offending in any given situation' (2000: 5). Studies of the 'situational foreground conditions' (Katz 1991) and the 'phenomenological context' (Jacob and Wright 1999) are therefore an important route to filling this gap. Cromwell *et al*. (1991) used the ingenious method of *staged activity analysis*, asking subjects to reconstruct burglaries they had committed, and sometimes going along with them to the actual sites to facilitate recall. Such methodology recognizes the 'situated' nature of human behaviour (Katz 1988). Getting research participants to say what is relevant very close to the commission of the act avoids the problems of retrospective, *post hoc* rationalizations and is more likely to capture significant emotional factors (e.g. Tice *et al*. 2001). Nevertheless, as Jacobs and Wright point out, 'decisions to offend like all social action do not take place in a vacuum' (1999: 150), and the study of the more immediate choices and motivations to commit crime should not be at the expense of attention to the more long-term plans and enduring motivations. As Shover (1996) heeds, the choice to offend or desist is one of a series of choices, some of which are more far-reaching, such as choice of identity and choice of lifestyle.

It is from a broader temporal perspective, taking account of exogenous influences on motivation, that involvement in and withdrawal from criminal activity are more likely to be understood (Farrell and Bowling 1999). As Maruna (2001: 17) has highlighted, giving up crime 'is not an event that happens, rather it is the sustained *absence* of a certain type of event'. A foray into the full biographical context may be required: Maruna argues that an explanation of desistance requires access to the self-narratives which ex-offenders develop to make sense of their lives. Such an approach is in keeping with a growing number of theorists who call for a longer-term perspective which allows for the dynamic interaction of social and subjective variables (e.g. Thornberry 1987; Bushway *et al.* 2001; Laub and Sampson 2001).

One early proposal for the employment of a dynamic, longitudinal model was made by Hood (1995: 19):

> Research on psychosocial interventions ... needs to be integrated with longitudinal studies of criminal careers. In other words, we need to develop an interactionist, more 'dynamic', research strategy in order to understand the varying impact of those factors including psycho-social interventions, which shape the reactions, choices and behaviours of those who have experienced penal sanctions.

The research to be described was an attempt to heed this call in a study of the dynamics of recidivism and desistance from the perspectives of property offenders as they moved from a prison sentence back into the community.

The Oxford study of recidivism

Researchers at the University of Oxford Centre for Criminological Research designed a two-year longitudinal study (Burnett 1992, 1994)[3] which concentrated on the detailed accounts of male property offenders as they progressed from imprisonment to re-entry in the community. The cohort comprised 130 men who had convictions for crimes of acquisition, including theft, fraud, robbery and taking without consent. They had between 3 and 14 previous convictions, indicating (according to risk of reconviction studies – e.g. Ward 1987) that they were at medium risk of reoffending. Those fulfilling this criteria, and who were close to their release dates, were selected from databases of inmates in nine prisons. The majority of interviewees were white (86 per cent), and in their 20s (76 per cent). The request to interview them before and after release in order to understand why some reoffended and others did not was relayed to them by prison officers and, presumably because it was a diversion from the prison routine, very few refused the initial interview.

There were three stages of interviewing. Following the first interview, which took place in prison shortly before their discharge date, there were two prolonged rounds of post-release interviewing. Round one took place four to six months after release and round two occurred 7–20 months after release. Altogether 109 (84 per cent) of the original sample were reinterviewed, including 57 who were reinterviewed on two occasions. Three of the men died during the follow-up period.

At the beginning of the second and third interview, the issues emerging in the previous interview were 'revisited' with the participants so that comparisons could be made with the present. A particular feature of the interviews was that, in all three meetings, the participants were asked to look back in time and forward in time as well as to explain their present perspective. On each occasion they were asked about their aspirations and expectations and what they saw as stumbling blocks to desistance from further offending. Specific questions were aimed at yielding information about their criminal intentions, what issues they saw as relevant to their offending or non-offending, what plans and strategies they had if any and what problems and prospects they faced.

Looking over the prison wall

Sample members were first interviewed shortly before their release from a prison sentence. Hood and Sparks (1970: 229) referred to both the initial and final part of a prison sentence as the time when the inmate is most likely to 'look over the wall', identifying with the outside community and thinking about what they will do after release.

To explore the relationship between their expectations of further offending and actual subsequent offending, a set of five related questions were asked in the pre-release interview:

1   Do you want to go straight?
2   Are you able to go straight?
3   On a scale of 0–100 how likely are you to commit an offence during the next 12 months?
4   If an opportunity arose to make money illegally how likely would you be to take it?
5   If an opportunity arose to make money illegally, and there were no risks of getting caught, how likely would you be to take it?

In the pre-release interviews, over 80 per cent said they *wanted* to go straight but only 25 per cent thought they would definitely be *able* to go straight (another 16 per cent thought they would 'probably' be able to achieve this). A small minority (5 per cent) said they did not want to go straight, the implications being that they preferred, or at least intended, to reoffend. Another 14 per cent expressed uncertainty about their wishes, often saying that what they wanted in this respect would be conditional on circumstances:

> Yes, I would like to go straight, but it is something you get caught up in. I can't read the future; it depends … I can't walk around the streets without money in my pocket. If I haven't got money in my pocket I've got to earn it, one way or another.

Wanting to desist was sometimes expressed as merely wishful thinking: 'I'd like to if I get the chance. You don't go out intending to carry on, but if things go wrong and you lack things, you seem to fall into it.' Many of those who said they would like to desist acknowledged straightaway that they would find it difficult, and indicated that they could only do so subject to particular conditions, such as obtaining employment, staying off drugs, being reconciled with a girlfriend or meeting some other prerequisite:

> If you are out of work and no money coming in, you have to do something – or the little ones would go hungry.

> I'd have to have the opportunities that would enable me to build the lifestyle I want without resorting to that kind of activity.

When participants were asked to explain why they wished and/or intended to stop offending, or why they were at least considering the idea, the majority mentioned negative aspects of imprisonment. About a quarter referred generally to unpleasant aspects of prison life or their objection to repeated prison experiences. A quarter stressed family factors, usually with regard to how prison was affecting their relationships. Some mentioned the deprivations for themselves, specifically missing contact with their loved ones and fear of losing their partners in the event of another period away, and others stressed the secondary effects for their partners or children:

> If I keep on, I'll lose my wife, so from that point of view I'm going to stop.

> If I was a single man, prison wouldn't have deterred me what-soever. But it has been more of a sentence for the wife, so not being single I see it differently.

Some had much clearer and more promising prospects than others. A large proportion (68 per cent) were without definite employment prospects, though half of these had plans for employment or thought their prospects of obtaining work were good. Nearly two-thirds (62 per cent) were unattached or were not intending to live with their wife or girlfriend. Just over half (55 per cent) had one or more children, although in a number of cases these were with previous partners and they were no longer in contact. Almost a fifth (17 per cent) were not sure where they would be living after release.

Participants were asked directly to state which obstacles or difficulties could result in them reoffending. A list of criminogenic factors was drawn up (loosely corresponding to a range of explanatory theories, from differential association theory to rational choice theory) and participants were asked whether any of those factors would make it more difficult for them to desist from reoffending, and then which, if any, factors would likely be their main difficulty. Their responses are shown in Table 7.1. Only nine of the men claimed they would be altogether free of difficulties in avoiding reoffending. The majority conceded that one or more of the factors listed to them could be stumbling blocks in attempts to go straight.

Lack of money was identified as a main obstacle considerably more often than any other item. Twice as many identified 'lack of money' as a stumbling block and identified a more profit-orientated motive: 'making money.' These two items contrast the motives of need and enterprise, a distinction often made by interviewees in their explanations of their previous offending. Around a quarter of the sample anticipated that most of the other items could be obstacles for them. At the pre-release stage, a similar proportion of participants identified a drug habit as a potential obstacle to going straight as had identified the use of alcohol as an obstacle, whether as the main difficulty or one among others.

The extent of uncertainty and doubt about their ability to desist was again indicated in participants' estimate on a 0–100 scale of the likelihood of them reoffending (property offences only). Twenty-nine per cent estimated a greater than 50 per cent chance of reoffending within 12 months from release; another 18 per cent estimated a 50–50 chance of

Table 7.1 Anticipated obstacles to desisting from crime

| | All obstacles | | Main obstacles | |
	$n = 130*$	%	$n = 130*$	%
Lack of money	76	58.5	36	27.7
Desire to make money	38	29.2	6	4.6
Police harassment	38	29.2	11	8.5
No alternative	37	28.5	9	6.5
Excitement/boredom	33	25.4	10	7.7
Alcohol	32	24.6	21	16.2
Drugs	32	24.6	20	15.4
Drift back to crime	31	23.1	2	1.5
Pressure from mates	30	23.1	7	5.4
Social prejudice	30	23.1	8	6.2
Anger/stress	30	23.1	11	8.5
Compulsion/temptation	26	20.0	8	6.2
Other	3	2.3	8	6.2
None	9	6.9	9	6.9

Note:
*Multiple answers possible.

recidivism. That is, virtually half the sample thought there would be an even chance or above-evens chance of them reoffending within a year of release. Well over half (63 per cent) indicated that they would be vulnerable to temptation if an apparently *risk-free* opportunity arose.

The interviewees were often reluctant to make the above predictions, preferring to reserve their judgement about how they would act and staying open to a change of perspective after their release from prison: 'This is how I feel now. Whether I can carry it out is another matter. You don't know what you are going to do until you get out there.'

Getting out to harsh reality

How many reoffended?

One objective was to compare the accounts of those who persisted in offending with those who desisted, based on their self-report. In the post-release interviews, the participants were asked: (1) what offences, if any, they had committed; and (2) if any offences had resulted in arrest or conviction. Forty-seven of the men (43 per cent) who were reinterviewed claimed that they had not committed further property offences, but six of these acknowledged other types of offences (including driving offences, disorderly conduct and offences of violence), none of which resulted in further custodial sentences. Given that this represented a departure from their previous conduct it was decided to include them, for comparative purposes, with the desisters. Sixty-two (57 per cent) of those reinterviewed claimed that they had committed property offences since release; some of these had also committed non-property offences (see Table 7.2).

A second distinction is between property offences resulting in court proceedings and those which do not. The use of self-report enabled inclusion of persisters who, at the time of interview, would have been desisters, according to official records. It is, of course, possible that some were falsely confessing to offences they had not committed, but it seems more likely that any false claims would have been in the opposite direction. Forty per cent of those who claimed to have persisted in offending had not been involved in court proceedings nor apprehended in connection with these offences at the time of interview. Furthermore, many of those who had been reconvicted had nevertheless avoided charges for other recent offences which they said they had committed.

In the following discussion, the 43 per cent who said they had not committed property offences up to the time of interview will be referred to simply as 'desisters', while the rest will be referred to as 'persisters'.[4] As in all previous research on recidivism, it was found that reoffending was related to age and to number of previous convictions. Two out of every three who were under 29 years of age had committed further property offences, while two in three of those aged 29 and over had desisted (see Table 7.3). The persisters also, predictably, had more

Table 7.2 Offences which did not result in a further custodial sentence

Desisters $n = 47$	(43%)	Persisters $n = 62$	(57%)
No offences	41	Court proceedings	37
Different type of offence	6	No court proceedings	25

Table 7.3 Reoffending related to age and number of previous convictions

	21–28 years ($n = 74$)	29–45 years ($n = 35$)
Persisters	49 (66.2%)	13 (37.1%)
Desisters	25 (33.8%)	22 (62.9%)

previous convictions than the desisters. Of the 23 men who had been serving their first custodial sentence when interviewed in prison, 61 per cent had desisted, while 38 per cent of those who had previously served sentences had desisted.

Expectations compared with outcomes

How predictive were their pre-release answers about possible criminal outcomes when matched against self-reported criminal outcomes in the post-release interviews? Answers to the five predictive questions (set out above) which had been asked in the pre-release interview were summed to produce a score of *desistance optimism*. These scores were divided into five categories of optimism: 'definite', 'optimistic', 'undecided', 'pessimistic' and 'sceptic'. As shown in Figure 7.1, this categorization was a good fit with self-reported desistance following release.

One hypothesis to explain these differences, which is compatible with a rational choice model, is that those who are open to the possibility of further offending are more likely to take up opportunities to reoffend. Following the decision model of Clarke and Cornish (1985) there is a degree of prior *readiness* to commit crime if factors seem to merit it. A second hypothesis, in line with strain theory, is that individuals' predictions of the likelihood of reoffending are aligned with the extent of personal difficulties anticipated. In order to explore these possibilities, a comparison was made of the social circumstances of persisters and desisters.

Figure 7.1 Pre-release desistance optimism and post-release criminal outcomes

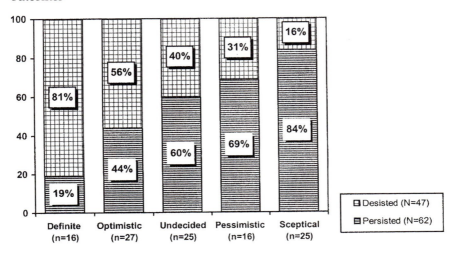

Social circumstances

Overall, there were more persisters than desisters with problematic or unsatisfactory circumstances. In summary, *prior to release*, similar proportions of both groups estimated employment and financial difficulties, but more persisters than desisters thought they might have accommodation and relationship problems and more indicated a possible drug problem. *Following release*, persisters were less likely to have employment, less likely to have satisfactory accommodation and stable relationships, more likely to be using 'hard' drugs and to have criminal associates, and more likely to be experiencing boredom and to have acted violently.

After getting out from prison more of the desisters had success in getting *jobs*. In later interviews many in both categories were unemployed but desisters were more likely to have looked for work or to have worked briefly. In both groups there was general scepticism about the likelihood of ever obtaining a job which would be acceptable to them, unless it was via self-employment. In response to this hopelessness, there was a tendency to develop a flexible, entrepreneurial approach to work. To some extent this entrepreneurial spirit was expressed by persisters in their criminal activity; this was a way for them to 'earn' money and to pay the bills. Desisters were more likely, instead, to engage in short bursts of casual employment.

Twice as many of the persisters as the desisters had *accommodation* problems after release. More of the desisters than persisters were living with *partners* following release, and more desisters expressed satisfaction with their relationships. More of the persisters did not yet have children (57 per cent compared to 43 per cent), and more persisters mentioned conflict with parents or other relatives. Meeting their partner or getting married were often given as the key reason for withdrawing from criminal activities – although some suggested they had only reached this position gradually ('Since I've been married, I've only done two sentences!').

At the post-release stage, there were considerably more desisters than persisters who acknowledged light or moderate use of *alcohol*, but the reverse was true for heavy drinking. *Drug abuse* was unquestionably a greater problem for those who persisted than for desisters. Following release, persisters were more likely to mention *criminal associates* than were desisters. In the pre- and post-release interviews, desisters seemed more prepared to resist pressures, rehearsing how they would respond, or referring to an understanding among co-offenders that family commitment justifies withdrawing.

Explanations and rationalizations

To which of these problems did the persisters attribute their subsequent offending? Following release, the reasons which persisters most frequently associated with their reoffending, in interview 2 and interview 3 respectively, were: lack of money (33 per cent and 50 per cent); making money (19 per cent and 25 per cent); financing a drug habit (15 per cent and 14 per cent); and need for excitement (15 per cent and 18 per cent). Comparison of obstacles anticipated prior to release shows that the desisters most frequently identified 'lack of money' and becoming 'angry or stressed' as their main obstacles to avoiding further offences (see Table 7.4). The most frequently identified main obstacles for the persisters had been drugs and alcohol but, much more than the desisters, they tended to identify a combination of several other factors as potential obstacles to going straight.

As Table 7.4 shows, those who persisted in offending were less optimistic about their ability to desist and, overall, they had more social difficulties. It is a challenge to remain optimistic when basic needs such as accommodation and relationships cannot be taken for granted. Were the persisters, therefore, simply being realistic given the magnitude of

Table 7.4 Pre-release anticipation of obstacles by post-release outcomes (%)

	Could be an obstacle			Main obstacle	
	Persisters *n* = 62*	Desisters *n* = 47*		Persisters *n* = 62*	Desisters *n* = 47*
Mates	33.9	14.9	Mates	8.1	4.3
Excitement	40.3	19.1	Excitement	9.7	4.3
Lack of money	72.6	63.8	Lack of money	19.4	36.2
Making money	41.9	25.5	Making money	6.5	2.1
Temptation	33.9	17.0	Temptation	4.8	8.5
Alcohol	30.6	25.5	Alcohol	21.0	12.8
Drugs	45.2	8.5	Drugs	24.2	6.4
Police	38.7	23.4	Police	8.1	6.4
Prejudice	43.5	19.1	Prejudice	8.1	6.4
Anger/stress	27.4	29.7	Anger/stress	4.8	14.9
Drift back	46.8	23.4	Drift back	3.2	—
No alternative	50.1	25.5	No alternative	8.1	6.4
Other	—	6.4	Other	1.6	6.4
None	3.2	12.8	None	3.2	12.8

Note:
*Multiple answers possible.

their problems? Or were there also subjective differences which could influence their subsequent criminal participation? Further distinctions derived from their accounts provide insight into the relative motivational weight given to beliefs and values on the one hand and social circumstances on the other.

In explaining their actions and motivations these property offenders made frequent use of stock phrases which may be reflective of personal strategies (McAdams 1994) and which reveal *rules of thumb* (Cromwell *et al.* 1991) or *standing decisions* (Cook 1980). Put together, such standing decisions provide a 'rough and ready' cognitive script, minimizing the need for careful forethought and evaluative self-reflection. Ex-convicts may leave prison with an underlying mindset which is supportive of either persistence or desistance, providing a structure for future action.

The following rationalizations, or standing decisions, supportive of persistence were recurrent in participants' accounts:

- *It's a case of having to if you're skint.* Offending provides a one-off or occasional solution when funds run out. This situation may arise regularly, with theft being used to make ends meet, or it may be held in mind as an emergency measure by an individual who is not committed to offending, and whose rationalization is: 'I'll do it if necessary.'

- *You have to get money from somewhere when you're on drugs.* A drug addict is caught in a spiral where his physical needs dominate his inclinations and large sums of money are necessary to purchase his supply. He decides that even if he was fit enough to obtain legitimate employment he would be unlikely to earn a sufficient amount. Alcoholic offenders are caught in a similar but probably less expensive spiral.

- *It's an earner.* Theft and other property offences are viewed as a regular source of basic income when it has not been possible to obtain legitimate employment, or when none of the available vacancies offers an acceptable alternative.

Rationalizations supportive of desistance include the following:

- *It's not worth the risk.* Another variant of this is 'There's too much to lose'. A risk is being taken which might result in imprisonment and this would be too high a price to pay. Even if an offence were to be carried off successfully, the amount gained would not justify the possibility of being found out and the consequences which could follow.

- *It's not fair on the family*. Offending risks imprisonment which results in separation from partner and children, or possibly a complete breakdown of personal relationships. Not only is the pleasure of being with them denied, but there is also the prospect of guilt and regret for the hardship and deprivation caused by being removed from the family. A related rationalization is 'I'll lose the wife if I don't stop.'

- *I just want to live a normal life*. A criminal identity and lifestyle have become irksome and may be seen as in conflict with self-concept. Freedom from the stress and anxiety of being constantly at risk of arrest is desired. The offender wants to explore whether alternatives are possible with a view to achieving a freer way of life.

A typology of persistence and desistance lifestyles

The accounts given in the interviews were analysed and compared, and various explanatory patterns emerged. The following typology (see Table 7.5) gives emphasis to whatever is distinctive about the motivational patterns but, of course, none of these are static or mutually distinctive categories. On the contrary, in rationalizations of behaviour an individual may switch between the motivations of one 'type' to another and the details given at time one and time two may reflect a shift from one lifestyle towards another.

Table 7.5 Patterns of persistence and desistance

Type	Pattern
Hedonists	Derive pleasure from crime and its outcomes and associated lifestyle
Earners	Use crime as employment to generate income or material gain
Survivors	Commit crime in order to meet basic needs or addictive cravings
Avoiders	Deterred from crime by risk of imprisonment and its personal effects
Converts	Reject crime in favour of alternative values and transformed lifestyle
Non-starters	Regard previous involvement in crime as anomalous and out of character

The relevant motivational patterns for persistent reoffending were concerned with, broadly, hedonistic experiences, earning money and with surviving. The *hedonists* were mainly motivated to offend by the general feeling of well-being which can be gained by various aspects of criminal involvement. They were attracted by the challenge of crime, 'the buzz' of adrenaline while carrying out a crime and the emotional highs following success, as well as the prospect of financial gain. The proceeds of crime finance an extravagant social life including parties and drug-taking. The highs derived from drugs and crime serve to camouflage possible feelings of depression, anxiety and low self-esteem (cf. Shover's description of 'life as party': 1996). The *earners* varied in their enthusiasm for offending and the intensity of their involvement but shared a view of crime as a viable money-making enterprise. Some saw crime simply as their regular job, equivalent to any other employment, while others were more opportunist or entrepreneurial, operating on an occasional basis when the prospects seemed good. The *survivors* were generally drug addicts or alcoholics, unhappily committed to a lifestyle of persistent property offending in order to finance their habit. Psychological problems and mental illness or substance addiction were underlying problems. Many were older and loners no longer in contact with family members. They were outsiders but their daily battle was to feed themselves or their addiction rather than to escape their marginalized existence.

The lifestyles of desisting ex-offenders in some cases overlap with persisting lifestyles and in others are a complete departure. This distinction depends on whether the consequences of conviction are being avoided as opposed to criminal activity itself. For *avoiders* imprisonment is the key issue. Either they have been deterred by a first or second period of imprisonment and have resolved not to go through that again, or they have experienced numerous prison sentences and have noticed time and opportunities running out for them (cf. the ageing criminals interviewed by Shover 1985). The smallest group in this sample, *non-starters*, were adamant that they were not 'typical thieves' or 'real criminals'. They had fewer previous convictions and claimed they had been wrongly convicted or asserted that any offences they had committed had been out of character and committed during an aberrant set of circumstances which would not recur. They insisted that they had no inclination to commit similar offences again. The *converts* were the most resolute and certain among the desisters. They had found new interests which were all-preoccupying and overturned their value system: a partner, a child, a good job, a new vocation. These were attainments which they were not prepared to jeopardize or which over-rode any interest in or need for property crime. Individuals fitting the profile of the converts seem likely to feature in in-depth studies of desisters (e.g. Leibrich 1993; Maruna 2001), perhaps because their self-reflection and clarity of outlook make it easy and rewarding for them to give detailed accounts.

Conclusions: the ambivalent path to desistance
This analysis of accounts and the emerging typology reveal that, behind the contrasting labels of 'persister' and 'desister', most property of-fenders are for a period in their criminal careers neither steadfastly one nor the other. Only the most committed in this typology, the *converts*, are unfaltering in their decision that crime can nevermore be an option for them. Prior to release from prison, ambivalence and uncertainty about the possibility of reoffending might be seen as symptomatic of being suspended from the process of getting on with life and not knowing what lies around the corner. However, continuing uncertainty about the future chances of them reoffending expressed in the post-release interviews suggests that ambivalent motivation is an abiding or recurring experience for former property offenders. Comparison between responses from one interview to the next illustrates how blurred the distinction between persisting and desisting can be. Even within a single interview some who gave a reasoned argument for desisting, which was expressed with determination and resolve ('I want to stop and I will, because …') back-tracked when considering how they would respond to a hypothetical, virtually risk-free opportunity ('Oh yes, under those circumstances I'd do it'). Ambivalence is also evident in self-contradictions made during the interviews if, for example, at one point arguing that prison is a salutary experience ('prison sorts you out: you realize it ain't worth it') and at another point in the same interview pointing to the logic of further offending (''cos I ain't got a job and I could get really fed up'). Sometimes the language of ambivalence was close to being oxymoronic ('I'm certain [desistance is] achievable providing I have the will-power'; 'There is zilch chance of me going back to it if things go as planned').

While some ex-convicts may seem to go through periods of drifting, apparently without firm commitments or plans, the state of being ambivalent is different from that of *drift* introduced by Matza in his seminal work *Delinquency and Drift* (1964). The ambivalent property offender, just like Matza's delinquent, is neither wholly committed to criminal nor conventional enterprises. However, unlike drift, ambiv-alence does not imply neutrality nor a state of being 'midway between freedom and control' (1964: 28) while lacking the drive to make choices.

Rather, ambivalence results from having opposing drives and desires in relation to crime and is 'a state in which one is pulled in two mutually exclusive directions or toward two opposite goals' (*The Penguin Dictionary of Psychology* 1995). Ambivalence arises from the knowledge that a choice could have either favourable or unfavourable outcomes and from simultaneous desires to act in two opposing ways: for example, to make easy money through crime *and* to avoid risks which could lead to incarceration. No criticism of Matza's definition of drift is implied by this comparison: the age difference is significant. The drifting young delinquent is discovering situations where a choices might be made but he or she has not, so far, been involved in mature reflection about values and the consequences of different actions. In contrast, the adult property offender is likely to have had the benefit of experience and to have formulated a sense of identity together with the values and goals which underpin choice. However, a chequered past may have impeded the development of a self-story and a clear sense of direction which would otherwise help to resolve ambivalence.

Implications for re-entry policy and practice

The motivational variations drawn from the men's explanations of what happened to them can help to unpack the paradox introduced at the start of this chapter. At one end of the continuum, those whose emerging identities, beliefs and lifestyles were incompatible with crime were the most adamant that they would not reoffend and their predictions were borne out by time. Those stalwarts, however, were a minority. For the rest, some degree of motivational conflict and ambivalence was evident: successful acquisitive crimes were viewed as a means to an end but getting caught could defeat those goals. The majority preferred not to go down the offending track but anticipated 'worst-case scenarios' which would justify them resorting to crime again. There was a 'readiness' (Clarke and Cornish 1985: 167) to become involved in certain types of crime if circumstances seemed to justify it. Given the typical social situation of people who get involved in criminal activity, effective intervention can never ignore factors, such as poverty and illness, which constrain free choice. However, just as Agnew (1995: 27) proposes for criminological theory, it is appropriate for more attention to be given within interventions to the 'factors which promote freedom of choice'.

A conclusion to be drawn from the finding that former property offenders struggle with ambivalent motivation is that counselling, though now out of favour, remains an appropriate method for working with offenders. Assuming rigorous professional standards, a one-to-one relationship between criminal justice worker and ex-offender can provide the ideal means whereby to tune into the issues underlying ambivalent motivations; to explore choices and opportunities and facilitate the formation of a non-criminal identity; and to promote self-determination. Counselling as an intervention has not been explicitly discredited by meta-analytical studies of What Works even though it has not emerged as one of the more effective methods for reducing offending (Palmer 1996).

Working with ambivalence

A key finding of this study is that desistance is a process which involves reversals of decision, indecision, compromise and lapses. In comparison with the unmotivated drifting which Matza (1964) suggested was applicable to the majority of young offenders, the repetitive acquisitive offender seems to sit on a pendulum of ambivalence, moving first towards desistance and then towards persistence as his or her orientation is swayed by the weight of alternative desires and rationalizations. There are strong parallels with the push and pull of addictive habits (e.g. Miller 1991; Barber 1995). The zig-zag path towards desistance (Glaser 1964; Maruna 2001) is one result of this ambivalence, alternative motivations encouraging the individual to shift from one direction to the other (see Chapter 5 this volume). If interventions are to facilitate the desistance process this ubiquitous state of ambivalence should be fully acknowledged and addressed.

Such ambivalence is characteristic of the *contemplation stage* of Prochaska *et al.*'s (1992) acclaimed model of change. This model has five stages leading to termination of a problematic habit or behaviour: pre-contemplation, contemplation, preparation, action and maintenance. It is assumed that change is gradual and that relapse is the rule rather than the exception. Interventions, therefore, need to be paced and adapted to suit the individual's position in the change process and to help him or her deal with lapses as a setback rather than regard them as evidence that his or her goals are unachievable. At the pre-contemplation stage, individuals do not perceive the behaviour in question as problematic or something they wish to stop doing. It is only at the contemplation stage, which is generally triggered by negative outcomes of the behaviour, that personal misgivings and dissatisfaction emerge. Although this approach has been developed for working with addictive behaviours, it clearly has some relevance for persistent property offending and has been adopted within some criminal justice intervention programmes. The model presupposes that it is appropriate to support the individual through all stages of the cycle, including relapses, even though the individual's commitment and motivation are in flux.

The experience of custody has been identified as a catalyst for contemplating desistance (Meisenhelder 1977; Cusson and Pinsonneault 1986). A period of imprisonment is therefore an appropriate opportunity for intensive one-to-one work in line with the contemplation stage of the Prochaska and DiClemente model – especially at the beginning of the sentence and in the run-up to release, when individuals tend to identify more closely with the outside community and to adopt pro-social attitudes (Hood and Sparks 1970). Examples of individual work to swing ambivalence in the direction of desistance include drawing up a *decisional balance sheet* of costs and gains from the criminal lifestyle and *motivational interviewing* to promote a desire for change and a belief in its possibility (for further examples, see Barber 1995: 72–91).

To move from the ambivalence of the *contemplation stage* to the firmer commitment and goal-setting of the *preparation stage* requires that the individual gains sufficient self-belief that he or she is able to act differently, as well as some optimism that the socio-structural circumstances will not defeat such personal change. The techniques of non-directive counselling (e.g. Rogers 1961; Mearns and Thorne 1999) are fundamental to motivational interviewing (Miller 1991) and to the promotion of self-respect and self-efficacy. The counsellor or, in this case, criminal justice worker does not express negative judgements or attempt to shame the individual but rather is warm and respectful, showing empathy and giving praise wherever appropriate. Arguments for change are not imposed by the worker but are identified by the individual in a setting which encourages him or her to think aloud, determine goals and make plans. The relationship between the worker and the individual becomes the safe 'place' where personal history can be revealed and where conflicting feelings and dark thoughts can be brought into focus and explored.

The resolution of conflict

The preceding argument for one-to-one counselling prior to release applies doubly so at the post-release stage when the individual may experience the disillusion of thwarted plans and shifts of mood accompanying setbacks. On a bad day, the best of intentions may slide into a devil-may-care abandonment. In dismissing the myth of the bogeyman, Maruna (2001) quotes Solzhenitsyn: 'the line dividing good and evil cuts through the heart of every human being.' It is little surprise then that criminal lawyers often present their clients as 'Jekyll and Hyde characters', echoing the self-descriptors of the people they represent and the descriptions given by partners and relatives. All people have a darker side and may experience opposition between the multiple selves they are capable of being. And we all experience the psychological conflicts which Szasz (1961) debunked as 'problems in living', particularly when our goals are frustrated. A recent example of this in the media spotlight was when the tennis player Goran Ivanisovich confessed to feeling divided within himself. His victory in becoming Wimbledon champion enabled him to regain personal integrity, and a press editorial captured this as follows: 'Ivanisovic has managed to conquer his darker side, the unruly and destructive part of his personality' (*Zagreb Vjesnik* July 2001). For the rest of us, smaller achievements or supportive discussions with someone who knows us well may result in similar gains.

Experiences of such inner conflict and mood swings were evident in accounts given in the post-prison interviews by ex-convicts in this study. Regretted lapses back into offending were attributed, in some cases, to overwhelming emotions such as anger or despair. Others had premonitions of a breaking point where they would give up on the effort to 'go straight' and go back to 'what I know best'. Indeed, Leibrich concluded following in-depth interviews with 48 New Zealanders about their experiences of giving up crime that 'the essence … of going straight is the resolution of conflict' (1993: 236). To reach this point, they had reassessed their lives and reviewed their values, but such assessment was often preceded by a catalyst or turning point, and the resolution of conflict depended also on how they had interpreted their situation. When people are struggling with inner conflict, if they can afford it, they often have recourse to counselling. Over the last few decades, gyrations in penological policy have tended to mitigate against the provision of counselling for those who perhaps have the most to gain from it.

The demise of one-to-one casework

Helping ex-offenders to identify, analyse and find solutions to their problems in living is precisely what probation officers have traditionally concentrated on doing. No one else is better placed to understand the phenomenological context in which individuals may be striving to avoid reoffending and to explore with them their transformative possibilities. In a bygone era this was sometimes referred to as 'the casework relationship' (Perlman 1957; Biestek 1961) or, borrowing from psychotherapy, a 'therapeutic alliance' (Storr 1960; Rogers 1961). There is some irony to be observed, therefore, in the recent recruitment of mentors within the US and UK criminal justice systems to form relationships with and influence offenders when, in the UK at least, this had been the central role of probation officers in accordance with their underlying mission statement of 'to advise, assist and befriend'. Similarly, pro-social modelling, which was always a more or less explicit component of social casework, is now picked out as a key ingredient in the What Works recipe (McGuire 1995).

It is especially ironic that criminal justice workers are now being diverted from counselling as a mechanism of change by the great steer towards cognitive behavioural groupwork. Probation work was long in need of an overhaul; past practice was shaped by the zealous specialisms of individual staff (Mair 1995) and one-to-one work was often atheoretical and unsystematic (Burnett 1996), but individual counselling may be the baby to be rescued from the muddy bathwater. Although the elements of the What Works agenda are sometimes listed as if set in stone, the authority of this so-called 'agenda' remains open to question and rigorous evaluation. According to commentators from within the UK, 'the claims made on behalf of meta-analysis go too far' even though those who have carried them out have tended to be cautious (Mair 1997), and 'the Home Office and the probation service have shown little hesitation in interpreting the findings of meta-analysis to be a ringing-endorsement of the cognitive behavioural approach as the definitive, universal treatment modality' (Gorman 2001: 3). Cognitive behavioural group programmes may be effective in reducing overall levels of recidivism (Vennard and Hedderman 1998) but neither groups nor the skills-based approach suit everybody. If the 'principle of responsivity', as one element of What Works, is to be upheld then one-to-one approaches should be promoted alongside groupwork.

Studies have shown that it is via their relationship with offenders that probation officers believe they do their most effective work (Leibrich 1991; Burnett 1996). In the days before 'joined-up services', person-centred, one-to-one work may have seemed an irrelevance in the face of, for instance, an individual's homelessness or dyslexia and, in the past, individual counselling may have been too loosely linked to the objective of desistance. However, these omissions are not intrinsic to individual counselling and therefore do not invalidate the approach. Indeed, the ambivalent motivation found in this study indicates that counselling can usefully be deployed to promote desistance by helping individuals resolve internal conflict and develop stronger rationales for desistance. It is the relationship element of one-to-one counselling which facilitates the candour and self-analysis which would generally be inhibited and inappropriate in a group setting.

The value of person-centred intervention

Interventions to resolve problematic behaviour have both a technical and a relationship domain (Kelly 1997), but the relationship domain is being swamped by the current concentration on cognitive-behavioural skills. A professional relationship has long been recognized as a powerful vehicle for change, enabling self-realization and personal growth (Rogers 1961) and facilitating an individual's potential for self-determination (Perlman 1975). There is a substantial body of research evidence which testifies to the value of the therapeutic relationship in contributing to positive therapeutic outcomes (for example, see Marziali and Alexander 1991; Sexton and Whiston 1994; Kelly 1997). Prochaska *et al.* (1992), in an analysis of therapeutic processes, found that a 'helping relationship' is one of the three most frequently identified change mechanisms across a range of theoretical approaches to counselling. Although the medical model which underlies much counselling was discredited from criminal justice following the 'nothing works era' and replaced by a justice model, the language of counselling need not be read as a backwards step towards pathologizing people who have committed offences. Quite simply, counselling can be helpful for the human condition. Most of us do not achieve significant change or accomplish projects without the support of other people. Giving up crime is a significant project and it would be amazing if an individual was to be denied a focused relationship to support him or her in doing that – not least because, within the 'risk factor prevention paradigm' (Farrington 2000), unhappy and broken relationships are a criminogenic risk factor while positive relationships are a 'protective factor'.

In his classic work on self-realization, Anthony Storr asserts that 'belief in the importance and value of the individual personality … is widely held as part of the liberal humanist tradition' (1960: 23). He notes that this view of the importance of the whole person over and above the presenting problem is reflected in criminal law: 'It is the criminal as a person who has to be dealt with; it is insufficient to punish the crime without reference to the person who committed it' (p. 24). This person-centred approach is in danger of being lost altogether even though rehabilitation may still be alive and reasonably well (Robinson 2001). There has been considerable theoretical debate on whether the objective of rehabilitation has been eliminated within contemporary penological policy. Robinson charts 'the evolution of a rationality of risk' in the UK probation service but finds that this development has been entwined with a revival of rehabilitation. Questioning 'the contention that the probation service has dispensed with its traditional rehabilitative optimism' (p. 1) and is now only concerned with risk management, she observes that rehabilitation is now different in character and, 'as Cohen (1985) predicted, it is now "offending behaviour" which is the target of intervention, rather than the "whole person" or any underlying conflicts or difficulties s/he may have' (p. 12). This is manifest in the large-scale movement to cognitive behavioural approaches which concentrates on social skills practices in a group setting at the expense of a person-centred approach founded on the development of a rehabilitative relationship.

Carl Rogers' (1961: 33) famous statement of the potential benefits of relationship has applicability beyond therapy in a medical or clinical setting: 'If I can provide a certain type of relationship, the other person will discover in himself the capacity to use that relationship for personal growth.' Through the development of trust and responses to the individual's initial disclosures the objective is for the worker to 'create an atmosphere of freedom [where the individual] can drop the false fronts, or the masks or the roles ... to discover something more basic, something more truly himself' (p. 109). When individuals do not enjoy harmonious and profound, rather than superficial, relationships in their personal life, or even if they do, a counselling relationship offers rich ground for personal pro-social growth. The following passage succinctly captures the potency of relationships, whether professional or otherwise, in enabling a person to get in touch with what is important to him or her and in achieving self-realization:

> The psychological process that drives human relationships is ... a dialogue of people's emotional systems with the social predicaments in which they find themselves. In the face of both these we often feel powerless ... This could be the reason why interpersonal relationships engage people more deeply than other activities, and why they have about them an 'existential' quality. They seem to engage what people are, not merely, in a more concrete and superficial sense, what they do. (Harré *et al.* 1985: 32)

Transformation through relationship and self-determination

According to the life-course perspective, offenders desist as a result of interactive individual, situational and community processes (Laub and Sampson 2001). The exogenous influences are all-important but so too is a change in personal conceptions and identity: 'Agency and structure are dialectically inter-related' (Farrall and Bowling 1999: 261). For the street robbers of their study, Jacobs and Wright (1999: 162) are sceptical about whether anything other than lengthy incapacitation would influence them to stop offending because their offending is intrinsically linked with their personal history, relationships and emotional life: 'being a street robber is … a way of behaving, a way of thinking, an approach to life.' Similarly, Shover (1996) found that, while they are being successful, thieves commit crime to perpetuate a way of life (life as party) which is experienced as pleasurable. The device of a typology, by which the lifestyles of *earners, hedonists* and *survivors* were depicted in this study, underlines that such lifestyles are not immutable characteristics of the people living them. They may be, and eventually are, replaced by alternative approaches to life, and new situational influences and identity transformations may impinge at any turn. Imprisonment, or court proceedings, may be the exogenous event to stimulate reflection and a renewed 'rationalization of crime' (Shover 1996: 164) and to motivate a fresh start. Maruna found that, for ex-offenders 'to maintain abstinence from crime, they need to *make sense* of their lives' (2001: 7). The availability of person-centred counselling at such critical times, providing the individual is willing to co-operate, will facilitate this reflection process and, perhaps, the formulation of 'a new script for the future' (Laub and Sampson 2001).

Key theories of motivation identify a need for self-efficacy – or a sense of being the cause of things and being self-determining – as a major motivating drive (Murray 1938). Crime may be chosen as the means to experience this. The sense of being in control during the commission of a crime can be a motivating factor over and above material gains for persisting in offending (Katz 1991) and successful crime provides a sense of personal and occupational competence (Shover 1996). On the other hand, Maruna (2001) found that an important characteristic of desistance narratives was the theme of being in control over their lives. Such experiences seem to be highly orientating, therefore, whether towards or against further crime. Maruna adds that 'an ex-offender may need to experience some level of personal success in the straight world before they realise that they do not need to offend to regain a sense of personal agency' (2001: 125). Again, a professional helping relationship is a potential mechanism for promoting self-agency: 'The humanistic concept of relationship – namely, in-depth, relational conditions such as empathy, congruence, and positive regard effectively facilitate indi-viduals' inherent potential for healing self-determination' (Kelly 1997).

The potential of individual counselling has been passed over in the drive to establish cognitive-behavioural programmes. Yet with its capacity to touch on the human qualities of subjectivity, self-reflectiveness and self-determination, it remains an expedient means of enabling personal development and decision at crossroads in a person's life. The erstwhile property offenders of the study described in this chapter often distrusted their ability to avoid reoffending despite their preference for a crime-free future. For those taking the zig-zag path of desistance, the opportunity for reflective discourse may be the key to moving them beyond ambivalence and the mere *wish* to desist to the *will* to desist and the self-efficacy to choose a satisfying 'straight' way of life.

Notes

1 This has been my own experience as a former UK probation officer and one which was shared by colleagues. Disappointing relapses by promising (both senses) supervisees is 'par for the course'.
2 A focus on subjectivity is by no means an omission of the social dimension in explanations of criminal conduct – nor any other human activity. It is a matter of common sense as well as sophisticated academic theory (e.g. Mead 1934; Giddens 1984; Harré *et al.* 1985; Bandura 2001) that what individuals do is indivisible from the society in which they live, and that human action – including avoidance of action and therefore desistance – is a complex, interactional reciprocal process (Thornberry 1987; Laub and Sampson 2001).
3 The findings reported in this chapter relate to research carried out in the early 1990s. More recently, reconviction data have been collected on the original cohort and a ten-year follow-up analysis is in progress (Maruna *et al.* 2002). The methodology of the original study was the basis for a subsequent study, also at Oxford, carried out by Stephen Farrall (see Chapter 3 this volume).
4 As observed by Maruna (2001) this is a false dichotomy because virtually all will become desisters at some point, and these two groups are therefore merely at different stages of the change process.

References

Agnew, R. (1995) 'Determinism, indeterminism, and crime: an empirical exploration', *Criminology*, 33 (1): 83–109.
Bandura, A. (2001) 'Social cognitive theory: an agentic perspective', *Annual Review of Psychology*, 52: 1–26.
Barber, J.G. (1995) *Social Work with Addictions*. Basingstoke: Macmillan.
Biestek, F. (1961) *The Casework Relationship*. London: Allen & Unwin.
Brown, I. (1998) 'Successful probation practice', in D. Faulkner and A. Gibbs (eds) *New Politics, New Probation? Probation Studies Unit Report* 6. Oxford: Centre for Criminological Research, University of Oxford, 57–76.

Burnett, R. (1992) *The Dynamics of Recidivism: Report to the Home Office Research and Planning Unit*. Oxford: Centre for Criminological Research, University of Oxford.

Burnett, R. (1994) 'The odds of going straight: offenders' own predictions', in *Sentencing, Quality and Risk: Proceedings of the 10th Annual Conference on Research and Information in the Probation Service. University of Loughborough*. Birmingham: Midlands Probation Training Consortium.

Burnett, R. (1996) *Fitting Supervision to Offenders: Assessment and Allocation in the Probation Service. Home Office Research Study* 153. London: Home Office Research and Statistics Directorate.

Bushway, S., Piquero, A., Mazerolle, P., Boidy, L. and Cauffman, E. (2001) 'A developmental framework for studying desistance as a process', *Criminology*, 39: 491–515.

Clarke, R.V. and Cornish, D.B. (1985) 'Modeling offenders' decisions: a framework for research and policy', in M. Tonry and N. Morris (eds) *Crime and Justice: An Annual Review of Research. Vol. 6*. Chicago, IL: University of Chicago Press.

Cohen, S. (1985) *Visions of Social Control*. Cambridge: Polity Press.

Cook, P.J. (1980) 'Research in criminal deterrence: laying the groundwork for the second decade', in N. Morris and M. Tonry (eds) *Crime and Justice: An Annual Review of Research. Vol. 2*. Chicago, IL: University of Chicago Press.

Cornish, D.B. and Clarke, R.V. (eds) (1986) *The Reasoning Criminal*. New York, NY: Springer-Verlag.

Cromwell, P.F., Olson, J.N. and Avary, D.W. (1991) *Breaking and Entering: An Ethnographic Analysis of Burglary*. Newbury Park, CA: Sage.

Cusson, M. and Pinsonneault, P. (1986) 'The decision to give up crime', in D.B. Cornish and R.V. Clarke (eds) *The Reasoning Criminal*. New York, NY: Springer-Verlag, 72–82.

Dweck, C.S. (2000) *Self-theories: Their Role in Motivation, Personality, and Development*. Philadelphia, PA: Psychology Press.

Farrall, S. and Bowling, B. (1999) 'Structuration, human development and desistance from crime', *British Journal of Criminology*, 39: 253–68.

Farrington, D.P. (2000) 'Explaining and preventing crime: the globalisation of knowledge: the American Society of Criminology 1999 presidential address', *Criminology*, 38: 1–24.

Giddens, A. (1984) *The Constitution of Society*. Cambridge: Polity Press.

Glaser, D. (1964) *Effectiveness of a Prison and Parole System*. Indianapolis, IN: Bobbs-Merrill.

Gorman, K. (2001) 'Cognitive behaviourism and the holy grail: the quest for a universal means of managing offender risk', *Probation Journal*, 48: 3–9.

Hagan, J. and McCarthy, B. (1997) *Mean Streets: Youth Crime and Homelessness*. Cambridge: Cambridge University Press.

Harré, R. and Secord, P.F. (1972) *The Explanation of Social Behaviour*. Oxford: Blackwell.

Harré, R., Clarke, D. and De Carlo, N. (1985) *Motives and Mechanisms*. London: Methuen.

Hood, R. (1995) 'Introductory report: psychosocial interventions in the criminal justice system', in *Proceedings of the 20th Criminological Research Conference, 1993. Council of Europe Committee on Crime Problems, Criminological Research*, 32: 11–19.

Hood, R. and Sparks, R. (1970) *Key Issues in Criminology*. London: Weidenfeld & Nicolson.

Jacobs, B.A. and Wright, R. (1999) 'Stick-up, street culture and offender motivation', *Criminology*, 37: 149–73.

Katz, J. (1988) *Seductions of Crime: Moral and Sensual Attractions in Doing Evil*. New York, NY: Basic Books.

Katz, J. (1991) 'The motivation of the persistent robber', in M. Tonry (ed.) *Crime and Justice: A Review of Research. Vol. 14*. Chicago, IL: University of Chicago Press.

Kelly, E.W. (1997) 'Relationship-centered counseling: A humanistic model of integration', *Journal of Counseling and Development*, 75: 337–45.

Kelly, G.A. (1955) *The Psychology of Personal Constructs*. New York, NY: Norton.

Kemshall, H. (1998) *Risk in Probation Practice*. Aldershot: Ashgate.

Lattimore, P. and Witte, A. (1986) 'Models of decision-making under uncertainty: the criminal choice', in D.B. Cornish and R.V. Clarke (eds) *The Reasoning Criminal*. New York, NY: Springer-Verlag, 129–55.

Laub, J.H. and Sampson, R.J. (2001) 'Desistance from crime', in M. Tonry (ed.) *Crime and Justice: A Review of Research. Vol. 28*. Chicago, IL: University of Chicago Press.

Leibrich, J. (1991) *A Study of the Probation Division's Perception of its Role in Reducing Re-offending*. Wellington: Department of Justice.

Leibrich, J. (1993) *Straight to the Point: Angles on Giving up Crime*. Otago, New Zealand: University of Otago Press.

Mair, G. (1995) 'Specialist activities in the probation service: "confusion worse confounded"?', in L. Noaks *et al.* (eds) *Contemporary Issues in Criminology*. Cardiff: University of Wales Press.

Mair, G. (1997) 'Community penalties and the probation service', in M. Maguire *et al.* (eds) *The Oxford Handbook of Criminology (2nd edn)*. Oxford: Clarendon Press.

Maruna, S. (1999) 'Criminology, desistance and the psychology of the stranger', in D. Canter, and L. Alison (eds) *The Social Psychology of Crime: Groups, Teams and Networks*. Aldershot: Ashgate.

Maruna, S. (2001) *Making Good: How Ex-convicts Reform and Rebuild their Lives*. Washington, DC: American Psychological Association.

Maruna, S., Le Bel, T., Burnett, R., Bushway, S. and Kierkus, C. (2002) 'Internal and external factors in desistance from crime'. Paper presented at the American Society of Criminology Conference, Chicago: November 18, 2002.

Marziali, E. and Alexander, L. (1991) 'The power of the therapeutic relationship', *American Journal of Orthopsychiatry*, 61: 383–91.

Matza, D. (1964) *Delinquency and Drift*. New York, NY: Wiley.

Matza, D. (1969) *Becoming Deviant*. Englewood Cliffs, NJ: Prentice Hall.

McAdams, D.P. (1994) 'Can personality change? Levels of stability and growth in personality across the life span', in T.F. Heatherton and J.L. Weinberger (eds) *Can Personality Change?* Washington, DC: American Psychological Association.

McGuire, J. (ed.) (1995) *What Works: Effective Methods to Reduce Re-offending*. Chichester: Wiley.

Mead, G.H. (1934) *Mind, Self and Society*. Chicago, IL: University of Chicago Press.

Mearns, D. and Thorne, B. (1999) *Person-centred Counselling in Action (2nd edn)*. London: Sage.

Meisenhelder, T.N. (1977) 'An exploratory study of exiting from criminal careers', *Criminology*, 15: 319–34.

Miller, W.R. (1991) 'What motivates people to change?', in W.R. Miller and S. Rollnick (eds) *Motivational Interviewing: Preparing People to Change Addictive Behavior*. New York, NY: Guilford Press.

Murray, H.A. (1938) *Explorations in Personality*. New York, NY: Oxford University Press.

Palmer, T. (1996) 'Programmatic and nonprogrammatic aspects of successful intervention', in A.T. Harland (ed.) *Choosing Correctional Options that Work: Defining the Demand and Evaluating the Supply*. Thousand Oaks, CA: Sage.

Perlman, H.H. (1957) *Social Casework: A Problem-solving Approach*. Chicago, IL: University of Chicago Press.

Perlman, H.H. (1975) 'Self-determination: reality or illusion?', in F.E. McDermott (ed.) *Self-determination in Social Work*. London: Routledge and Kegan Paul.

Piliavin, I., Gartner, R., Thornton, C. and Matsueda, R. (1986) 'Crime, deterrence, and rational choice', *American Sociological Review*, 51: 102–19.

Prochaska, J.O. and DiClemente, C.C. (1984) *The Transtheoretical Approach: Crossing the Traditional Boundaries of Therapy*. Homewood, IL: Dow Jones/ Irwin.

Prochaska, J.O., Norcross, J.C. and DiClemente, C.C. (1992) 'In search of how people change: applications of addictive behavior', *American Psychologist*, 42: 1102–14.

Rex, S. (1998) 'Promoting effective supervisory relationships', in D. Faulkner and A. Gibbs (eds) *New Politics, New Probation?*. Probation Studies Unit Report 6. Oxford: Centre for Criminological Research, University of Oxford, 77–90.

Robinson, G. (2001) 'A rationality of risk in the probation service: its evolution and contemporary profile', *Punishment and Society* (forthcoming).

Rogers, C.R. (1961) *On Becoming a Person*. Boston, MA: Houghton Mifflin.

Sexton, T.L. and Whiston, S.C. (1994) 'The status of the counseling relationship: an empirical review, theoretical implications, and research directions', *The Counseling Psychologist*, 22: 6–78.

Short, J.F. (1997) 'The level of explanation problem revisited: the American Society of Criminology presidential address', *Criminology*, 36: 3–36.

Shover, N. (1985) *Aging Criminals*. Beverley Hills, CA: Sage.

Shover, N. (1996) *Great Pretenders: Pursuits and Careers of Persistent Thieves*. Oxford: Westview Press.

Shover, N. and Thompson, C.Y. (1992) 'Age, differential expectations, and crime desistance', *Criminology*, 30: 89–104.

Storr, A. (1960) *The Integrity of the Personality*. Harmondsworth: Penguin Books.

Szasz, T. (1961) *The Myth of Mental Illness*. New York, NY: Harper & Row.

Thornberry, T.P. (1987) 'Toward an interactional theory of delinquency', *Criminology*, 25: 863–91.

Tice, D.M., Bratslavsky, E. and Baumeister, R.F. (2001) 'Emotional distress regulation takes precedence over impulse control: if you feel bad, do it!', *Journal of Personality and Social Psychology*, 80: 53–67.

Tunnell, K.D. (1992) *Choosing Crime*. Chicago, IL: Nelson-Hall.

Vennard, J. and Hedderman, C. (1998) 'Effective interventions with offenders', in P. Goldblatt and C. Lewis (eds) *Reducing Offending: An Assessment of Research Evidence on Ways of Dealing with Offending Behaviour*. Home Office Research Study 187. London: Home Office, 101–19.

Ward, N. (1987) *The Validity of the Reconviction Predictability Score*. Home Office Research Study 94. London: HMSO.

Chapter 8

Desistance from crime: is it different for women and girls?

Gill McIvor, Cathy Murray and Janet Jamieson

Introduction

Traditionally, criminological research has concentrated on attempting to understand the aetiology of offending, with a view to identifying appropriate measures aimed at preventing young people from becoming involved in crime. However, offending is, essentially, an age-related phenomenon and most young people eventually 'grow out of crime' (Rutherford 1986). An enhanced understanding of the processes that accompany or promote the cessation of offending may therefore inform the development of more effective responses to young people who have already begun to offend. Recent research (e.g. Shover 1985; Burnett 1992; Hubert and Hundleby 1993; Leibrich 1993; Graham and Bowling 1995; Rex 1999; Maruna 2001) has consequently focused upon uncovering the circumstances and processes involved in desistance from crime.

Desistance from offending is now widely acknowledged to be a complex process (Leibrich 1992; Sommers *et al.* 1994; Shover 1996). While transitions such as leaving home, getting married, finding work and assuming family responsibilities have been shown to be associated with desistance (Sampson and Laub 1993; Laub *et al.* 1998) so too have individual choice and decision-making been found to be integral to the commitment not to reoffend (Maruna 2001). Farrell and Bowling (1999) have emphasized the interplay of structure and agency in the process of disengagement from offending, while Maruna (2001) has highlighted the role of both ontogenetic and sociogenic forces in this process.

Previous research also suggests that the process of desistance may be different for men and women. Young women, who are of course less likely to offend in the first place, seem to desist sooner than their male counterparts (Graham and Bowling 1995). Sampson and Laub (1993) have suggested that the realization of adult transitions is mediated by individual contingencies and that the meaning attached to these transitions – and hence their potential to encourage desistance – differs between women and men.

This chapter examines this issue of gender differences in the experience of desistance by drawing upon existing literature and upon the further analysis of data from our study of young people and offending in Scotland (Jamieson *et al.* 1999). This study – 'Understanding Offending Among Young People' – focused upon the choices made by young people of different ages with respect to their decisions to resist involvement in, desist from and persist in offending behaviour. In doing so, it took account of the relative importance of a range of factors – including social circumstances, personal characteristics and the formal intervention of the criminal justice system – for the choices the young people made.

In-depth interviews were conducted with a total of 276 young people (138 male and 138 female) in three age groups: 14–15 years, 18–19 years and 22–25 years. These ages were selected because they appear to represent significant points at which young people make choices about offending. The samples were drawn from two Scottish towns that had crime rates close to the national average. The issues explored in the interviews include: education; employment; use of leisure and lifestyle; drug and alcohol use; offending; relationships with family, friends and partners; neighbourhood, community and society; values and beliefs; victimization; identity; and aspirations for the future. A qualitative approach was considered most appropriate because of the exploratory nature of the study and the need for flexibility and sensitivity. Furthermore, in-depth interviews allowed respondents to talk in their own 'frames of reference' which in turn allowed the meanings and interpretations they attributed to events and relations to be understood (May 1993). As Maruna (2001: 33) argues, 'analyzing the subjective experience of going straight can only strengthen criminology's understanding of the roles of social bonds and aging in the desistance process'. Some additional material was, however, collected through the administration of questionnaires using a laptop computer: this included the nature and frequency of substance use, propensity towards risk-taking and self-esteem – factors which have been shown to be associated with offending by young people.

How desisters compared with resisters and persisters

Prior to being interviewed, the young people in our study completed a self-report questionnaire about their offending behaviour. Responses were used to allocate the young people to one of three categories on the basis of the recency and seriousness of their self-reported offending. Young people were categorized as resisters (92) if they had never offended, as desisters (75) if they had offended in the past but not in the previous 12 months and as persisters (109) if they had committed at least one serious offence or several less serious offences in the previous 12 months. The classification of young people sometimes had to be reviewed in the light of further information provided in interviews. For instance, some young people admitted to 'offences' that could not strictly be defined as such, with the behaviour being an omission (for example, borrowing a bicycle without asking the owner's permission first) rather than the deliberate commission of a delinquent or criminal act. The categories were, moreover, permeable and were appropriate only at a given point in time: resisters and desisters may have subsequently become persisters and persisters may have become desisters at subsequent points in their lives.

Despite the fluidity of the categories employed, and the difficulties that have been acknowledged to exist in achieving a workable definition of desistance (e.g. Maruna 2001), a remarkable degree of consistency was observed in the experiences, views and attitudes of young people within each of the categories. Desisters almost invariably occupied a middle position between resisters and desisters. This was true, for example, in their views about the seriousness of a range of offences and the degree to which they reported they would engage in a range of risk taking or impulsive behaviours. Sometimes desisters were more similar to resisters and other times they more closely resembled young people who continued to offend. Desisters were more likely than resisters (though less likely than persisters) to consider that some types of offending were acceptable, to take alcohol and drugs, to 'hang about' in public spaces, to have been involved with the police and to express negative attitudes towards them. They were closer to persisters in being more likely than resisters to have friends and a family member who had offended.

Where desisters resembled resisters most closely was in their general attitude to offending. Desisters and resisters generally construed offending in broad terms as immoral, futile or both, whereas few persisters considered offending to be wrong as such, emphasizing instead that this was conditional upon a variety of factors including the seriousness of the offence or the circumstances of the offender:

Woman: I don't suppose it can be justified, but I think a lot of it could be explained – why people do offend and the reason behind it.
Interviewer: Right, and what sort of explanations would you be talking about?
Woman: Drugs, drunken madness, poverty. (Female, oldest age group)

I can understand it, but I can't understand people robbing old women and things like that. I've been strung out myself. As I say, I was on it [heroin] for a few years and there was days when I was pure ill and never in my life would I go out and rob an old woman. (Female, oldest age group)

It depends how drastic it is. You know if it's going to be something like breaking into a house or something like that, I don't feel that's right because you wouldn't like it happening to yourself. (Male, youngest age group)

Even some of the persisters who believed that all offending was unacceptable added caveats – for example, 'I suppose not really, not acceptable, but people do it; it still happens'.

Desisters and resisters were also more likely to attribute offending by young people to their upbringing or family background while persisters most often attributed it to young people's use of or, more usually, addiction to drugs. With respect to their perceptions of the acceptability (or otherwise) of offending, the location of desisters in relation to resisters and persisters changed with age, with desisters in the youngest age group more closely resembling resisters and those in the oldest age group more closely resembling persisters. A similar pattern was apparent in relation to drug use, with the pattern of drug use among desisters in the youngest age group being similar to that among resisters. In the oldest age group, however, desisters were as likely as persisters to have used a range of recreational drugs, with the patterns of drug use among desisters and persisters being distinguishable largely by the more prevalent use of opioids and opiates among the latter. Finally, while resisters, desisters and persisters in the youngest age group demonstrated similar levels of self-esteem, resisters and desisters in the older two age groups had higher self-esteem than persisters did in these age groups. These age-related differences in the location of desisters relative to resisters and persisters suggest that the process and nature of desistance are likely to differ with age.

Young people did, indeed, offer different reasons for desisting at different ages. For example, desistance among boys and girls in the youngest age group was often associated with the consequences – actual or potential – of offending, or with a growing recognition – attributed to increased maturity – of the pointlessness or immorality of continued involvement in offending behaviour. Increased maturity was likewise invoked as a reason for desisting by young people in the middle age group, though this was often linked to the transition to adulthood, as characterized by events such as getting a job, going to college or university, entering into a relationship with a partner or leaving home. Among the oldest age group, desistance was more often said to have been encouraged by the assumption of family responsibilities, especially among young women, or by a conscious lifestyle change. Finally, persisters in the youngest age group were more optimistic about their ability to desist while, for older respondents who may have become more entrenched in patterns of offending and drug use, desistance was rarely considered to be an immediate or achievable goal. As one young man explained, 'it's just the drug scene. I can't stay away from it and I never will'.

The transitory nature of involvement in offending is highlighted in Matza's (1964) theory of delinquency and drift whereby individuals 'drift' into and away from offending. Shover (1996: 122) has shown that periods of desistance may often be followed by further offending and that 'many, particularly those with criminal identities, may reduce the frequency of their offenses but continue committing crime for months or even years'. The interviews with persisters tended to bear this observation out. Many described attempts they had previously made to stop offending, which had met with varying degrees of success. Many also recounted current plans to stop offending. One of the most striking features of these accounts was the relative optimism of the youngest age group of persisters, who were more likely than the older groups to say they had desisted or planned to desist. By comparison, older respondents, while often acknowledging that desistance was something they wished to achieve, were less inclined to say they were no longer offending or that they planned to stop in the immediate or foreseeable future.

Gender and desistance

Previous research which has focused upon the causes of offending has concentrated almost exclusively upon males, who at all ages are more likely than females to come into contact with the criminal justice system as a consequence of their offending. Moreover, the fact that females are significantly less likely than males to engage in offending behaviour has resulted in attempts to define and explain female criminality with reference to constructs which are not usually invoked in similar attempts to understand offending by men. In an analysis of Scottish statistics, Asquith and Samuel (1994) identified a broadly similar relationship between age and the incidence of offending for men and women, even though the difference in the actual number of convictions between men and women was large. This led them to argue that the gender difference in number of convictions tends to obscure an age-related pattern of offending consistent among young men and young women:

> The pattern which emerges from these data provides quite convincing evidence that for females, as with males, crime is very much a youth-related phenomenon in Scotland ... To overlook and ignore this pattern ... helps sustain the myth of female criminality as individualistic, pathological and essentially non-social. (Asquith and Samuel 1994: 81).

More recent figures suggest, however, that although convictions are more common among both young men and young women in their late teens and early 20s, women's convictions tend to show a less marked age-related pattern than was previously believed to be the case (Scottish Office 1998). Possibly this is the result of an increased incidence of drug use and associated offending among women in Scotland.

Several UK studies have suggested that women are likely to desist at an earlier age than young men (Graham and Bowling 1995; Flood-Page *et al*. 2000). Flood-Page *et al*. (2000) found that while rates of self-reported offending were similar among boys and girls at 12–13 years, the peak age of self-reported offending for girls was 14 years and for boys was 18 years, leading them to conclude that 'females grow out of all types of anti-social behaviour at an earlier age than males' (p. 10). In our research we also found evidence that girls' involvement in self-reported offending declined between 14 and 15 years of age, while boys' offending at the same age became more serious (Jamieson *et al*. 1999: 10).

Overall, it appears that young women tend to desist from offending earlier than do young men. This might be because a 'chivalry factor' continues to operate in respect of girls (though not in respect of women). In other words, girls may be more likely than boys to evade formal processing by the juvenile justice system, despite committing roughly similar crimes. Through the avoidance of being labelled as a result of this formal processing, girls may find it easier than boys to desist. However, desistance is, according to Graham and Bowling (1995), both a social and cognitive process. This might imply that in order to stop offending it is necessary first to acknowledge the behaviour. If this is the case – and it is open to debate – the apparent level of denial found among the female respondents might have been expected to have served as an impediment to their ability to desist.

Findings such as these suggest that the factors and processes associated with desistance may differ between young men and young women. Though research on desistance has concentrated primarily upon men, a few studies have included both sexes (e.g. Leibrich 1992; Graham and Bowling 1995; Uggen and Kruttschnitt 1998; Maruna 2001) or have focused solely upon women (e.g. Sommers *et al.* 1994; Katz 2000). Sommers *et al.* (1994) have suggested that the processes and 'turning points' associated with desistance among female street offenders are similar to those associated with desistance among men. Our study and others suggest, however, both that a variety of factors may influence decisions to desist and that these factors may differ in their salience between men and women.

In the remainder of the chapter the key themes that emerged from the accounts of desistance related by young men and women in 'Understanding Offending Among Young People' will be considered and located within the wider literature on gender and desistance from crime.

'Maturation'

A common explanation offered by people who have stopped offending is that they 'grew out of it' or 'grew up'. In our study this theme was often manifested in the view that offending was 'not worth it', signalling a weighing up, albeit often neither explicit nor necessarily conscious, of the benefits and costs of crime. For example:

> I'm more mature now and I understand that like smashing a school window now it would cost the school money and money is important for education instead of paying for school windows. (Male, youngest age group)

> Probably I'm different and feel stronger and know that if I did have a future that [offending] would harm me. (Female, youngest age group)

A similar process has been documented by Shover (1996) and by Graham and Bowling (1995), though the latter have suggested that this may not be sufficient to enable desistance to be sustained. For this to happen, appropriate attitudinal changes may also be required: that is, crime must be recognized as morally wrong and likely to impact adversely upon the lives of others.

While explanations of desistance linked to 'maturation' were advanced by young people of both sexes in 'Understanding Offending Among Young People', young men tended to couch their explanations in broadly utilitarian terms, while young women more often alluded to the moral dimension of crime. This is illustrated in the following responses:

> You really don't want to be committing offences especially in the job I'm in [...] If you're going to commit offences and get caught for them it's going to hurt your prospects for the future no matter what you do for a whole number of things, maybe getting loans or anything like that. (Male, middle age group)

> I know it's wrong. When I was stealing, one of my friends got caught and just what she had to go through, going to the police station. And then you think about the manager and how he feels when someone takes his stuff, and I think it's wrong. (Female, youngest age group)

Unlike the more criminally involved women in the study by Sommers *et al.* (1994), for whom 'shame' apparently played little part in their decisions to desist, young women in our sample often associated offending with a profound sense of guilt or shame (see also Leibrich 1992). For example: 'I used to feel really guilty and I used to think that everybody knew. Every time anybody looked at me I thought "they know what's happened, they know what I've done" ... I went through a lot, a lot of guilt' (female, oldest age group).

A 'relational' dimension (Gilligan 1982) was therefore more often apparent in the accounts offered by young women, while those of young men tended to be more individualized in nature. A similar pattern was also evident in young people's accounts of being the victims of crime. Young men were more likely to focus upon the formal interventions that followed the incident while young women more often focused upon the emotional experience and expressed empathy with and sympathy towards other victims as a result:

Victims as in people that have had beatings and things like that? I suppose nowadays it's not so bad because they've got a – they've got a – I can't remember what it's called, but you get compensation money if you're a victim these days. One of my pals got a doing last year or something like that, got his nose broke like that, got £2,000 for it. I suppose it makes up for it in a way. (Male, youngest age group)

It was a fairly minor thing that happened to me, but I suppose it can help you understand how somebody who suffered a more serious crime would react and feel. The feeling of helplessness and all that, it must be awful. (Female, middle age group)

I think being involved in domestic violence is – well I've always seen other people suffering from domestic violence but I think until you experience something yourself, you don't read right into it. You don't know so much about it until you experience it yourself. I wouldn't say it's changed me crimewise. It hasn't changed my attitude to crime or anything like that, but it's changed my feelings towards victims and stuff like that because I understand it more I suppose. (Female, oldest age group)

Transitions

A number of significant lifestyle transitions have been found to be associated with desistance, and these may be cumulative in their effect (Rutter *et al.* 1998). They include leaving school, starting work, leaving home, getting married or settling into a relationship and having a family. Ironically, while the studies which have identified these factors have, on the whole, been conducted with male populations, Graham and Bowling (1995) found that, in general, these indicators of social development seemed to be related to desistance among young women but not among young men. They attributed this to the finding that young men in their sample tended not to 'grow out of crime' until their late 20s.

In 'Understanding Offending Among Young People', we found that both male and female research participants identified similar events as being associated with their decision to stop offending. In addition, related factors such as the fear of losing their job (identified also by Leibrich 1992) and a concern not to jeopardize their future chances by accruing a criminal record were also prevalent. As one male respondent in his late teens explained: 'But you worry about it, you know, because if you had something like a bigger record you'd have to start bringing it up at job interviews and I think I'd be worried if I started doing that, if you get caught in a sort of spiral of bigger things.'

For this reason, reaching 16 years was a turning point for some young people in Scotland, since after this age any offences with which they were charged would usually be dealt with by the (adult) criminal justice system, resulting in the possibility of a conviction. This was emphasized, in particular, by the professionals (police officers, social workers and teachers) who were also interviewed as part of our study. While a police warning or an appearance before a children's panel was considered sufficient to deter many young people from further involvement in delinquency, professional respondents most commonly made reference to the impact made upon young people by their transition from the children's hearings system to the adult criminal justice system at 16 years of age:

> There's some guys and girls at school who for bravado offend to show off to their friends, go to the children's panel and they just shut their ears when this is on. But when they go to court for maybe one or two times they suddenly realize this is a slippery slope here, and they could stop offending. I think the coming of age – the 16 year old thing – is a barrier for a lot of kids to stop offending. (Police officer)

> They get into a pattern of offending when they're a juvenile and they know the system backwards. And they know that as soon as they get to three months before their 16th birthday it all goes to the fiscal [public prosecutor]. And that's when you can start getting fined. Its with the 'big boys' now – you can go to jail. (Police officer)

Graham and Bowling (1995) have argued that leaving home, especially for boys, may escalate rather than reduce involvement in offending if the young person lacks the necessary maturity and resources to cope effectively in the adult world. Leaving home may, however, be associated with desistance by young women, especially if it corresponds with their transition to parenthood. Many commentators have speculated that teenage motherhood may partly facilitate desistance among young women (Rutter *et al.* 1998). For instance, Graham and Bowling (1995) have argued that having children imbues a sense of responsibility which is accompanied by greater attention to the needs of others and greater cognizance of the consequences of one's own behaviour.

This relationship was confirmed in our own Scottish study and in Leibrich's (1992) New Zealand research. The following are illustrative of the views of young mothers in our study:

Since I had Y [child], I've no done nothing bad apart from smoke a joint now and again. (Oldest age group)

I realized I've got the wean [child] to think about. I cannae just think about myself all the time. I've got to put him in front of me. (Oldest age group)

The assumption of parental responsibilities was also identified for some young men as important to decisions to stop offending. For example, one young man commented: 'I've settled down with the girlfriend and the wean [child]. I've got to think again about who I'm hurting.' However, young men more often associated desistance with other family responsibilities that they considered essential for eliciting continued support and assistance from families. One young man, who appreciated re-entry to the family home and the renewal of family relationships, commented:

I thought to myself if I keep this up I'm going to end up killing my Ma, you know, because she has heart problems and all that [...] My sisters used to not bother with me when I was on the smack [heroin]. They would even walk by me on the street. It was that bad at one time, you know. But now they are a lot happier with me. (Oldest age group)

Women in our study, as in the research by Graham and Bowling (1995), articulated their concern that they might lose their children if they continued offending and were imprisoned as a result. For example:

Say I get caught, I've been told by the social worker next time I get lifted by the police my kids will get took away. (Female, oldest age group)

I couldn't afford to take the risk. I mean at the end of the day if I was going to do anything stupid ... if I ever ... got locked up or anything like that, what about the kids? Who is going to look after them? It all falls back, this is what holds me back, this is what sort of keeps my head on my shoulders. (Female, oldest age group)

The influence of having children upon women's desistance from offending may well be culturally determined. Katz (2000) found that becoming a parent was associated with desistance among white women in her sample, but not among women from minority ethnic groups. She suggested that this may be because white women are more likely to define their worth in terms of relationships with partners and children, while women from ethnic minorities are more likely to define themselves in relation to kinship networks, neighbourhoods and work.

Relationships

It is well established that peer groups represent one of the most powerful influences on offending among young people. Consequently, it is not surprising that the 'neutralization' of peer influences has been associated with desistance from offending. As Graham and Bowling (1995: 70) concluded, 'disengaging from delinquent peers, whether consciously or by chance, is a necessary condition for desistance and may occur in a number of ways'. For instance, Graham and Bowling (1995: 70) have suggested that leaving school offers girls a particular opportunity to 'relinquish ties with delinquent peers and start a new life'.

In our 'Understanding Offending Among Young People' research, numerous instances were recounted in which desistance had been facilitated by 'breaking away' from offending friends. For example:

I wasn't with that group of people anymore ... if I was still hanging about with [them] ... I probably would have done a lot more trouble. (Female, middle age group)

I don't bother with them ... I just want to stay away fae [from] them because they're always out getting smack [heroin] constantly. (Male, oldest age group)

Young women were more likely than young men to have taken active steps to dissociate themselves from anti-social peer groups, by seeking out alternative friendship networks or by spending less time socializing with those who continued to offend. Among young men, a change in peers appeared more often to be combined with other transitions such as moving to another neighbourhood, going to college and starting work.

These findings are consistent with the basic tenets of differential association theory. For instance, Warr (1998) argued that the explanation for the apparent correlation between marriage and desistance is that, once married, individuals are likely to spend less time with delinquent or criminal peers. He suggests that a similar process may account for the relationship between desistance and other transitions such as going to college or finding work.

Several young men in our study linked desistance to a wish to avoid damaging (or further damaging) family relationships or to the assumption of responsibilities towards partners or families. On the other hand, for young women in our sample, ending a relationship with a partner often represented an opportunity to dissociate themselves from crime. One young woman, who had been encouraged to offend by an ex-partner, explained:

> I think I stayed with him more out of fear than anything else because he was quite violent with me ... I broke up with him at Christmas and I met my husband in the April and we lived together for six months before getting married and in those six months I changed completely. (Oldest age group)

Female persisters in our sample had often been introduced to drug misuse and associated offending by partners who used drugs. The partners of female persisters also appeared, from their accounts, to be involved in relatively serious offending, including house-breaking, drug dealing, reset and armed robbery.

Lifestyle changes

Leibrich (1992: 288) concluded from her study of former probationers that the first step towards desistance is a conscious decision to 'go straight' that may be triggered by an event or by 'a sudden clarity of insight – seeing an old situation in a new way'. Sommers *et al.* (1994) also found that the process of desistance tended to be precipitated by a crisis of some kind which caused the women to re-evaluate their lifestyles, to redefine their identities and to foster relationships with non-offending friends. For these women, the initial resolve to desist was followed by their publicly disclosing the decision, engaging in new behaviours and becoming integrated into new social networks. Desistance from crime, therefore, was associated with lifestyle change.

In our study, the most dramatic feature of the lifestyles of young people who had continued offending into their late teens and early 20s was their misuse of (and in most cases addiction to) drugs. Offending was associated with drug use among all the women in their early 20s and most of the young men. These young people saw no prospect of giving up offending until they were able to give up drugs. Male and female respondents recounted similar struggles to stop offending and come off drugs, even though the routes into offending and drug use appeared to differ between young men and young women. Male respondents in our sample had usually begun offending before becoming addicted, whereas the female respondents tended to start offending only after they began using drugs.

Discussion

This chapter began by speculating that differences might exist between women and men in the process of desistance from crime. However, it appears that in many respects the process of desistance may be similar for young men and women, with the familiar themes of maturation, transitions, changed lifestyles and relationships being pertinent for both groups. These findings are, moreover, broadly consistent with Shover and Thompson's (1992: 97) assertion that 'the probability of desistance from criminal participation increases as expectations for achieving friends, money, autonomy, and happiness via crime decrease'. Age, and more particularly, the transitions associated with it, may be a more important determinant of desistance than gender.

It also appears, however, that the process of desistance may differ in some respects between young men and young women. In 'Understanding Offending Among Young People', female respondents were, for example, more likely than their male counterparts to cite moral as opposed to utilitarian rationales for stopping offending and were more likely to emphasize the importance of relational aspects of this process. The latter included the views of parents, experiences of victimization, the assumption of parental responsibilities and dissociation from offending peers. Young men, on the other hand, more often emphasized personal choice and agency in their decisions not to offend. In this respect our findings are similar to those reported by Graham and Bowling (1995).

One of the most striking findings in 'Understanding Offending Among Young People' was that desisters almost invariably occupied the middle position between resisters and persisters in respect of a range of factors. As this held across the whole sample of young people, it suggests that at least in some respects there is a commonality in the experience of desistance that transcends gender and age. It is particularly interesting that desisters resembled resisters most closely in their general attitude to offending (which they regarded as immoral, futile or both), rather than in their behaviour. At the time of the study the desisters were desisting, yet they were still closer to persisters than resisters in their behaviour, for example in their 'hanging about' public spaces, contact with the police and having friends who offended. This suggests that attempts to reduce or stop young people's offending might usefully focus on achieving both attitudinal and, more particularly, behavioural change.

Nevertheless, across all three age groups in 'Understanding Offending Among Young People', many female persisters were keen to be viewed as desisting, even if they acknowledged having recently offended. This, we suggest, may reflect the existence of socially disapproving attitudes towards female offending, whereby women are judged not only in terms of the criminal act itself but also in accordance with their family, sexual and interpersonal relationships (Hudson 1988). As a recent Scottish Office report on female offenders (1998: 6) notes: 'Whilst offending may be a socially inclusive experience for many men and they may gain prestige amongst their friends for their criminal behaviour, this is rarely the case for women and this may be a partial explanation of why so few women offend.'

As Worrall (1990) has indicated, the woman who offends is viewed as having broken both the law and the 'gender contract.' Assigning the offending to the past rather than acknowledging it as a current or future reality may enable young women and girls better to cope with the tensions which may arise when, on the one hand, society encourages increased gender equality and, on the other, continues doubly to condemn young women who step beyond their traditional gender roles. Recognizing the social construction of women's offending is therefore particularly critical to understanding the meaning and process of desistance among young women who offend.

References

Asquith, S. and Samuel, E. (1994) *Criminal Justice and Related Services for Young Adult Offenders*. Edinburgh: HMSO.

Burnett, R. (1992) *The Dynamics of Recidivism*. Oxford: University of Oxford Centre for Criminological Research.

Farrall, S. and Bowling, B. (1999) 'Structuration, human development and desistance from crime', *British Journal of Criminology*, 39 (2): 2–267.

Flood-Page, C., Campbell, S., Harrington, V. and Miller, J. (2000) *Youth Crime: Findings from the 1998/99 Youth Lifestyles Survey. Home Office Research Study 209*. London: Home Office.

Gilligan, C. (1982) *In a Different Voice*. Cambridge, MA: Harvard University Press.

Graham, J. and Bowling, B. (1995) *Young People and Crime*. London: Home Office.

Hubert, R.P. and Hundleby, J.D. (1993) 'Pathways to desistance: how does criminal activity stop?', *Forum on Corrections*, 5 (1).

Hudson, A. (1988) 'Boys will be boys: masculinism and the juvenile justice system', *Critical Social Policy*, 21: 30–48.

Jamieson, J. McIvor, G. and Murray, C. (1999) *Understanding Offending Among Young People*. Edinburgh: HMSO.

Katz, R.S. (2000) 'Explaining girls' and women's crime and desistance in the context of their victimization experiences: a developmental test of strain theory and the life course perspective', *Violence Against Women*, 6 (6): 633–60.

Laub, J.H., Nagin, D.S. and Sampson, R.J. (1998) 'Trajectories of change in criminal offending: good marriages and the desistance process', *American Sociological Review*, 63 (2): 225–38.

Leibrich, J. (1992) *Straight to the Point: Angles on Giving up Crime*. Dunedin, New Zealand: University of Otago Press.

Maruna, S. (2001) *Making Good: How Ex-convicts Reform and Rebuild their Lives*. Washington, DC: American Psychological Association.

Matza, D. (1964) *Delinquency and Drift*. New York, NY: Wiley.

May, T. (1993) *Social Research: Issues, Methods and Process*. Milton Keynes: Open University Press.

Rex, S. (1999) 'Desistance from offending: experiences of probation', *Howard Journal of Criminal Justice*, 38 (4): 366–83.

Rutherford, A. (1986) *Growing out of Crime: Society and Young People in Trouble*. Harmondsworth: Penguin Books.

Rutter, M., Hiller, H. and Hagell, A. (1998) *Antisocial Behavior by Young People*, Cambridge: Cambridge University Press.

Sampson, R.J. and Laub, J. (1993) *Crime in the Making: Pathways and Turning Points through Life*. Cambridge, MA: Harvard University Press.

Scottish Office (1998) *Women Offenders – a Safer Way: A Review of Community Disposals and the Use of Custody for Women Offenders in Scotland*. Edinburgh: Scottish Office.

Shover, N. (1985) *Aging Criminals*. Beverly Hills, CA: Sage.

Shover, N. (1996) *Great Pretenders: Pursuits and Careers of Persistent Thieves*. Boulder, CO: Westview Press.

Shover, N. and Thompson, C.Y. (1992) 'Age, differential expectations and crime desistance', *Criminology*, 30 (1): 89–104.

Sommers, I., Baskin, D.R. and Fagan, J. (1994) 'Getting out of the life: crime desistance by female street offenders', *Deviant Behavior*, 15 (2): 125–49.

Uggen, C. and Kruttschnitt, C. (1998) 'Crime on the breaking: gender differences in desistance', *Law and Society Review*, 32 (2): 339–66.

Warr, M. (1998) 'Life-course transitions and desistance from crime', *Criminology*, 36 (2): 183–216.

Worrall, A. (1990) *Offending Women: Female Lawbreakers and the Criminal Justice System*. London: Routledge.

Part IV
Desistance-focused Reintegration Research

Chapter 9

Beating the perpetual incarceration machine: overcoming structural impediments to re-entry

Stephen C. Richards and Richard S. Jones

Introduction

In this chapter we introduce the convict perspective and a structural analysis of prisoner re-entry to the community. We then discuss the economic and legal consequences of incarceration, qualitative methods used in our study of Iowa convicts, our findings, the perpetual incarceration machine, programme recommendations and beating the penal machinery. We conclude with an esoteric discussion of descent and ascent: a means mentally to overcome the material structures of the incarceration machine. As former penitentiary prisoners we learnt mind over matter and the need to struggle against the oppression of determinist structural barriers.

Our research study attempts to answer the following questions. Why do so many ex-convicts experience rearrest and reincarceration? What are the social-structural variables, impediments and obstacles that contribute to recidivism? Specifically, what insights into the structural problems of prison release explain parole failure? How do convicts beat the machine?

Convict perspective

The convict perspective is built upon the experience of captivity, ethnographic research and the need to give voice to the men and women who live behind prison walls. The Convict Criminologists (e.g. Richards and Ross 2001; Ross and Richards 2002, 2003) – a growing group of former prisoners now employed as criminology and criminal justice faculty at different universities – are developing their own literature. Research and publication by this group (e.g. Irwin 1970, 1980, 1985; Jones 1995; Richards and Jones 1997; Richards 1990, 1995, 1998; Newbold 1982/85, 1989, 1991, 2000; Austin and Irwin 2001; Richards *et al.* 2002; Austin *et al.* 2003; Richards and Ross 2003; Terry 1997, 2003) should be viewed as a dramatic attempt to critique, update and improve the critical literature in the field. For example, we do not use the terms 'inmates' or 'offenders', as these words suggest statistical categories, and are used by correctional authorities to dehumanize persons. We prefer prisoners, convicts and persons convicted of criminal offences. Thinking about prison and re-entry, we conceptualize problems and possible solutions from the viewpoint of prisoners.

A structural analysis of prisoner re-entry to the community

From a convict perspective, the structural realities of prison conditions and re-entry to the community (Richards 1995) are the issue, and not the criminal or deviant behaviour of individuals. We suggest that criminal careers are not necessarily chosen but may result from incarceration and reincarceration that are predicated on the structural problems experienced by prisoners when released from prison. In effect, many prisoners are never allowed a fair opportunity to return home and start a new life. Instead, these persons are processed through correctional stages where they are structured to fail, return to prison and, over time, become institutionalized.

Controlling for individual differences and deficiencies, how does the rule-resource structure of prison release contribute to work release and parole failure? For example, consider a hypothetical sample of 100 innocent men or women, without criminal records, psychological disorders, alcohol or drug abuse problems, or deficiencies in educational or vocational training. Now imagine a mad criminologist, without any concern for human decency or professional ethics, designing a nightmare double-blind experiment whereby these respectable citizens are arrested for a serious felony, convicted and sentenced to serve ten years in a penitentiary. Serving time in prison they are considered by convicts and staff to be 'Square Johns' (Irwin 1970: 32–5) who had families and employment before their incarcerations, and do not learn and internalize criminal identities while in prison. We predict that these men, upon leaving prison, will have the same rate of parole failure and subsequent reincarceration as a conventional non-experimental population of parolees. Considering this hypothetical sample, what structural variables, as opposed to individual behaviour, may explain parole failure?

The purpose of this study was to explore what structural impediments, as opposed to individual deficiencies, may contribute to parole failure and recidivism. The research was guided by three theoretical propositions that derive from Giddens' structuration theory (1984, 1987, 1990, 1991):

1   Prisoners upon release, depending upon the length of time spent in prison, may have little memory traces of societal rules and resources (memory of social structure) with which to reciprocate in the practice (social integration) of day-to-day life (routinization). These men experience the disjuncture between two different structurations of time and space (prison and the free world) as a lack of confidence and trust (ontological security) in the structure they re-enter. Conversely, society may react without confidence and trust to prisoners who wear a stigmatized and spoiled identity (Goffman 1961, 1963).

2   Prisoners upon release, even when they are able to 'pass', may carry with them memory traces of the rules and resources (structure) acquired in prison back to the streets.

3   The speed and complexity of modern society impose additional structural impediments or barriers to ex-prisoners' re-entry and reintegration into the community.

Convicts, scholars and practitioners are frustrated by the high rate of parole failure and recidivism. Unfortunately, recent policy developments have only made prisoner re-entry more difficult for persons released from prison. These policies have resulted in what Austin and Irwin (2001) called 'the rising tide of parole failures', which they explained as the result of parolee misconduct, technical violations, drug testing and close parole supervision. In contrast, we focus on how the structure of time and space, and rules and resources, may contribute to parolee programme failure.

Our research study looked at the experiences of convicts in the Iowa state prison system as they were transferred from medium and maximum-security institutions to correctional half-way houses in Des Moines. Qualitative research methods were used to explore the experiences of prison convicts with prison release and re-entry to the community. Our study asked prisoners and correctional staff to comment on the problems of prison release, work release, re-entry to the community and recidivism. The focus was on structural impediments to parole success, defined as economic and legal barriers to prisoner re-entry to the community.

Economic and legal consequences of incarceration

The public does not understand that a prison sentence carries both direct and indirect consequences. The direct consequences of incarceration, which may be pervasive and profound, include what Sykes (1958) termed the 'pains of imprisonment.' These include being deprived of liberty, material comfort, heterosexual relationships, autonomy and security. Convicts may lose nearly everything dear to them, including the intimacy of family and friends. Most of their worldly possessions are forfeited, loaned or stolen. They may have their homes, farms, businesses and material possessions claimed by relatives, repossessed by the bank or confiscated by the government. Eventually, they lose their spouses and children.

The indirect or collateral consequences of incarceration may not be evident to prisoners until they are released from prison. The collateral consequences of criminal conviction (Allen and Simonsen 1995) include disabilities, disqualifications and legal restriction. In a study of state statutes Burton *et al.* (1987: 52) found collateral consequences of a felony conviction were:

> In some sixteen states (nearly one third of the jurisdictions surveyed), courts may terminate parenting rights upon conviction or incarceration of a parent. (2) More than half (twenty-eight states) permit divorce for conviction or imprisonment of a felony. (3) Some 30 percent of the jurisdictions permanently bar convicted felons from public employment in their home states, unless pardoned or restored to full citizenship. (4) If one is a felon in nineteen states, one may not hold public office. (5) Almost every state forbids a felon from possession of a firearm. (6) Only eight states require the felon to register as a former offender, and only four states continue the practice of civil death.

These legal structural impediments to successful re-entry to the community restrict the ex-prisoner to a structure of diminished resources.

Historically, the legal status of prisoners has been defined by civil death statutes. Johnson (1990: 155–6, 168) discussed civil death:

When we sentence criminals to prison we suspend their civil lives, rendering them civilly dead until they are deemed worthy of return to the society of the living. Civil death entails the loss of one's freedom and of the attendant benefits of civil life in the free world ... Prisoners, until fairly recently, were viewed as the legal equivalent of dead men ... They were *civilites mortuus*, and their estates, if they had any, were managed like those of dead men.

Civil death (Davidenas 1983: 61; Allen and Simonsen 1992: 6, 273–4) implies that their worldly legacy is claimed or inherited by others; a prisoner's property is confiscated in the name of the state (a common practice of the federal government); a man's wife is declared a widow and is free to remarry; and a 'dead' person is disqualified from signing contracts or conducting business affairs.

Many prisoners leave prison with barely enough money to survive a few days. According to Lenihan (1974: 4–6): 'Most State governments give each releasee clothing, transportation, and "gate money," ranging from $10 to $200 – the median is $28. Fifteen states do not provide transportation; six do not provide clothing; three give neither; and two give no money.' Today, in Iowa and many other states, prisoners are issued $50 gate money and a bus ticket.

Convicts are released from prison with considerable debts and financial liabilities. These debts are a consequence of being locked up for years and being forced to work at prison wages, usually only pennies per hour. With these meagre earnings, they must provide for their personal needs, for example, commissary, legal expenses and collect phone calls to family. Released from prison, the ex-convict has little if any money and is typically hit with delinquent bills that have built up for years, including court costs and fees, fines, restitution, tax deficiencies, child support and domestic family bills.

Considering the research on parolees securing employment, it is no surprise that many persons return to prison. The relationship between employment, crime, imprisonment and recidivism has been the subject of much empirical analysis (e.g. Greenberg 1977; Janovic 1982; Chirico and Bales 1991; Zimring and Hawkins 1991). In a market economy, unemployment marginalizes individuals and may contribute to high rate of imprisonment and parole failure (Welch 1996: 50–2). Pownell (1969: 49) reported that federal male parolees experience three times the rate of unemployment of the general population; Tropin (1977) estimated the national rate of unemployment for all ex-offenders at three time the rate for non-offenders. Dale (1976: 323) suggested that ex-convict unemployment is related to the rate of recidivism: 'This high unemployment rate is reflected directly in the rate of recidivism. Of the more than 100,000 released from prison each year, 70 percent will return to prison – 30 percent within a year after release.' Recent studies (Dickey 1989; English and Mande 1991; Richards, 1995; Richards and Jones 1997; Richards 1998; Austin *et al.* 2001; Austin and Irwin 2001) also suggest that unemployment contributes to community programme failure and recommend priority be given to job development assistance.

Generally, ex-convicts are unlikely to receive any prison training in marketable skills, employees are reluctant to hire them and they have great difficulty in filling out employment applications that inquire about arrest and conviction records. While on parole they must okay their employment with their parole officers who are required to verify employment by calling or visiting the parolees' work site. This may lead to the termination of employment.

Restrictive laws and policies provide obstacles for ex-convicts in the labour market. The unemployment rate of ex-convicts may be due to discrimination and laws prohibiting their hire. Smith (1984: 5) reported: 'The American Bar Association (1973) speculated that the reasons for an unusually high (36 percent and higher) unemployment rate among ex-offenders are not only their lack of skills but laws, regulations, and practices which prohibit certain jobs to those with a criminal record.' Stanley (1976) discussed three barriers to ex-convicts securing legal employment: licensing restrictions; civil service rules and practices; and bonding requirements. A study by the American Bar Association (Hunt *et al.* 1973: 5) found '1,948 separate [state] statutory provisions that affect the licensing of persons with an arrest or conviction record'. Ex-convicts are required by state statutes to prove 'good moral character' to receive an occupational licence for the following: restaurant work where alcohol is sold; bartender; chauffeur; plumber; physical therapist; teacher; tree surgeon; dry cleaner; midwife; funeral director; doctor; lawyer; stock broker; car sales person; insurance agent; barber; cab driver; and child care worker. As Stanley (1976: 152) indicated, 'There are lists pages long of occupations for which a license may be denied if the applicant has committed a criminal offense'.

Ex-convicts may fare no better in public sector employment. Miller (1972) reported they faced formidable obstacles in securing government employment. Stanley (1976) suggested that civil service laws were worded to deny ex-convicts employment opportunities. Most cities, counties, states and the federal government do not hire ex-convicts for many job categories. Criminal records are used to deny ex-convicts employment as policeman, fireman, teachers, garbage collectors, secretaries, clerks, and to prevent enlistment in the military. Ironically, one innovative programme, funded by the US Department of Labor, the 'Model offender program', was unable to hire ex-convicts as employment counsellors because of restrictive regulations.

More recently, a growing number of universities are using criminal records to reject student applications for admission, student loans and employment. University systems now ask 'Have you ever been convicted of a felony ?,' on applications for admission and employment. Applicants are being denied admission to both undergraduate and graduate programmes. The same 'felony question' may preclude professors being hired as faculty.

Bonding companies routinely denied bonding to ex-convicts. This practice effectively excluded them from many jobs, including truck driving, furniture moving or employment that required handling currency or operating a cash register, such as fast food or retail sales. Businesses may be concerned that employing felons will increase their insurance premiums.

In summary, the direct and indirect consequences of incarceration created legal and economic difficulties for prisoners who served time in prison and upon release to community facilities. Economic impediments include:

1 problems with securing employment in both the public and private sectors (barriers to employment may include criminal records, restrictions on occupational licensing, bonding and civil service requirements);
2 imposition of court fees and fines, restitution, lawyer bills and child support;
3 years of imprisonment that result in the accumulation of various unpaid consumer bills;
4 the relative poverty of prisoners released as measured by their 'gate money,' assets and debts; and
5 the rate of unemployment as compared with the general population.

Legal impediments include the loss of civil rights and collateral consequences of criminal convictions.

Qualitative methods used in our study

The original study (Richards 1995; Richards and Jones 1997) of prisoner release from Iowa prisons and return to the community in Des Moines was conducted in 1992. In this chapter we discuss the methodology and finding and revisit our discussion and update our recommendations. This research was conducted by two ex-convicts (both Iowa State University PhDs) observing prisoners upon their release from prison to work-release facilities and parole. As former penitentiary prisoners familiar with the cultural context and symbolic meanings of the prison world we have some insight into prison release and problems encountered. We also make no pretence to value-free objectivity (Weber). The data in this study are open to different interpretation, depending upon both the analysis and analyst.

Understanding prisoner experience requires a methodology that gives convicts a voice to report their problems with the many stages of custody. Convicts do prison time and, on a given day, pass through prison gates to continue their sentences in community facilities. A new life is supposed to begin when the convict walks out the prison gates.

We interviewed men released from prison, following them from the prison gates to their designated correctional half-way houses. First, we visited the prisons to learn about pre-release programmes and procedures. Secondly, we stood outside the prison gates and waited for random prisoners to walk out. 'Hi, I'am a ex-convict sociologist studying prison release. Do you mind if I ride the bus with you to Des Moines and ask you a few questions?' Along the way, when the Greyhound stopped at a truck stop, we bought the just released prisoners meals and smokes. Once the men relaxed and decided we were not police, although they still did not have a clue what a sociologist was or believe we were ex-cons, they were talkative, asking as many questions as they answered. When the bus arrived in Des Moines, the men were required to report immediately to the community half-way house.

Thirdly, in an attempt to understand how community facilities operated, we spent long evenings at three correctional half-way houses visiting with both prisoners and staff. Over the months we also observed correctional staff and prisoners in prisons, half-way houses and parole offices. Having collected initial observations, programme reports and official permission to conduct prisoner interviews, we then decided systematically to survey prisoners using an open-ended questionnaire. Our criterion for selection of men was that they were convicted felons who had served more than one year in prison. As it turned out, most of the interviewees were recidivists who have served more than one prison sentence and a considerable part of their adult life in correctional institutions.

Fourthly, 2–4-hour interviews were conducted with 30 male prisoners on site in person with audio-taped questions and answers. A number of men were interviewed twice, and several group interviews were also completed. These interviews were conducted late into the evenings, sometimes past midnight and on weekends, over a six-month period at one prison, two residential work-release centres, a house of hospitality for ex-convicts, parole and probation offices and the offices of human service providers. Correction staff at these sites graciously provided office accommodation. All interviews were private and confidential without interruptions from either staff or clients. The prisoners, without exception, were cordial and eager to discuss prisons, prison release and their future plans with ex-convict researchers.

After a few initial interviews, it became apparent that the men had their own stories to tell, regardless of our research protocol. As a result, we consciously attempted not to control the interviews. The vulnerable status of work-release prisoners and their precarious foothold in the community while residing in a correctional facility with controlled movement dictated that we not jeopardize them personally. We did not ask compromising questions about criminal records, court cases, drugs, alcohol or illegal activities. However, discussion of these subjects was initiated by the prisoners.

We decided not to review either criminal or prison records of prisoners. These records, including pre-sentence investigations (PSI), court records, police records and central correctional files, are official records of stigmatization. Criminal history record information is used by statutory provision to deny felons the right to purchase firearms, to refuse bail, to upgrade criminal offences, to enhance sentences for offenders with prior convictions, to provide for mandatory sentences for habitual felons, to deny probation, as evidence in pre-sentence reports, to decide correctional classification and to affect parole eligibility. Thus criminal history records were instrumental in the processing of prisoners through every stage of the criminal justice system. Consequently, it is not surprising that some prisoners would be threatened by an outside researcher reviewing their records. Prisoners complained that official records were used both to enhance and sustain criminal sanctions; they are part of their punishment.

Interviews of correctional staff provided an opportunity to get background information on both prison release and work-release programmes. As the study progressed, we were able to check contradictory or conflicting information by comparing prisoner and staff responses.

Findings

Theoretically, Iowa operated a prison system where prisoners were processed through a series of structured environments of diminishing security levels, as they gradually progress to release. They were transferred from prison to community half-way houses operated by the Department of Corrections. These facilities were secure facilities, with locked windows and doors, staffed by uniformed officers, with controlled movements and frequent 'counts.'

The prison population studied consisted of men who individually had served time in a number of different prisons (maximum, medium, minimum security) before being transferred to a work-release facility. As they completed their prison time they were provided with an opportunity to serve the last 3–6 months in work release which provided them with a chance to adjust in stages to working and living in the community. Upon successfully completing the work-release programme the men were eligible for parole. They would still be in 'constructive custody' for a number of years until they finished parole supervision.

Gate money

Prisoners were released from prison to work release with five dollars 'gate money,' a bus ticket and $50 release money from which the cost of their 'prison blues' was deducted. Two prisoners interviewed together discussed release money:

> *First prisoner*: Out of the money allotment for clothes [$50] I bought two pairs of their jeans and a shirt. And basically it ain't like I went down to the clothing room, I got the clothing I already had up in my locker.
> *Interviewer*: How much did that cost you?
> *First prisoner*: The pants were fifteen, the shirt was seven, and they made me pay for my boots.
> *Interviewer*: Did you have any of that $50 left?
> *First prisoner*: About $10 or $12, something like that.
> *Second prisoner*: Did you get out in winter time man?

First prisoner: It was March, sort of winter.
Second prisoner: Did they make you buy the coat?
First prisoner: Yea, thanks man. The coat came along too. The coat and the boots.
Second prisoner: If you don't buy the coat they'll make you go without one.
Interviewer: They give you $50?
Second prisoner: That you never see. You don't see the money. If you got personal clothes they still won't give you the money if you don't want to wear the state clothes. It used to be they took you downtown and you bought straight from the store. But now they don't do that. It ain't like they take you to the clothing room and give you new stuff for the money. It's what you been wearing. And it's stuff you been wearing for a while, working in and everything.

The balance of the fifty dollars was forwarded to the men's institutional account at their intended destination, the work-release facility, where it was applied to their first week's rent bill.

Clothing

These men walked out of prison wearing old, worn-out prison uniforms, carrying a cardboard box containing their personal belongings, with five dollars gate money in their pockets. Upon arrival at the work-release centre most of them were 'stone broke' until either their family arrived to provide them 'walk around money' or their prison account money was delivered by mail, which may take a few weeks or more. Many of them received loans from the work-release centre to tide them over while they looked for work, waited for their first real pay cheque, or pursued alternative means to securing street money.

Why are these men exiting prison wearing prison uniforms? One community corrections employee discussed the problem:

They come in with no clothes. He came in [referring to one prisoner in a group interview] with no shoes. January 24th and no shoes no coat, T-shirt and a pair of pants. Coming from prison, one guy from Oakdale came in with, in December, cut off shirt, one lense in his glasses, not two. They did get his hearing aid cleaned so he did have that. Pair of pants that's it, no coat. And we are seeing more and more of that. We are seeing more and more come in with nothing. And they are even talking about cutting the money they get when they leave [prison]. That's rumors from the budget cuts.

Another community corrections employee responded to our question: 'How long has it been that you've been seeing them walk in here wearing prison blues?'

> Well they have always done that, oh yeah, forever. Even when they dressed people out they really didn't dress them out in clothing that was really appropriate. You could pretty much pick them out in a crowd no matter what. I'm not sure it has to be that way but that's the way it's always been. The shoes are a big give-a-way most of the time.

The prisoners left prison wearing 'prison blue' uniforms and penitentiary boots. It is amazing they were not arrested by the police as escapees. They arrived at the work-release centres without appropriate clothing to wear when applying for employment. The same community corrections employee explained:

> If they could get a stock of clothing that was varied enough that would fit in, I think that probably would help. I certainly don't like to see them come in here [wearing prison blues] because that's one of the first things we have to deal with. The work release prisoner says, I don't have appropriate clothing to job search.
> I don't know what the answer to that [street clothes] is. At some point in time they need to address that, whether it be at the institution or give us enough money and resources here to be able to do it, one or the other. But it needs to be addressed, that is a problem. If we had a pre-release center that certainly would be the appropriate place to deal with those kinds of issues.

The amount of 'gate money,' release clothing and bus tickets were only some of the issues that need to be addressed.

Inadequate preparation for release

The prisoners also said they did not have sufficient notification and time psychologically to prepare for their transfers from prison to community work release. Some of these men had spent years in the penitentiary and were surprised to learn they were being released. The director of a work-release facility stated:

> What I see happening is there is a waiting list [at the prisons]. I don't know that there is a hell of a lot of work that goes on with that

individual prior to the time that he is to be released. Has that counselor really sat down and tried to work with and prepare that guy for release? I don't think so. They are jerking a guy out of a cell or off his work detail and saying, 'Here pack your stuff you are going to Newton, your bus leaves in an hour.' That's the kind of thing I see happening. That's the stories we hear.

Correctional staff reported that, upon arrival at the work-release centres, the prisoners appeared to be in a euphoric trance, happy to be out from behind the wall but unprepared for the challenges before them. The same director of a work-release facility explained:

There is not a heck of a lot of time for that individual to get a mind set about what he is going to try to do or try to accomplish while he's on work release. Maybe that somewhere along the line did take place but then with our waiting list we got with the half-way house maybe that was three months ago. He still has to get that mind set going to say, 'Okay, you know I've got to do this, I'm going to do that, I'm going to really try to do this, I'm going to try to avoid that.' He is probably thinking about that on the way here on the bus. And then we bring him in here and nail him with all the rules and regulations in an orientation and he's just spinning. We know that that's a problem.

'Spinning' refers to the state of mind the prisoners were in upon arrival at the work-release centre. They have been transported from prison, with its rules and regulations, to a new environment, the work-release facility, with an entirely new set of rules and specific obligations. Upon arrival at the work-release centre they are confused and anxious, even a little frightened. Some of these men, particularly those who served a long time in the penitentiary, had not been required to pay rent, purchase food or look for employment in years.

They have no money when they arrive at the half-way house

Leaving prison the convicts are issued with a bus ticket to Des Moines and $50 gate money minus what they are charged for prison-issue clothing. In effect, they ride the bus with $20–30 in cash, mere pocket money to pay for meals.

Getting off the bus and entering the community half-way house facility, they are wearing their prison uniform and carrying a cardboard box with their meagre personal possessions. Locked up in prison they were unable to save money because of low prison wages and the court-ordered deductions (for court fines, restitution, child support) from their monthly pay. Most of the interviewees reported their penitentiary wage as one dollar per day or 12.5 cents an hour, for a total of 20 dollars a month. One prisoner reported:

> Two dollars was top pay [per day]. I was making twenty-five cents an hour top pay. The pay we get up there [prison] now is just ridiculous, it's nothing to live on. You have to have your people send you money in. If your people out on the streets don't have it then you're screwed.

Out of this 20 ($1 a day for 20 days) to 40 dollars ($2 a day for 20 days) a month, convicts were required to pay for their own cigarettes, paper, envelopes, stamps, commissary food and collect phone calls. Typically, convicts estimate it takes at least $100 a month to pay for their expenses while in prison. Iowa prisoners were forced to depend on their families to make up the difference.

Most of these prsioners, as a means of survival, relied upon money from home that arrived as US postal money orders and was added to their commissary accounts. These cheques mailed from family and friends, are cashed by the institution and used to pay court-ordered restitution. The convicts told us the prison authorities forged their signatures and cashed cheques made out to them. One prisoner said: 'If my family had intended to pay my restitution they would have mailed their check to the court.' They saw this practice as the prison stealing from their families.

Visits in prison

Seven of the thirty men in the study received no visits at all while they were incarcerated. A number of others reported considerable anxiety about the visits they did receive. One prisoner recalled his visiting days:

> I remember a lot of days like that. My visits would be the next day, and the day before I would get real quiet. On the day my visit was coming I always got real nervous. And I never understood why because I had known this girl for ten years. When it was time to go visit her I would always get real nervous. I'd get nervous to the point where my hands would shake.

Some of these men refused visits while others had no family or friends that were interested in or able to visit them. A number of men referred to their families' low income as the reason why the latter did not visit their sons, husbands and fathers in prison; other men preferred that their families not visit them because of the degrading treatment they would receive from penitentiary staff. The number of visits a convict receives per year may be related to the length of his sentence and number of prior incarcerations. Prisoners serving long sentences (ten years to life) or who have served a number of prior sentences may lose their community ties and have fewer visits per year.

Most significant needs

We asked the prisoners what were their most significant needs upon release from prison. The most frequent responses were money (24 men), job (23 men), new friends (18 men), job training (13 men) and education (13 men). The convicts now at the community half-way house were desperate for money and willing to take nearly any employment. A number of them were concerned that, after working all week, they had no money to give their wives to pay house bills. An even more pressing problem were demands for money from the correctional authorities.

The programme is all about money

The men reported being under constant pressure from the staff to work for money that would be deducted from their pay cheques to pay for mandatory rent and restitution. Money was needed immediately to comply with work-release centres' rules that they pay weekly rent, purchase institutional sheets (15 dollars is deducted from the money that arrives from the prison or their first pay cheque), and provide for their own food and transportation. The prisoners called the correctional staff 'collection officers' because they felt they were more concerned with collecting money for the state than providing assistance to their residents.

The correctional counsellors were ordered to collect money from each man. Prisoners paid four, seven or twelve dollars a day rent for their bed in a work-release centre, depending on the facility and their status; and $120, $210 or $360 rent a month plus a 20 per cent deduction for restitution from their paycheques. The rent was for a bed or bunk in a dormitory or four-man room in a controlled movement facility and did not include food. Most of the prisoners quickly fell into debt to the work-release centre for back rent. In some cases, their resentment of correctional staff handling their pay cheques and deducting for rent and restitution dampened their interest in legitimate employment. Some of the men who worked 40-hour weeks complained they had little money to purchase food, clothes or presents for their children. One prisoner voiced his resentment:

> You leave the penitentiary on a Tuesday, you come here, and you're broke for the whole week or two till they send your money from the penitentiary. What kind of shit is that? Ya know, I mean a man come home from the penitentiary they don't even give you gate money. They give you five dollars [and] bus fare. You got rent to pay, bus tokens to pay for. They make you buy sheets. They give us two sheets, pillow case, face towel, and a bath towel, and charge us fifteen dollars. And it ain't like do you want it, you got to take it. There ain't no option. They do that and that ain't right.
>
> We coming straight from the penitentiary, they trying to take our money. And then you get your money, okay my money just come [from the penitentiary], I owe for sheets, owe for bus tokens, I owe for my rent. You're automatically two weeks behind in rent, see what I'm saying. Then your counselor, I don't where, they get the power to take your money and spend it like they want to. I didn't ask to come here and be put in the hole by your all program. Ya all know that when I come here it would take a while for me to find a job.

Even if they do locate employment, in their first few weeks at the work they find themselves in debt for rent, sheets and bus tokens. Every week that passes without working puts them deeper in debt to the programme. This debt contributes to the tension and bad feeling that exists between the staff and some of their less than successful clients. Men who are unable or unwilling to find work, usually at minimum wage, and who do not have the resources to pay restitution and work release rent are restricted to daily release only to look for work, or sent back to prison.

One prisoner reported: 'I ain't going to do time and pay for it too. You don't have to pay that restitution.' The problem was if a prisoner was unable to find employment, and failed to pay half-way house rent or monthly restitution payments, he would be punished by being returned to prison. During the weeks we were interviewing, a number of men were 'cuffed up' and transported back to the state penitentiary (maximum security) or reformatory (medium security) when they refused work or complained about rent and restitution.

The prisoners had accumulated considerable debt, including restitution, court cost and fees, back child-support bills with the county and miscellaneous domestic bills. The debt ranged from a few hundred dollars to tens of thousands of dollars. A few of them also owed back taxes, complete with fines and interest that built up while they were incarcerated. They were subject to a 20 per cent deduction from their pay cheques that started in prison and continued through work release and parole and would later face garnishment of their pay.

Paying for public defenders

Many of the men complained bitterly about being assessed legal fees for court-appointed lawyers. At the time that their court cases were being decided (by their public defenders pressuring them into pleading guilty) they were unaware that they would be assessed attorney fees. None of them understood how they could be charged legal fees for public defenders. A prisoner stated: 'Court costs, reimbursement to the place we broke into, the stuff that we took. It's really weird, it's suppose to be free [public defender], when you lose [plead guilty] you have to pay.'

Court-appointed lawyers collect their fees for services rendered to indigent clients through the imposition of court costs on those who plead guilty; the fees are collected by the state and paid to the attorneys. Seasoned prisoners, those who had been through the court system more than once, were not surprised they were pressured by public defenders to plead guilty. Defendants who plead not guilty and demand a trial are not assessed legal fees.

Prison losses

Prisoners experienced a dramatic reduction in material resources as the result of serving prison time. The sample of 30 work-release prisoners in this study reported losing the following as a result of their prolonged removal from the community during their incarceration: 11 reported losing a marriage (divorced while in prison); 8 reported losing homes or farms, either by bank repossession or divorce; 17 lost cars upon going to prison; 10 had their furniture disappear; and 11 reported not being able to locate their clothes upon release. The most commonly reported loss was employment, with 17 losing the jobs they held prior to incarceration.

Employment: working for the man

When the prisoners did find a job they were not even allowed to even receive their own pay cheques. They would work all week and never see a pay cheque. The men were directed to apply for employment at local companies that were part of the 'state programme' and already prepared to hire them. The rule was that half-way house prisoners' pay cheques were mailed to the facility and cashed by staff. If by some chance they found a job on their own, the employer would then have to comply with state rules: mail the employee's pay cheque to the correction facility. Still, come pay day they may have been reluctant to mail the pay cheque to the state, especially as this did little to improve employee morale.

Most of these companies paid minimum wages, were desperate for new employees and would hire nearly anybody who could walk, talk and show up on a regular basis. The typical job was fast food or telemarketing where the men could report everyday at the same address. The men were not allowed to work in construction, in door-to-door sales or in transportation jobs where they were off site and could not be monitored closely. They were usually not allowed to work cash registers, handle money or drive while employed. None of the interview sample attended school or college.

The work-release centres required prisoners to take the first available job. At the time of the interviews, 23 of the 30 men were employed. The unemployed men had either just arrived from prison, were disabled, recently laid off or had had their employment terminated. Most of the men, with the exception of the disabled and impaired, who may require assignment to sheltered workshops, did find employment. But they were limited by their interrupted work histories, the missing years in their work records, the requirement that they disclose their place of residence to prospective employers, employment application questions about criminal records and other legal restrictions to the lowest-paid occupations. They took minimum-wage dead-end jobs: laundries, food service, car washes, day labour, service stations, hotel service, low-paid factory, temporary labour or telemarketing.

Many of them expressed dissatisfaction with the low pay and working conditions of the jobs they worked. Most of them had worked at jobs before going to prison that paid considerably better than their present employment. Prior to going to prison, the men averaged wages over ten dollars an hour with a number of them working union construction and factory jobs. Arriving at the work-release centres they averaged only $5.50 an hour, with only one man of the 30 receiving a wage that was significantly above the minimum wage. As a group, the work-release prisoners were being paid approximately half the hourly wages they made before going to prison.

Few of the men who were employed managed to save any money while they were at the half-way house. Because they were only able to find low-wage employment, much of their pay cheques went to pay for their keep, with little left over. Few of them were able to save the money they would eventually need upon leaving the half-way house to pay for security deposit and first-month rent on a private apartment.

Summary: the perpetual incarceration machine

In 1988 the total population prison population in Iowa was 2,890. By 1989 this population had grown to 3,322, an increase of nearly 15 per cent. In 1989 there were 2,913 total admissions and 2,481 total releases. At this rate the state will have to build a new medium-size prison every year to keep up with the anticipated increase in incarceration. Of these 2,913 new prison admissions, only 1,156 were new court commitments, while 570 were revoked probation, 650 were parole violators, 56 were shock probation returns, 205 were escape returns, 139 were work-release returns, 38 were OWI returns and 99 were other admissions. For 1989, over half of all prison admissions were former prisoners returned on either new criminal charges or revocation of community custody. These revocations of probation, work release and parole were largely due to increases in programme violations rather than new convictions for felonies or aggravated misdemeanours. In effect, the state's prison population continues to climb as the result of prison-release failure, as reflected in the rate of community custody revocation.

Direct and indirect or collateral consequences of incarceration are reflected in the rules and resource structure prisoners encounter upon leaving prison. Felons as ex-convicts are subject to a plethora of bewildering restrictions upon release from prison, as stipulated by the rules of, first, work-release facilities and then parole. These rules are predicated on the requirements of custodial supervision and not the needs of the released prisoners. At the same time that these men are subject to parole rules and regulations they have experienced a dramatic decrease in personal resources.

Iowa operated a perpetual incarceration machine, a system of institutional facilities designed as human warehouses for the return of damaged goods. Prisoners are released to work release or parole with little preparation for success. Over 50 per cent of the men will fail work release, and nearly 70 per cent fail parole and eventually return to prison. Many of these parolees are being returned to prison for status offences as they have violated the rules and regulations of their community custody status. The prison system is perpetuating growth as a result of its own institutional failure properly to prepare prisoners for release. The system is a revolving door that shuffles prisoners from one level of custody to another, from probation to prison, from prison to work release and parole and from parole back to prison.

Revisiting the original 1992 study: the Iowa prison system in 2002

Since we first conducted this study in 1992 (Richards 1995; Richards and Jones 1997), the situation for prison release in Iowa and the USA has deteriorated. The last ten years of prison admissions proves our thesis stated above. The Iowa prison system has grown by nearly 300 per cent in less than 10 years, to over 10,000. This was accomplished by building new facilities that are now nearly all overcrowded, with the entire system 20 per cent beyond legally rated capacity (Iowa Department of Corrections Home Page 2001). We predict that if we return to Iowa in 2012, the prison population will again be larger. The Iowa prison population, like those across the country in numerous states, continues to grow because of its failure to rehabilitate, educate, train and prepare prisoners for successful re-entry to the community.

Nationally over the last two decades, the prison population has tripled from 500,000 to 1.8 million (Irwin *et al.* 2000: 135). Today in the USA over 500,000 men and women exit prison every year (see Austin *et al.* 2001). Nearly 50 per cent of prison admissions are women and men being returned as the result of the effects of incarceration and community programme failure.

Further, we also predict that the national prison population will continue to grow as a result of mandatory minimum sentences, so-called truth in sentencing laws, repeat offender statutes and the continued failure of prisons to 'do corrections'. Unfortunately, prisons today have become human warehouses with fewer programme opportunities (educational or vocational) and resources to train prisoners to be productive citizens. As the prison population increases, along with the average length of sentence, this convict hypothesis becomes more evident: the more time in prison and the higher the security level, the more institutionalization and less chance for successful return to the community.

Programme recommendation updates

Our observations and interviews at work-release facilities convinced us of three essential facts:

1   Prisoners have not been properly prepared for release to work-release facilities.
2   Work-release prisoners need a carefully planned 'staged release programme'.
3   There is a need for better communication and programme continuity between the prisons and the work-release centres.

Prisons need exit programmes that properly prepare men for release. This programme should include expanded visitation privileges, home furloughs, and family and employment counselling. The pre-release programme should arrange for the prisoners to have driver's licences and social security cards before leaving prison. Prisoners with outstanding consumer or tax debt could receive legal counselling on filing for bankruptcy. They should be supplied with a set of clothes appropriate for their employment search and sufficient gate money to meet their needs for at least 90 days.

All prisoners should have a detailed pre-release plan prepared while on community furloughs. This may be a work-release or parole plan. The plan should include specific reference to family, place of residence and employment or school. Social workers or parole officers should be assigned to take these men home for a first visit with their children and spouses or ex-spouses. This provides the man and his family with a professional observer if assistance or intervention is required.

A pre-release programme needs to be one step in a carefully planned programme of staged release that includes prison vocational and education programmes, the pre-release programme, and work-release facilities that allow the men (or women) to attend colleges or universities. The director of a work-release facility explained:

> I think that that needs to be a natural progression in the chain again. From there it needs to slow down, bring it back in there, let's do those steps, let's hammer those things into these people, let's work with them. Get it to a natural progression again. Get it going again. We did that years ago. We did it and we had a seventy-some percent success rate. We are not doing it now. We are getting a fifty-some success rate. And believe it or not we are working harder than ever with people, working with resources that we have never worked with before, in manners that we have never done before. We are knocking our brains out and getting less pay back. The system is just not working properly.

A carefully planned programme of staged release requires increased funding, a commitment to helping prisoners, community co-operation and a steady flow of information and feedback between the prisons, community corrections and conditions on the street. Community corrections cannot be funded on the 'cheap' (Gibbons 1986) or at the expense of prisoners, without a high rate of predictable programme failure.

We recommend an ongoing effort be made to improve communication and co-ordination between this pre-prison release programme and the work-release centres and parole offices. As the situation now exists, convicts have a better understanding of the correctional system than some of the staff. Prisoners have lived and experienced the succession of correctional stages, while most correctional staff have only worked in prison or community corrections and do not have a comprehensive understanding of the system as a whole. One community corrections employee stated: 'I don't know what they tell these people. I don't know who does what in the prison system. But I will tell you there is very little communication between the institutions and community based corrections.' This lack of communication between the prisons and community corrections does not allow for effective prison release planning and implementation. We recommend that the Iowa Department of Corrections encourage staff to apply for positions both inside and outside the prison, as a means of acquiring experience with different stages of the correctional system.

Another recommendation concerns the need for work-release facilities that operate with less supervision. Few work-release clients require the intensive supervision of controlled movement facilities. Some prisoners may benefit from a less structured work-release centre that is operated informally, on an honour plan. We suggest that the Department of Corrections may want to visit and tour less restrictive work-release centres currently operated by the federal government and non-profit agencies.

For example, the Salvation Army manages modest motels and hotels all over the country occupied by both state and federal prisoners and homeless families. Typically, prisoners prefer these facilities because the Salvation Army provides services (counselling, help in finding employment and housing) and little correctional supervision. Generally, the house rules are simple and there is no provision for drug testing or collection of restitution. The prisoners are treated no differently from the homeless. The Salvation Army correctional contracts provide for state and/or federal payments (so many dollars per day per prisoner) that support a community shelter that provides rooms, food and services for the prisoners and hundreds of homeless families each year.

Another less restrictive facility, located on 6th Avenue in Des Moines, Iowa, is the Hanson House of Hospitality operated by Criminal Justice Ministries. This group home for men released from prisons operates without any government funding. Hanson House charges nothing for rent and food and has successfully assisted over a thousand former prisoners with their re-entry to the community.

All states should consider funding residential and counselling services administered, operated and staffed by ex-convicts. Only ex-prisoners know and understand the difficulties of leaving prison and re-entering the community. Their expertise is an available resource rarely utilized and desperately needed if we are ever to make a dent in the rate of recidivism.

Further, these findings suggest that the states need to rethink the public defender system. In this study of Iowa prison release we did not ask work-release prisoners questions about the court system. However, in nearly every interview we conducted, when asked about court-ordered restitution, the men complained bitterly about being assessed for court-appointed attorneys. We recommend that the present system of appointing and paying for public defenders be investigated. We suggest that this is a topic for further legislative and academic study, and possible legal action.

Courts are now handing out multiple sentences, what Morris and Tonry (1990) call 'punishment packages', that include prison time and alternative sentencing. Prisoners complain that they understood probation, restitution and community service to be alternatives to incarceration. Community supervision (for example, probation or court-ordered treatment for substance abuse) was developed as a means to divert minor or first-time offenders from prison. Financial sanctions, such as court-imposed fees, fines and restitution, were intended to reimburse the state for administrative and judicial costs, compensate the victims of crime and teach the defendant civic responsibility as an alternative to prison.

Unfortunately, the State of Iowa's attempts to extract money from prisoners may be structuring community programme failure. While assessing fees, costs and restitution orders may appear to serve as a means of paying part of the state expense for operating courts and prisons, it may be counterproductive in the long run if it contributes to increased status violations, recidivism and subsequent incarcerations.

In Iowa prisons, the prisoners were paid (top pay) a dollar a day for work. Under a new programme where 20 per cent is deducted from prisoner pay, commissary accounts and cheques received from family and friends, the total sum of funds collected from Iowa prisoners does not amount to more than $30,000 a month (Hovelson 1992). This collection of $30,000 a month works out at an average of $10 a month for 3,000 prisoners. Considering all the court, prison, community corrections and parole staff time devoted to collecting restitution payments from prisoners, we doubt the effort is worth the trouble. States may save money (the salaries paid to state employees required to collect restitution) by terminating the collection of restitution from prisoners. Research is needed to compare the cost of restitution collection and the funds received as a means of evaluating the present policy.

Even if the collection of restitution from prisoners was profitable for the state, it may not be the best use of staff resources. Why are state court and correctional professionals being employed as bill collectors? Prisoners complain that correctional counsellors are more concerned with collecting restitution than providing counselling. Considering the emphasis put on collecting restitution by prison authorities, it is not surprising that Iowa convicts refer to correctional counsellors as 'collection counsellors'. We recommend that the practice of deducting restitution and rent money from prisoner paycheques be terminated. We suggest that work-release facilities negotiate banking services with local banks for the benefit of their clients. Prisoners could deposit their own pay cheques in a saving account that would accrue interest. This would provide the prisoners with an opportunity to save money for re-entry, for housing, transportation, education and employment.

Another policy recommendation concerns restoring prisoners' civil rights. States might consider installing voting booths in all their prisons. The restoration of voting rights to felons and prisoners may have interesting repercussions for prison conditions and correctional budget demands. For example, if prisoners could vote, politicians may suddenly become interested in providing increased budgets for prison educational and vocational programmes. At the very least, restoring voting rights to prisoners would encourage state politicians to visit prisons. This may result in dramatic improvements in the food service, reductions in overcrowding and increases in general funding for maintenance and repair of facilities.

States might consider a programme that waives the first year of tuition at state-supported schools and universities for men just released from prison. The state would save money by sending men to school, including college, rather than back to prison. It now costs, depending on the state and level of security, from $15,000 to $30,000 a year to keep a woman or man in prison. The taxpayers could save millions of dollars by transferring thousands of prisoners to live in dormitories on state university campuses. At least provided with an opportunity to get a college education, we know that we would not only save money on the cost of incarceration but also we predict for these prisoners that fewer would return to prison. Instead, they would get an education, find a job and pay taxes like the rest of us.

The state could use correctional funding to build dormitories on community college and university campuses. Higher education would serve as an incentive for some prisoners to reform, relieve prison overcrowding and lower recidivism. We suggest the prisoners be released early from prison to attend college, with their first year of room and board paid for by the state. If they violate the law or flunk out of school they return to prison. Ex-convict college graduates could be employed as academic and lifestyle mentors.

We recommend that states close the 'big house' prisons and replace them with smaller facilities. Penitentiaries are outdated, a relic of the nineteenth century. Modern prisons should be small, with populations of 200 or less. One correctional counsellor suggested: 'If you had unlimited resources you could plunk one of them down here for 100 people. And I still think that it takes probably less money to do it that way than to build a gigantic prison, and probably going to be more productive in the long run.' Small facilities provide the staff with an opportunity to get to know the prisoners, their names, their needs and their ability for self-improvement.

Finally, we recommend that prison and community programme administrators have their personal employment performance review graded by how much they reduce recidivism. It is no longer good enough simply to be evaluated by how they manage their budget, prevent escapes or maintain an orderly institution. No warden should keep his job if he or she cannot deliver the goods: design and deliver programmes that reform prisoners and lower the rate of return. One trip through the machine should be enough for most people.

Discussion: beating the penal machinery

Revisiting the original 1992 study, we have checked our finding by interviewing additional prisoners in prisons and community facilities over the last 10 years. Numerous prisoners have related to us how they were victimized by the perpetual incarceration machine. They described how they were returned to prison for petty programme violations – for example, refusing to pay restitution or rent, work a minimum wage job or failure to abide by half-way house rules.

Reflecting how poor public policy and mean spirited legislation contribute to parole failure and recidivism, we have renamed community corrections 'community punishments' (Richards 1998). Prisoners may see these community programmes as simply a collection of correctional businesses operated for private profit or to provide local employment (Welch 1996: 49–50). Convicts now dread half-way houses as facilities designed to frustrate their attempt to 'go home'. In a similar fashion, they fear parole supervision as they do not expect to be able to comply with the rules and restrictions and 'walk down paper' successfully. Instead, they may elect to refuse reassignment to a half-way house, and even parole release, and wait in prison for mandatory release at the completion of their sentence. Many of these men and women no longer trust community programmes to give them a fair deal.

A related problem is that prison administrators are not being held responsible for their inability to 'do corrections'. They do not adequately assume responsibility for properly preparing prisoners for their re-entry to the community. The result is a correctional system that continues to grow at an alarming rate as it consumes a growing percentage of scarce public resources. Meanwhile, our inner cities deteriorate, school systems go without adequate funding, economic development waits and taxpayers pay the bill.

Unfortunately, the emphasis has always been on parole failure, recidivism and career criminals, with too little attention paid to the ex-convicts who 'make good'. Correctional authorities and scholars have failed to document success stories. There has been virtually no effort to interview convicts who have returned to the community to lead law-abiding lives. Recent academic publications have begun to fill this gap in our understanding (Jones and Schmid 2000; Maruna 2001; Richards and Ross 2001; Ross and Richards 2002).

Still, despite the odds, it is possible to beat the system and avoid returning to prison. The perpetual incarceration machine is a slow-moving bureaucratic force, a mechanical animal with metal teeth and claws, but easily defeated by those that are able to move beyond its reach. The secret is to learn from incarceration, to transcend the experience through personal transformation.

Conclusion: descent and ascent

Departing from our study, we have elected to close by speaking to ex-convicts about descent and ascent. From a convict perspective, beating the perpetual incarceration requires more than programme recommendations. Prisoners cannot wait for prisons to improve or community punishments to recede. Instead, they 'do their own time', avoid reimprisonment and must learn to rise above the chaos and confusion of the criminal justice machinery. A person descends when he or she goes to prison and then, if he or she can muster the intellectual or spiritual desire to remake him or herself, he or she ascends from the shadows to rejoin the world. This is also our opportunity to remind the reader that convicts are human beings, each more or less pieced together from the lessons and struggles of life. If corrections is to mean anything, the person who enters prison is somebody new and improved upon his or her release.

The co-authors of this chapter are both ex-convicts who transcended the humiliation and pain of incarceration. This required much more than re-entry to the community, finding a job, a place to live and avoiding rearrest. To transcend the prison experience a person must honestly understand who he or she is and what he or she wants to be, and do the work to accomplish the change. Returning to our hypothetical sample, even 'innocent men', after serving time in a penitentiary, have serious work to do if they ever hope successfully to regain freedom and rejoin conventional society.

In deference to the reader, it is time for us to show you the way home. Solzhenitsyn (1975: 619) writes: 'A duel with years and with walls constitutes moral work and a path upwards if you can climb it.' Amid the broken and helpless, some men grow wings. Cervantes, Victor Hugo, Alexander Dumas, Tolstoy, Dostoevsky and Solzhenitsyn were prisoners. Did they not grow wings to ascend? Dr Albert Schweitzer tells a story of being imprisoned with his wife by the French government in 1914, for the duration of the First World War. Upon arrival at the prison in the French Pyrenees, he experienced a feeling of *déjà vu*. He found the entrance foyer to the prison somehow familiar. Then he remembered a painting of the exact same entrance foyer that hangs upon the wall of his parent's Alsatian home. This was of a painting by Vincent Van Gogh, painted by the artist when he was a prisoner in the same French prison a hundred years before. Did Schweitzer learn his famous philosophy, respect for life, in prison? Did Van Gogh learn to paint vivid colours while incarcerated in a drab confinement?

Descent eventually levels off. After all, how far can a person free fall?

Eventually you hit bottom. After the first or second year of imprisonment, a convict, illusions gone, begins to understand his fall from the world. As Chekhov said: 'Soul searching – that is what's truly needed for correction' (Solzhenitsyn 1975: 628):

> And on the whole, do you know, I have become convinced that there is no punishment that comes to us in this life on earth which is undeserved. Superficially, it can have nothing to do with what we are guilty of in actual fact, but if you go over your life with a fine tooth comb and ponder it deeply, you will always be able to hunt down that transgression of your for which you have received this blow. (Solzhenitsyn 1975: 612)

Descent leads to soul searching and, for some convicts, the acknowledgement of their mistakes in life.

These transgressions, acknowledged or not, usually have little to do with the legal code. A prisoner, with years of time to think, can't help but to think of his family, children and friends. Searching his soul, he remembers the times of his own impatience or inconsideration for the needs of others. Living with so many other men, sharing their pain, witnessing their soul searching, reshapes a man. Other men learn from imprisonment to accept the modesty of non-material existence.

The unique beauty of prison is the equality of environment. Convicts live in an almost communal society where there is little social differentiation, no money other than rolls of coins and cigarette cartons, and little if any opportunity to escape each other. Prisoners dress alike, personal property is severely restricted, men share common quarters and there are no social class distinctions.

This simplicity, although enforced by the regimented environment, has its own lesson to teach: that feelings of security are a function of a person's mental state and not a collection of his or her material possessions; that a person can be happy with less. After a few years, a prisoner may learn tolerance for other men. Sharing cells or rooms together they learn to respect other men for their differences. For example, convicts are amazingly tolerant of homosexuals and, despite media stories of racial gangs, most prisoners develop close relationships with prisoners of other racial and ethnic groups. It could even be argued, although no academic has thought to research the topic, that prison is the most racially integrated environment, with convicts the most sophisticated in their acceptance of diverse racial cultures, as they have shared the horror and humiliation of captivity.

Living in this collective of degraded humanity may transform some individuals and inspire new beginnings. Provided that the time to be served has an ending (are not life sentences), a convict, if he is fortunate, may learn to appreciate his environment. Given the opportunity for reading, study and reflection, ascent may occur. Ascent is a function of a person rising, growing wings, being reshaped as a new person. The old person remains, but transformed. This transformation, or meta-morphosis, like Kafka's 'hunger artist', is the result of suffering, of soul searching and rebirth. No alcohol, drugs, sex, money or egotistical social status sets the stage for creative rebirth. Reduced to a common denominator by descent, by reduction to humility, the prisoner is reshaped again by ascent:

> And as soon as you have renounced the aim of surviving at any price, and go where the calm and simple people go then imprisonment begins to transform your former character in an astonishing way. To transform it in a direction most unexpected to you. And it would seem that in this situation feelings of malice, the disturbance of being oppressed, aimless hate, irritability, and nervousness ought to multiply. But you, yourself do not notice how, with the impalpable flow of time, slavery nurtures in you the shoots of contradictory feelings. Once upon a time you were sharply intolerant. You were constantly in a rush. And you were constantly short of time. And its months and its years, behind you and ahead of you – and a beneficial calming fluid pours through your blood vessels – patience. You are ascending. (Solzhenitsyn 1975: 610–11)

References

Allen, H.E. and Simonsen, C.E. (1995) *Corrections in America*. New York, NY: Macmillan.

American Bar Association (1977) 'The legal status of prisoners', *The American Criminal Law Review*, 14: 376–629.

Austin, J., Bruce, M. A., Carroll, L., McCall, P.L. and Richards, S.C. (2001) 'The use of incarceration in the United States. American Society of Criminology National Policy Committee. *Critical Criminology: An International Journal*, 10 (1): 1–25.

Austin, J. and Irwin, J. (2001) *It's About Time: America's Imprisonment Binge*. Belmont, CA: Wadsworth.

Austin, J., Richard, S.C. and Jones, R.S. (2003) 'Prison release in Kentucky:

convict perspective on policy recommendations', *Offender Programs Report*, 7 (1): 1, 13–16.

Burton, V., Cullen, F.T. and Travis, L. (1987) 'The collateral consequences of a felony conviction: a national study of state statutes', *Federal Probation*, 51 (4): 52–60.

Chiricos, T.G. and Bales, W.D. (1991) 'Unemployment and punishment: an empirical assessment', *Criminology*, 29 (4): 701–24.

Dale, M. (1976) 'Barriers to the rehabilitation of ex-offenders', *Crime and Delinquency*, July: 322–37.

Davidenas, J. (1983) 'The professional license: an ex-offender's illusion?', *Criminal Justice Journal*, 7 (1): 61–96.

Dickey, W.J. (1989) *From the Bottom up: Probation and Parole Supervision in Milwaukee.* Madison, WI: Continuing Education and Outreach, University of Wisconsin Law School.

English, K. and Mande, M.J. (1991) *Community Corrections in Colorado: Why do Some Clients Succeed and Others Fail?* Denver, CO: Department of Public Safety, Colorado Division of Criminal Justice.

Giddens, A. (1984) *The Constitution of Society: Outline of the Theory of Structuration.* Berkeley, CA: University of California Press.

Giddens, A. (1987) *Social Theory and Modern Sociology.* Stanford, CA: Stanford University Press.

Giddens, A. (1990) *The Consequences of Modernity.* Stanford, CA: Stanford University Press.

Giddens, A. (1991) *Modernity and Self-identity.* Stanford, CA: Stanford University Press.

Goffman, E. (1961) *Asylums.* Garden City, NY: Anchor Books.

Goffman, E. (1963) *Stigma: Notes on the Management of Spoiled Identity.* New York, NY: Simon & Schuster.

Greenberg, D.F. (1977) 'The dynamics of oscillatory punishment process.' *The Journal of Criminal law and Criminology*, 68 (4): 643–51.

Holt, N. and Miller, D. (1972) *Explorations in Inmate-family Relationships. California Department of Corrections, Research Division, Report* 46.

Hovel, J. (1992) 'Paying back victims: prisoners' restitution doubles since spring', *Des Moines Register*, June.

Hunt, J., Bowers, J. and Miller, N. (1973) *Laws, Licenses, and the Offender's Right to Work.* Washington, DC: American Bar Association, National Clearinghouse on Offender Employment Restrictions.

Iowa Department of Corrections (2001) 'Daily statistics (8/7/2001). Home page, (available at http://www.doc.state.ia.us/statistics.asp).

Irwin, J. (1970) *The Felon.* Berkeley, CA: University of California Press.

Irwin, J. (1980) *Prisons in Turmoil.* Boston, MA: Little, Brown.

Irwin, J. (1985) *The Jail.* Berkeley, CA: University of California Press.

Irwin, J., Schiraldi, V. and Ziedenberg, J. (2000) 'America's one million nonviolent prisoners', *Social Justice*, 27 (2): 135–47.

Janovick, I. (1982) 'Labor market and imprisonment', in A. Platt and P. Takagi (eds) *Punishment and Penal Discipline.* San Francisco, CA: Crime and Justice Associates, 105–12.

Johnson, R. (1990) *Deathwork: A Study of the Modern Execution Process.* Pacific Grove, CA: Brooks/Cole.

Jones, R.S. (1995) 'Uncovering the hidden social world: insider research in prison', *Journal of Contemporary Criminal Justice*, 11: 106–18.

Jones, R.S. and Schmid, T.J. (2000) *Doing Time: Prison Experience and Identity among First-time Inmates.* Stamford, CT: JAI Press.

Lenihan, K.J. (1974) *The Financial Resources of Released Prisoners.* Washington, DC: Bureau of Social Science Research.

Lenihan, K.J. (1975) 'The financial condition of released prisoners', *Crime and Delinquency*, July: 226–81.

Maruna, S. (2001) *Making Good: How Ex-convicts Reform and Rebuild their Lives.* Washington, DC: American Psychological Association.

Miller, H.S. (1972) *The Closed Door: The Effect of a Criminal Record on Employment with State and Local Public Agencies.* Georgetown, SC: Georgetown University Law Center.

Morris, N. and Tonry, M. (1990) *Between Prison and Probation.* New York, NY: Oxford University Press.

Newbold, G. (1982/5). *The Big Huey.* Auckland: Collins.

Newbold, G. (1989) *Punishment and Politics: The Maximum Security Prison in New Zealand.* Auckland: Oxford University Press.

Newbold, G. (1991) 'What works in prison management: effects of administrative change in New Zealand', *Federal Probation*, 56 (4): 53–7.

Newbold, G. (2000) *Crime in New Zealand.* Palmerston North, NZ: Dunmore.

Pownell, G.A. (1969) *Employment Problems of Released Offenders.* Report to the US Department of Labor.

Richards, S.C. (1990) 'The sociological penetration of the American gulag', *Wisconsin Sociologist*, 27 (4): 18–28.

Richards, S.C. (1995) *The Structure of Prison Release: An Extended Case Study of Prison Release, Work Release, and Parole.* New York, NY: McGraw-Hill.

Richards, S.C. (1998) 'Critical and radical perspectives on community punishment: lesson from the darkness', in J.I. Ross (ed.) *Cutting the Edge: Current Perspectives in Radical/Critical Criminology and Criminal Justice.* New York, NY: Praeger, 122–44.

Richards, S.C. and Jones, R.S. (1997) 'Perpetual incarceration machine: structural impediments to post-prison success', *Journal of Contemporary Criminal Justice*, 13 (1): 4–22.

Richards, S.C. and Ross, J.I. (2001) 'The new school of convict criminology', *Social Justice*, 28 (1): 177–90.

Richards, S.C. and Ross, J.I. (2003) 'Convict perspective on the classification of prisoners', *Criminology and Public Policy*, 2 (2): 243–52.

Richards, S.C. Terry, C.M. and Murphy, D.S. (2002) 'Lady hacks and gentlemen convicts', in L.F. Alarid and P. Cromwell (eds) *Contemporary Correctional*

Perspectives: Academic, Practitioner, and Prisoner. Los Angeles, CA: Roxbury, 207–16.

Ross, J.I., and Richards, S.C. (2002) *Behind Bars: Surviving Prison*. Indianapolis, IN: Alpha.

Ross, J.I. and Richards, S.C. (2003) *Convict Criminology*. Belmont, CA: Wadsworth.

Smith, R.R. (1984) 'Reported ex-offender employment in American adult corrections', *Journal of Offender Counseling, Services and Rehabilitation*, 5–13.

Solzhenitsyn, A. (1975) *The Gulag Archipelago. Book III-IV*. New York, NY: Harper & Row.

Stanley, D.T. (1976) *Prisoners Among Us: The Problem of Parole*. Washington, DC: The Brookings Institution.

Sykes, G.M. (1958) *The Society of Captives*. Princeton, NJ: Princeton University Press.

Terry, C.M. (1997a) The function of humor for prison inmates', *Journal of Contemporary Criminal Justice*, 13 (1): 23–40.

Terry, C.M. (1997b). *The Fellas: Overcoming Prison and Addiction*. Belmont, CA: Wadsworth.

Tropin, L.A. (1977) Testimony before the US House Judiciary Subcommittee on Crime. 27 September.

Welch, M. (1996) 'Critical criminology, social justice, and an alternative view of incarceration', *Critical Criminology: An International Journal*, 7, (2): 43–58.

Zimring, F.E. and Hawkins, G. (1991) *The Scale of Imprisonment*. Chicago, IL: University of Chicago Press.

Chapter 10

With eyes wide open: formalizing community and social control intervention in offender reintegration programmes

Faye S. Taxman, Douglas Young and James M. Byrne

Introduction

The responsibility for preparing inmates for return to the community has generally been delegated to institutional corrections. In some systems, this role is shared with parole agents, although their involvement with offenders before release is usually limited to one meeting. The general purpose of this meeting is to focus on aspects of the inmate's plans that can help the agent monitor compliance with release conditions. In practice, transitional services provided by prison or parole staff often amount to helping the inmate draft a 'paper plan' for his or her return to the community. Detailed and realistic release planning is left to the offender, who must find a place to live and a steady job, while re-establishing family and other social connections under a new, crime-free identity. The implied assumption is that offenders can comfortably make these preparations from their prison cells, build upon the lessons learnt from incarceration and readily pick up whatever positive pieces they left behind (Taxman *et al.* 2003).

The sheer volume of offenders returning to the community – nearly 600,000 a year in the USA – has spurred a renewed interest in the re-integration process. Due, in part, to the disregard shown by correctional institutions for this process, scholars and practitioners have turned to community justice models to tap another set of social controls – albeit informal ones such as family, religion, cultural and community groups – to assist transition and re-entry. Compared to reliance on conventional and formal institutions, the new models reflect a 'good society' where the community assumes a central role in supporting the returning offender (Taxman *et al.* 2003). In assimilating deterrence and restorative justice concepts, community justice models demand that the community, formal justice agencies and the offender share the responsibility of successful reintegration.

Over the last several years the community justice model has grown as a means to refocus on how 'crime and justice affect community life' and the 'actions that citizens, community organizations, and criminal justice systems can take to control crime and social order' (Karp and Clear 2000: 324). Efforts to employ different elements of the community justice model are evident in a number of pilot initiatives on prisoner re-entry mounted in recent years. Fostered by the US Department of Justice, these include re-entry partnership initiatives, re-entry courts and weed and seed-based programmes. Although partnerships among formal institutions – corrections, parole, police, service providers – were most prominently featured in plans for these initiatives, several of them recognized the central role of community in the re-entry process, and sought to build on that role.

In this chapter we describe and assess the 'Re-entry Partnership Initiative' (RPI) in light of the community justice model and examine the critical contributions of informal social controls to any organized efforts by formal social control agencies to support offender re-entry. The researchers were responsible for conducting a process evaluation of the RPI for the National Institute of Justice in 2001 that measured fidelity and soundness of the approach based on current knowledge in the field. The evaluation involved site visits, stakeholder interviews, network analysis surveys and system documentation. This evaluation provides a platform for exploring the viability and contributions of a re-entry–community justice model (further information about the evaluation can be found in a series of articles published by the authors or at www.bgr.umd.edu). First, we trace the predominant themes in corrections and sanctioning that have emerged in recent decades as a backdrop to the contrasting model of community justice. The role of community organizations and citizens as the central complement to institutional initiatives focused on re-entry is then discussed. This chapter concludes with a discussion of some of the issues underlying the use of informal social controls to accompany re-entry practices. In particular, we outline some of the historical barriers that have hampered prior efforts and are likely to impede progress unless strategic and targeted attention occurs. We also outline a research agenda to test whether this new model can achieve the ultimate goal of specific deterrence, or controlling individual offender criminal behaviour.

Corrections and community reintegration

Historically, prison and parole systems shared the responsibility for the offender's transition from prison to the community. In an era where the goal of sentencing was rehabilitation (1950s–1960s), correctional systems often provided transitional beds and half-way houses for offenders on their way back to the community. In the 1970s, transitional services took on the form of pre-release and work-release programmes and, more recently (1980s), day reporting programmes were implemented in a few jurisdictions. In these various models, the offender was 'half-back' – under correctional custody, but free to work and move about the community for part of the day; behaviour was monitored, most often during the evening hours. The offender could begin to work, earn money and make arrangements for basic shelter and clothing needs, while also seeking to obtain long-term employment and re-establish relationships with family and friends. Institutional corrections were typically responsible for placing the offender and operating the half-way facility; transition to the community was achieved by the offender with varying parole support and supervision.

These and other rehabilitation-oriented efforts were blunted when one of the first analyses of correctional practice was widely interpreted as showing that 'nothing works'. This review of 220 studies of correctional practice, including parole, half-way houses and other innovations, concluded that few programmatic efforts made a difference in terms of offender recidivism (Martinson 1974). Most noted within this work was that most programmes were not implemented as planned, undermining their ability to affect offender outcomes. In practice, offender programmes provided little in terms of treatment or services and, in the case of half-way houses, widely publicized stories about crime rings operating from a few houses tainted their image and the public's taste for transitional programming. During this same period, John Irwin (1970) completed his work, *The Felon,* which described the steps that offenders must pass through to become a member of society, and detailed the structural obstacles and internal psychological barriers that typically overwhelm such efforts. Irwin concludes that few offenders actually 'make good' because most are ill-equipped to meet the extraordinary demands of navigating the reintegration process.

The work of Martinson and Irwin contributed to growing questions about the feasibility of rehabilitation to achieve the goals of changing offenders. At the same time, retributionist philosophers were arguing that rehabilitation was an inpractible aim and it was time to adopt a more realistic goal of sanctioning – retribution. Under this model, the purpose of sentencing was 'just deserts' or an 'eye for an eye', where the slate is cleaned once the offender completed his or her term of incarceration. Even though Martinson later refuted the earlier claims that nothing works (Martinson 1979), by the 1980s just deserts and incapacitation were the accepted cornerstones of sentencing policy.

The field of corrections easily shifted to the change in political landscape. Many corrections staff were already reluctant to provide rehabilitative services because they felt that offenders were undeserving of help because they had violated the tenets of society; few correctional wardens had a favourable attitude to these services (Pogrebin 1978). The public policy shift was readily integrated in a new institutional mission that now focused on prison safety and the management of incarcerated populations to reduce disruptive behaviour. With the move towards punishment and incapacitation, resources for correctional education, vocational training and treatment steadily declined both in prison and in the community. Changes in the system for delivering substance abuse treatment services occurred during the same era (1980s), which reduced the quantity of treatment services available in the community. The scarcity of treatment services added to the attitude that offenders are somewhat different from other drug abusers, and that legally coerced offenders are less likely to do well in treatment.

These changes also brought into question the need for parole services for returning offenders. Parole was perceived as a tool of the justice system to reward good conduct that appeared to conflict with the retributionist perspective of holding offenders accountable for their actions (Burke 1996). Under the guise of 'truth in sentencing', the 1980s and 1990s witnessed massive changes in parole decision-making, with the federal system and states moving from indeterminate systems where parole release was premised on good conduct in prison to determinate sentencing and largely non-discretionary release. By 1999, mandatory parole release was the predominate form of release from prison, accounting for over 41 per cent of all releases (Hughes *et al.* 2001). In total, 15 states have abolished discretionary parole release and five other states have partially abolished it for certain types of offenders.

The move away from rehabilitation was also assimilated quickly in many parole agencies, with parole officers taking on a strong law enforcement orientation. As zero tolerance and offender accountability became the catchphrases of the day, parole policy and practice increasingly embraced warrants, arrests and sending back to prison 'technical violators' – parolees who had violated the technical conditions of release. In recent years, parole violators account for nearly 40 per cent of all prison admissions. Churners – offenders who move from prison to community and back to prison – create new challenges for reintegration (Beck and Harrison 2001; Lynch and Sabol 2001).

With years of increases in prison commitments of all kinds and, more recently, longer stays behind the walls, the prison population had risen to 1,321,137 adults by 2000 or 1 out of 90 adults. With the pace of prison construction falling behind the steady growth in sheer numbers of inmates, crowding became increasingly routine, further reinforcing the focus on prison safety and inmate management over transitional services and other programming. States scrambled to find sufficient correctional bed-space for the offender population that continued to drain available resources for transitional and other services that were deemed luxurious. As treatment and service costs were cut, classification units gained resources to better manage the flow of offenders among the facilities and achieve the twin goals of minimizing disruptive behaviour and maximizing cell and bed efficiency. Providing inmates with education, vocational training or substance abuse treatment, or mental healthcare in prison, and subsequently matching them with appropriate, available programmatic resources upon release to the community are now, at best, secondary aims in most correctional systems. The demise of correctional programming has occurred at the same time that parole and probation units are serving nearly 4.6 million offenders with the same or limited resources (Petersilia 2000).

Countering the trend away from rehabilitation and the 'nothing works' thesis is a growing body of research literature that documents the success of some corrections interventions, and identifies programme practices that are reliably associated with reduced recidivism and other favourable outcomes (Sherman et al. 1997; Simpson and Knight 1999; Taxman 1999). Some of the most consistent findings about effective programmes have focused on prison-based substance abuse treatment and continuing care models linked to community treatment. The importance of transition services and post-release aftercare in reinforcing gains made in prison has been underscored in this research (Simpson et al. 1999; Simpson and Knight 1999; Wexler et al. 1999). Findings from the Delaware Therapeutic Community [Key/Crest], Amity and TCU models with similarly strong aftercare programmes have demonstrated that the recidivism rates of those who partake in the transitional and community services are lower than inmates who attend only the prison phase of the programme (Simpson et al. 1999). Besides highlighting the value of programmes focused on reintegration, research-based literature on 'best practices' also includes many more specific lessons for the structure and content of offender re-entry programmes. We discuss these in a later section of this chapter.

Despite this empirical support for specific interventions, programme services still struggled to gain favour in the 1990s. This partly reflects the precarious nature of success in this context – even with the volumes of detailed descriptive information on effective practices and programmes (e.g. NIDA 1999; see the Center for Substance Abuse Treatment's treatment improvement protocols (TIPS)). More often than not, correctional systems fail in trying to implement and operate these programmes. Many things can and will go wrong in offender programming, including client identification and assessment, recruitment and training of staff, re-employment of correctional staff, the balance between punitive versus therapeutic sanctions, aftercare and the use of coercion in service delivery systems (Taxman 1998; Farabee et al. 1999; Taxman and Bouffard 2000). The common thread in implementation problems remains the same: concern that offenders are undeserving of rehabilitation programmes and services (Duffee and Carlson 1996) and that such services are not the core mission of the corrections or parole agency.

While hesitancy certainly exists about the potential for correctional programming based on the struggles of implementation, recent attention to the issues of desistance from criminal offending behaviours in academic research has fostered a renewed interest in service delivery models and programmatic ingredients designed to deter offender behaviour. One major advancement is the conceptualization that desistance is a process that moves someone from deviant to conforming behaviour, and that such behaviour seldom 'terminates'. Instead there is a change in both the rate and frequency of offending behaviour and this gradual change constitutes the process of desistance. In their book *Crime in the Making*, Rob Sampson and John Laub (1993) develop the theory of informal social controls to explain offending behaviour as part of a life course. Most importantly the scholars illustrated how developmental transitions such as employment, military service and marriage affect involvement in criminal behaviour, even for delinquent youth. A number of other studies during this period of time contributed to an understanding that desistance from crime is gradual and reaffirmed the importance of social bonds. Horney et al. (1995) illustrated how employment, marriage, and other bonding life circumstances impacted involvement in criminal behaviour. Similarly, Laub et al. (1998) found that 'quality marital bonds' influenced gradual declines in involvement in offending. Warr (1993) found that marriage reduces the time spent with delinquent peers and exposure to high-risk situations. The emphasis on informal social controls – the institutions in our society that wed an individual to pro-social behaviour – had some appeal to the ever-growing concern about the authority and power of social control agencies such as 'law and order' law enforcement personnel, tough-minded supervision staff and judges who are sceptical about the effectiveness of correctional treatment. The importance and value of this research contributed to a renewed interest in how to integrate the concept of informal social controls into social interventions (see Chapter 3 this volume).

Community justice: new ventures in community corrections

Popular themes of offender accountability, competency development and concern for victims were bound together in the 1990s in a new rationale for sentencing – restorative justice. Restorative justice seeks to be responsive of society's needs and concerns for public safety, while ensuring that offenders make the most of time spent serving the sentence. Under the model, offenders must be held responsible for their behaviours, including addressing harms to victims. It is also premised on the notion that the offender, by going through the sanctioning experience and returning with more skills, can be useful and productive in society. The focus on the community essentially provides the platform to begin to conceptualize the issues about informal social controls as part of a reparative model, one that works on the offender and the community. Community justice grew, in part, out of the restorative justice movement, while encompassing a broader perspective:

> Community justice broadly refers to all variants of crime pre-vention and justice activities that explicitly include the community in their processes and set the enhancement of community quality of life as a goal … Its central focus is community-level outcomes, shifting the emphasis from individual incidents to systemic patterns, from individual conscience to social mores, and from individual goods to the common good. Typically community justice is perceived as a partnership between the formal criminal justice system and the community, but communities often autonomously engage in activities that directly or indirectly address crime. (Karp and Clear 2000: 324)

Variants of the community justice model have been developed in recent years in virtually all aspects of the criminal justice system, including community policing, prosecution, defence, courts and sanctioning systems (Goldstein 1990; Rottman 1996; Stone 1996; Corbett et al. 1999;

Bazemore 2000). The dominant feature in each of these models is the engagement of the community and a respect for, and reliance on, the power of informal social controls. In the words of Karp and Clear:

> formal social control by police and the courts is a thin layer in a much thicker foundation of institutions and cultural practices that produce social order. The thin blue line is buttressed by the important work of families, schools, churches, civic organizations, and others in the creation of law-abiding citizens and safe public places. (2000: 330)

In this model, the promotion of public safety and quality of life in the community are compatible goals of equal value. And the means of achieving these goals rest on as much *or more* with the community as with formal governmental organizations and structures. This stands in contrast to the pattern of development in corrections over the past 25 years, where institutional and bureaucratic goals and actions took precedence over those of the community. The recognition that the community has a role in the correctional and reintegration process is a step forward towards reinvigorating the emphasis on returning offenders.

'Re-entry Partnership Initiative' (RPI): a community justice model for re-entering offenders

Informal social controls, community justice and continuum of care are three concepts that evolved in the last decade that have influenced the conceptualization of reintegration. Prior efforts have focused on transitional services only, or the point at which offenders return to the community. The realization was that re-entry is a process of re-integration that involves prior to and returning to the community, and after the prison sentence, and that throughout this process there are critical programmatic components that ease the transition to the next part of the process. The community and informal social controls can be integrated into the offender-processing model. The question that looms is how best to put together this process to ensure integrity in the design.

Much of the following draws from a process evaluation we conducted to assess the development and implementation of eight pilot 'Re-entry partnership initiatives' (RPIs) started under the guidance of the Office of Justice Programs (OJP) of the US Department of Justice. To be designated an RPI site, states had to agree to build a re-entry infrastructure emphasizing the collaborative involvement of corrections, probation/ parole, law enforcement, victim organizations, treatment agencies housing agencies and other community groups. While OJP provided technical assistance to the sites, they received no federal funds for either planning or operations. Each site was on its own to define, develop and implement a partnership suitable to the sociopolitical environment of the state and selected locality for the initiative. The eight jurisdictions – although unique in organizational context, staffing levels, target populations and programme design features – developed initiatives that reflect a consensus view of re-entry as a structured process that spans incarceration and community release. The eight sites selected as model re-entry partnership initiative programmes during 1999 by OJP are as follows: Baltimore, Maryland; Burlington, Vermont; Columbia, South Carolina; Kansas City, Missouri; Lake City, Florida ; Las Vegas, Nevada; Lowell, Massachusetts; and Spokane, Washington.

Figure 10.1 provides an overview of the key steps in the offender re-entry process for RPI, which falls into three distinct but intertwined phases: institutional, structured re-entry and community reintegration. The model depicted reflects components of the model developed by Altschuler and Armstrong (1994) for intensive aftercare services to high-risk juveniles returning from residential placement, except it directly integrates informal social controls into the process. Altschuler and Armstrong view aftercare as a continuing process that begins at the point of entry to the institution, prepares the youth and family for return to the community and provides seamless supervision and support during the period of transition and while under custody in the community.

Echoing some of the principles of intensive aftercare and other integrated service models, the best RPI sites have attempted to implement programmes that centre around a system of boundary-less case management, where the collective efforts of justice agencies, service providers, family and other community supports are devoted to enhancing the offender's accountability and productivity in the community. These efforts seek to strengthen the offender's stakes in becoming a contributing member of the community in such roles as parent, partner, neighbour and worker. The stakes are enhanced through the building of relationships with community members who are vested in the offender's progress as a productive citizen. The central features of these relationships are the informal social controls that can engage the offender in the process of reintegration. Through a mix of support, monitoring and sanctions, informal social controls can work in a complementary fashion with formal control efforts.

241

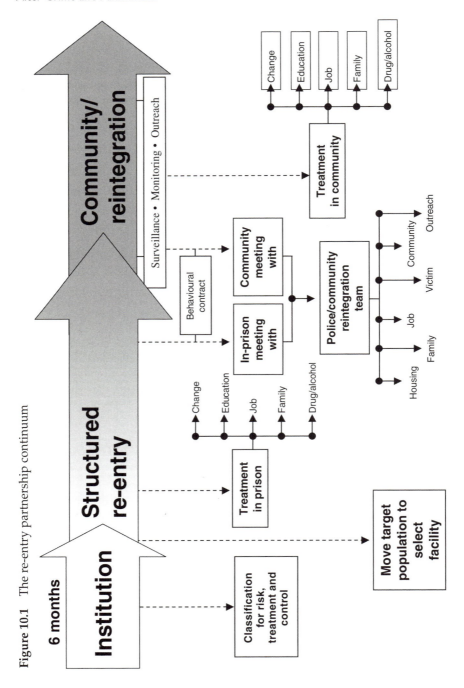

Figure 10.1 The re-entry partnership continuum

Phase I of the RPI re-entry model is the traditional *institutional phase* where the offender is assessed, classified and placed in an appropriately secure facility, and ideally receives services that address identified needs. In our view, the most advanced re-entry programme would be oriented around preparing inmates for returning to the community from the outset of their prison stay. Unfortunately, most inmate classification and placement systems are driven by short-term priorities – maintaining security and maximizing use of scarce correctional space. At the institutional phase, the challenge re-entry presents is to balance these immediate, pragmatic concerns with the long-term goals of increasing public safety and reducing recidivism. Regardless of when the corrections department can begin the process, the goal of this initial re-entry phase is to create an individual treatment plan based on a valid and systematic assessment of the offender's risk, needs and strengths. Assessments should be updated as needs are addressed (or not) during the institutional stay. Described further in the next section, a complete pre-release assessment should inform a detailed transition and re-entry service plan followed by the offender and monitored by both institutional and community representatives.

Once an individual is identified and selected to participate in the re-entry programme, the *structured re-entry phase* begins. Transcending organizational and physical boundaries, structured reentry begins in prison and carries over into the first month or so in the community. The crossing of organizational boundaries is important because it ensures that the focus is on the community phase instead of the institutional commitment. This period is characterized by increasing the intensity of preparation for release, formalizing basic elements of the reintegration plan and establishing stable connections in the community. The goal is to develop a realistic plan to minimize risk of failure upon re-entering the community. The core plan must first ensure that basic survival needs are met at release – food, shelter and a legitimate source of financial support. Meeting these basic needs has become more of an issue in recent years as changing sentencing practices have led prisoners to endure longer periods of incarceration and isolation from the community; offenders have also lost access to prison education, treatment and services (Mumola 1999; Taxman *et al.* 2002c) due to diminished resources and public perception that such services are unnecessary.

Preparing for release is greatly facilitated by moving offenders to facilities near the communities to which they will return and placing them in treatment programmes devoted to re-entry – programmes that might provide opportunities to rehearse new behaviours in realistic community settings, sensitize offenders to victims, build motivation and readiness for change and prepare the offender for this role in the community. Before release, offenders meet with community supervision agents, local service providers, police, victim advocates, family members, and other members of the community. Several RPI sites have developed innovative models that ensure involvement of community representatives in re-entry, in the form of guardians (Washington), advocates (Maryland) or reparation panels (Vermont and Missouri). Along with family members, pro-social peers, local ministers and others, these community members are the agents of informal social control that can powerfully affect the re-entry process. In initially engaging with the offender, they seek to extend a sense of welcome and the understanding that the offender will be accepted in the community as long as norms are maintained. For programmes that target unconditional releasees who leave prison with no supervision requirements, community attachment is a potentially valuable approach to link offenders to pro-social activities.

During structured re-entry, offenders sign behavioural contracts that set priorities, specify supervision requirements and service participation and detail sanctions for not complying with the contract. As soon as possible after release they meet with the same community member and others (or in some cases a reparation panel); together they reassess and update the re-entry plan, seeking stabilization during the first 30 days in the community.

Phase III of the RPI process begins in the second month after release and continues until the termination of the supervision period. In the *community reintegration* phase, the focus shifts to sustaining gains made in the initial release period, refining and maintaining the re-entry plan and achieving independence from the formal case management process. Traditionally, the responsibility for reintegration has resided with the resource-poor supervision agency – parole or probation. RPI has helped realign this responsibility, sharing it among partnering agencies and the community. Non-governmental service agencies, faith-based and neighbourhood organizations, family members and local residents shoulder more of the efforts than under more traditional correctional approaches. These representatives help define and articulate community values to the re-entering offender, and facilitate compliance with those values. At the same time, formal social control agencies – corrections, parole, probation, police – continue to attend to the offender while seeking to enroll informal social control agents to be partners in the reintegration phase.

The community reintegration phase incorporates a wide range of offender change strategies. Resources will be made available for offenders who need skills training (e.g. jobs, education), family or individual counselling, substance abuse treatment, housing and/or health care. In the best RPI programmes, planners have recognized the importance of establishing a seamless system of services for offenders that ensures continuity between institutional and community-based programming. For offenders on conditional release status, this phase of the programme involves formal surveillance and control activities on the part of supervision agents. For unconditional releases, surveillance and control responsibilities fall to community police officers, volunteer guardians, reparation panels or other neighbourhood representatives. By working hand in hand with community organizations and representatives, the partnerships provide a collective presence that offenders have not experienced before. As one corrections commissioner explained to a group of programme clients, the RPI is not about waiting for them to fail, it is about preventing failure.

Evidenced-based practices underlying the offender re-entry process

Alongside emerging principles and practices associated with community justice, the recent accumulation of knowledge about What Works in corrections has served as an effective counterpoint to prevailing dismissive beliefs about offender rehabilitation (Sherman *et al*. 1997; Taxman 1999). Like the principles of community justice, this knowledge – from studies of substance abuse treatment, contingency management, intermediate sanctions, comprehensive, system-wide interventions and theoretical research on developmental issues – can be applied directly to re-entry programme development. Figure 10.2 provides a list of empirically based principles relevant to re-entry that are derived from nearly 30 years of research on correctional (Sherman *et al*. 1997; Taxman 1999) and substance abuse and mental health treatment interventions (Simpson *et al*. 1997; NIDA 1999; Surgeon General 2000). The era of stand-alone programmes, whether in prison or in the community, is closing as studies show the need for integrated, complementary programming, provided over relatively long durations (Taxman 1998; NIDA 1999; Simpson and Knight 1999). The growing consensus is that behaviour change is possible if offenders are provided with tailored, sequential programming that addresses their individual needs.

Research has also indicated that the timing of interventions can affect their effectiveness in achieving behaviour change and reducing the

Figure 10.2   Evidence-based principles of re-entry programming

---

- *Informal social controls* (such as family, peer and community influences) have a more direct effect on offender behaviour than formal social controls (see, e.g., Byrne 1990; Gottfredson and Hirschi 1990).

- *Duration* of the intervention is critical to offender outcomes. Behaviour change is a long process that requires a minimum of 12–24 months. The period of incarceration and reintegration provides a sufficient period to bring about change.

- *Dosage* of the intervention is critical to change. Intensity and frequency are important to assist the offender in making critical decisions that affect the likelihood of success. Intervention units should be matched to offenders' risks and needs, and their readiness for change. Often, intensive interventions are more effective when they are preceded by treatment focused on building offender motivation and advancing their readiness for change (Simpson and Knight 1999; Taxman 1999). Intensive services should be followed by support services provided during stabilization and maintenance periods to reinforce treatment messages (NIDA 1999; Surgeon General 2000).

- *Comprehensive, integrated and flexible* services are critical to address the myriad needs and risk factors that affect long-term success. Offenders typically present diverse deficits and strengths, and programmes are effective when they can meet the multiple needs of individuals. Valid assessment tools should be used to prioritize needs, and services must be integrated so there are not competing demands and expectations placed on offenders.

- *Continuity* in behaviour-change interventions is critical (Taxman 1998; Simpson *et al*. 1999). Interventions, either in prison or in the community, should build upon each other. Pitfalls to avoid are incompatible clinical approaches or inconsistent messages to offenders.

- *Communication* of offender responsibility and expectations is necessary. A behavioural contract that articulates the structured re-entry and community reintegration process is an effective tool for conveying these expectations and consequences for non-compliance (Silverman 1996; Taxman *et al*. 1999).

- *Support* mechanisms are critical to long-term success. Support mechanisms can involve the family, community and informal agencies (e.g. religious organizations, Alcoholics Anonymous, spouse support groups, etc.). The support mechanism links the offender and the community and provides the ultimate attachments (NIDA 1999).

> • Offender *accountability* and responsibility are key. A system of sanctions and incentives must ensure that the offender understands expectations and rules, and the offender should take part in the process of developing these accountability standards. The offender must be held accountable for actions taken both in prison and the community; the partnership should support constructive, pro-social decisions.

likelihood of recidivism (Taxman 1999). Programme interventions that are part of the structured re-entry process should complement positive psychosocial changes that the offender undergoes in making the transition to the community, while addressing the profound changes and challenges faced by newly released offenders. Focus groups held with programme participants in several of the RPI sites revealed that they confront four common themes:

1 The offender's role in society (e.g. stigma).

2 The offender's acknowledgement of the harm he or she has done to family and community.

3 The offender's doubts about becoming a self-sufficient, self-supporting and contributing member of society.

4 The offender's uncertainties about acknowledging the need for help, and utilizing support and community services to address physical, social and psychological needs central to successful reintegration (Taxman *et al*. 2003c).

In our experience, offenders readily articulate these issues (Taxman *et al*. 2003c), particularly the concerns about structural barriers that impede their ability to navigate through their life. It is evident that the best intentions of partnering agencies will be undermined if their re-entry programmes do not bridge the gap between these agencies' perceptions and beliefs about what is best for the offender, and the knowledge, experience, beliefs and feelings of the offender. In some RPI sites, for example, programme designers assumed offenders would be willing to participate in free community-based services on demand. They were surprised when almost no one took them up on the offer. As a result, the programme planners had to establish interventions during institutional and structured pre-release phases that focused on building offender motivation and readiness for change, to provide a foundation for the reintegration phase. In some cases, programme developers also had to empathize with their potential clients and recognize that offenders' past experience with law enforcement, supervision agencies and treatment providers left them dubious about the real intentions of these agencies and staff. To give the RPI partnerships any chance at success, re-entry programme staff will have to convince clients that the intent is to support their reintegration in the community; efforts to find fault, increase revocations or speed a return to the justice system will only undermine the re-entry goals.

Implementing the model: challenges of moving from theory to practice

In contrast to the wealth of information from recent correctional research that is applicable to re-entry initiatives, virtually none of this literature has considered a community justice perspective, beyond axioms about the relative power of informal social controls (over formal controls) on offender behaviour. In this section on re-entry implementation issues, we draw broadly from literature in areas that have track records in community justice (policing and to a lesser extent prosecution and courts) and, more specifically, from the initial experience of the RPI sites. The RPI record underscored the challenges of building new models that mixed bureaucracies and communities, formal and informal agents of control (see the collection of articles by Byrne *et al.* 2002; Taxman *et al.* 2002a, 2002b; Young *et al.* 2002). It is evident that those planning and operating re-entry programmes must do so with eyes wide open, anticipating issues, carefully monitoring the fits and starts that characterize complex, innovative initiatives, and building the capital needed to support the venture through difficult periods. Here we discuss some questions and concerns that require the attention of re-entry planners. As discussed earlier, implementation issues have contributed to the swinging pendulum in corrections. While the RPI model offers new promises, it is with some caution that jurisdictions should proceed to prevent repeating history and, more importantly, to consider the infrastructure needed to sustain a reintegration process that emphasizes informal social controls as the main element of reintegration.

Who is the community?

There sometimes seems to be as many answers to this question as there are agencies that align themselves with community justice. As in other parts of the justice system, the re-entry programme's definition of community is critical because it determines who is invited to the table – who from outside the usual circle of formal control agencies will join the partnership that comprises the re-entry initiative. Community identity is also important in this context because it determines the values and norms of the area to which the offender is returning, which can impact the goals of reintegration. In pragmatic terms, norms translate into rules about acceptable behaviour (e.g. moral issues such as cohabitation, religious issues such as attendance at services, etc.), monitoring practices and decisions about the use of sanctions and rewards. In involving the community, formal agents of control must fully explore these issues, identify differences with their own policies and practices, and seek common ground and consensus.

These and related issues reflect particular attention because of the fragile economic conditions endemic to many offenders' neighbourhoods. Many offenders are returning to communities that lack social capital. These communities are often described as suffering from public neglect, crumbling physical infrastructures and inadequate human and social resources. These conditions beg the question about the readiness of the community to be an active participant in the reintegration of the offender. Re-entry planners and practitioners must have answers to this question – they must go beyond the broad picture and invest the time and effort needed to identify and engage community elements that have the resources to be full partners in the re-entry process. To be effective, community representatives must have the strength and capacity to identify controls, carry out monitoring and sanctioning roles, advocate for the offender in the acquisition of resources and provide instrumental support when needed.

Definitions of community also include the local sociopolitical environment and its affect on re-entry policy and practice. This usually involves creating some role for local stakeholders – elected representatives, leaders of civic or business associations, religious leaders, school administrators – in re-entry initiatives. Several RPIs found the process of engaging many stakeholders (particularly politicians and business leaders) followed a predictable course. Initially they would express resistance to the idea of a re-entry programme, reacting negatively to any notion of offenders residing in their community. When they were informed that this had *always* happened – that these were mothers, husbands and sons of locals residents who inevitably must return to homes in the community – they nearly always saw the logic of efforts to support and speed their reintegration, and became valued advocates for the programme.

But community is much more than local designated leaders or abstract notions of norms and values. Perhaps the most powerful agents of informal social control, and those most critical to the course of offender re-entry, are family and friends. This view is part and parcel of our working definition of community (Young *et al.* 2002). In the context of re-entry, we believe that community is best viewed as *people who, by virtue of their natural (extra-legal) relationship with the offender, have the greatest potential impact on the offender's behaviour, or are most affected by that behaviour.* In this view, community is relative and specific to the individual offender. The definition implies that critical features of the community are the geographical area in which the offender resides and those who live and work in that area have a stake in the offender's impacts on them and the area. The definition is intentionally functional; it implies that re-entry programme developers should aim to engage the best exemplars of community – those most affected by and most influential in – that individual's re-entry (Young *et al.* 2002: 8). The inclusion of the family as a member of the community raises a series of issues regarding the health and well-being of that unit, and how to engage the family into the community. The family is an untapped resource although, in other efforts to include the family, the family dynamics are unknown. Much work is needed in this arena to consider the related issues.

Who do community representatives represent?

This is another question that strikes at the core of the community justice model. All eight RPI sites created roles for private community agencies, most often as service providers to clients after release. Four of the eight RPI sites included community representatives in a major operational role and, in two of these, the representatives were paid staff of community agencies that, in most cases, had contracts with the criminal justice agency that led the initiative. The community organizations involved in the sites were all private, non-profit groups and varied considerably, from mental health and substance-abuse treatment providers to church-based groups and housing coalitions. In only two sites, however, was the community represented by uncompensated citizens – specifically, residents recruited from the neighbourhoods to which RPI clients were returning.

The sites' reliance on paid staff of contracted agencies calls into question the independence of these staff, and the extent to which their community role is compromised by financial ties to their employer, and that organization's ties to the sponsoring public agencies. The involvement of these staff, on the other hand, has important benefits. While contractual relationships affect the integrity of the community justice model, they also represent the re-entry programme's use of professionals who bring specialized knowledge and experience to their role. Contractual support is part of the reality of ensuring that the community is involved in offender assessment, monitoring and service provision on a daily basis. It is also the mechanism to ensure that the community staff are qualified to provide the offender with professional assistance since many of the offenders are in need of professional services, not merely a support system. Effective re-entry programmes are premised on the community, or its representative, to be an active participant, and it is unreasonable to assume that such a role can be accomplished on a volunteer basis. Even more importantly, it is unreasonable to expect that professional services can be delivered by volunteers on the basis of a 'kindness of the heart' model. And, to prevent the history of corrections from repeating itself, the trend towards volunteer staff, particularly staff without professional qualifications, undermines the initiative to improve overall services.

Programme planners, none the less, should attend to the integrity of these initiatives and create roles for community partners who can maintain their independence from the influence of governmental agencies. A potential solution – but one underused in the first generation of RPI plans – is to engage offenders' family members in these key community roles. A functional family can provide the support mechanisms that an offender needs, particularly in the areas of housing and emotional support. The family is seldom brought into the mix in a formal process for addressing re-entry issues; instead, the tendency is to assume that the family can reunite without the support of others. In the past such efforts have not been facilitated by the process with the offender assuming more of a role in reintegration. The RPI model positions the family to assume more of the responsibility for addressing adjustments with the offender and providing a stability in the re-entry process. Alternatively, and certainly an item for the future, is the need for re-entry to focus on the family as the unit of service. By extending the family as a unit of service, the re-entry efforts will focus on improving the overall social capital of an area. The benefits will be multiplied by not only one – the offender – but by the members of the family and potentially the extended family. Such a community approach may fit well within a wellness model underlying the community justice model (Young et al. 2002).

Is the offender a member of the partnership?

Programmes can create different roles for the offender in re-entry, including as a member of the re-entry case management team. The role of the offender in the RPI is open to interpretation, and it is often affected by the community's values about offenders. While formal justice agencies (and particularly parole officers) often dictate this role, the partnership can redefine the role. The tenets of behavioural management techniques purport that offenders, like clients in other services, tend to play a more proactive role in programmes with a strong community presence. Well organized communities may assume a more inclusive humanistic perspective, accepting the offender as both partner and benefactor, whereas less developed and organized communities may view the offender as a passive recipient of their re-entry efforts. Stated simply, community norms can designate the returning offender as a contributing member, another resident, a visitor or an outcast. Successful partnership initiatives will transform the perception of the offender as an outcast to a contributing member.

Writings on the community justice model actually give little attention to the offender and his or her role in activities flowing from the model. The restorative justice model, however, emphasizes assisting the offender to become a more competent citizen and providing him or her mechanisms to repair harms committed in the community. Behavioural management models are similarly focused on offenders assuming responsibility for directing their destiny. Effective re-entry programmes seek to empower the offender to change behaviour. While some of the RPI sites self-described themselves as such, most did not create active roles for their clients in developing, monitoring and modifying transition and release plans. Only two jurisdictions included the offender as an active participant in formulating and committing to a re-entry behavioural contract.

The community can, as always, play an even more influential role in providing a sense of empowerment and, more fundamentally, a feeling of acceptance as a peer and fellow citizen. Focus groups conducted with offenders in five RPI sites confirm that offenders are sensitive to the challenges of starting anew, free of stigma and prophecies of failure. Offenders' greatest concern seemed to be a sense of belonging. Emotional barriers of re-entry – uncertainty, apprehension, fear – need to be acknowledged and addressed by re-entry programme partners, particularly community members. Recent federal and state laws have only made this a more difficult sell. At the federal level, a growing number of restrictions preclude the offender from obtaining student loans, residing in public housing, employment in certain professions and civic participation (e.g. voting). Some states' practices of broadcasting names, addresses and faces of offenders over the Internet give similar messages. In the end, these adversely affect the ability to locate suitable housing, rejoin family members in their choice of residence and earn a living; perversely, these practices probably reduce public safety. Re-entry initiatives must obviate some of the structures that constrain offenders as they try to 'make good' (Taxman *et al.* 2002a). Community representatives can most effectively alleviate related anxieties. But the question the remains whether the community can alleviate these societal barriers in a sufficiently meaningful way.

Are service provisions suitable for offenders?

Despite the best efforts of re-entry partners representing both formal and informal sources of social control, offenders may fail in re-entry because they do not get the services they need. More than 60 per cent of the offender population in prison does not have a GED or high-school diploma (Bernstein and Houston 2000). Many offenders are pigeon holed into low-wage markets, where they are increasingly threatened by competition from workers with college degrees. Substance abuse prevails in the offender population, with nearly 35 per cent of all offenders reported to be in need of treatment services and many more reporting frequent use of illicit substances (Taylor *et al.* 2001). Nearly one in five offenders in prison have some need for mental health services (many of whom are medicated in prison but have trouble obtaining services upon release) (Beck and Maruschak 2001).

Together, this paints a picture of enormous need for both prison and community-based services that must be addressed to ensure public safety. On paper, most re-entry programmes effectively identify these needs and describe continuum-of-care models – from prison to community – that form the core of their service provision. However, with restrictions on the number of available in-prison treatment programmes (whether it be for substance abuse, mental health, vocational training or educational services), the ability to create that service continuum is limited. The inherent difficulties of making connections between in-prison and community-based programming add to the challenge. Recent studies validate the importance of the continuum of care (Taxman 1998; Simpson *et al.* 1999), and yet other discussions highlight the difficulties that systems have in providing for contiguous treatment experiences (Farabee *et al.* 1999; Taxman and Bouffard 2000). Re-entry sites must conduct service inventories and analyses to assess the availability and effectiveness of linkages that meet the identified needs of offenders both pre- and post-release.

Conclusion: a postmodern model of re-entry?

Until recently, involvement of formal criminal justice agencies in offender re-entry took one of three forms: non-existent, nominal or, at best, bureaucratic. The intellectual, academic grounding of these policies and practices was provided by the 'nothing works' empirical literature and arguments for the punitive, just-deserts philosophy of sanctioning. In turn, these fuelled the intuitive inclinations of many corrections staff and administrators, who felt that offenders were undeserving of efforts aimed at the goal of rehabilitation. This was coupled with the dubious concerns about the feasibility of the treatment programmes. Recent federal and state laws severely restricting the civil rights of offenders speak to the lasting, cumulative power of these approaches.

The RPI model in many ways responds to the likely failures of existing offender transition and reintegration programmatic efforts and represents a notable departure from this past quarter century of policies. The emphasis on an offender-processing model embraces community justice tenets where the community and justice agencies are partners in the process. The eight sites of the RPI project went a step further to develop consensus and collaboration from multiple public agencies, along with the community, on key programme practices – assessment, treatment, case management, supervision and sanctions/rewards. The model moves from compartmentalized services to novel efforts to communicate and share responsibilities in oversight, operations and service provision. The boundary-less notion is to cut across organizational lines to create a service delivery system based on the client, not the agency. The newest development is that multi-agency teams have pioneered techniques that are feasible. Assessment, services and compliance can occur through these teams that even involved representatives of the community. This advancement is notable and one that was unforeseen at least two decades ago.

Added to the mix is the involvement of the community and informal agents of social control, and to a large extent the change in philosophy that offender reintegration is not merely an exercise of justice agencies but a true partnership with the community to change the balance of controls from formal to informal. This dramatic shift extends the partnerships beyond intergovernmental memorandum of understandings (MOUs) to encompass community members with few (or no) formal ties to institutions. This formation represents the postmodern hybrid of the model re-entry partnership. It also brings into the picture the natural systems that provide social and psychological supports reinforcing pro-social behaviour. The willingness of RPI sites and other jurisdictions to undertake this shift in approach underscores their frustration with the results from conventional re-entry models where the justice system dominates. Moving beyond the boundaries of the justice system is inherently a risky adventure. The justice agencies will have to relinquish control besides acknowledging the limits of formal social controls. A number of issues related to 'supervision' or the maintenance of rules (e.g. avoiding criminal behaviour, possession of illicit substances, possession of alcohol, curfews, etc.) have yet to be negotiated. And of even greater concern is the potential processes when the community 'gives up' or determines that an offender is undeserving. The model presumes that offenders will conform based on the support from the community (Sampson and Laub 1993) – this has yet to be tested, and it is based on life-course research that presumes bonding during the developmental years. Irwin's insights nearly 35 years ago suggest that even the community justice model may not be appropriate for all offenders; it provides a rude awakening about the difficulty of long-term behaviour change. As noted by Maruna (2001) in his recent book, the issue is that offenders may not go straight, they may merely go crooked as part of the reforming process. His work also highlights that incorporating a 'new person' image is an important component of reintegration but the question remains as to how a person progresses towards this image, and how informal social controls contribute to this progression. Experiences of offenders with foster care and juvenile detention facilities may predispose the offender not to welcome the arms of the community, and perhaps even to find these arms even more anxiety producing which creates more psychological distress for the offender. More research is needed to address many unanswered questions.

The new model presents a research agenda that underscores an examination of the individual–community interaction and its impact on individual criminal behaviour. From a structural perspective, one overriding issue is the role of the community and how that role materializes. The differences between a 'natural' system (e.g. faith, community groups, etc.) and a contractual service is yet to be determined, both in terms of the ability of the community group to achieve desired goals (e.g. reduced crime, community safety, attachment to community, etc.), to maintain an ongoing relationship with the offender regardless of other efforts (e.g. with or without funding, change in personnel/volunteers, etc.) and to assist the offender with stabilization efforts. From a community justice perspective, the system goals of improving the social capital in the community, improving the service delivery system and affecting the next generation of services are all research issues that have yet to be explored. From the individual perspective, the impact of informal social controls that are not 'naturally' provided (e.g. family, religious groups, etc.) on offender behaviours is an area where further research is needed. The available research on informal social controls shows great promise for the future but it is uncertain whether the nature of the informal social control personally affects differential outcomes (Laub and Sampson 2001). Even more intriguing is the question of whether the linkage between the formal and informal social controls can, overall, affect the rate of offenders who 'make good'.

New models open up new opportunities to explore how justice and community agencies can work together in the process of reintegration. Part of the exploration is to understand the concept of reintegration, or integration, where the offender assumes a pro-social role in the community. As more partnerships evolve, so will the ability for research opportunities flourish in the area of understanding the models of desistence, and how different formal and informal social control variables contribute to these individual trajectories. It is in these individual trajectories that the promise of successful re-entry and transition can materialize.

It is appropriate to return to re-examine the lessons learnt from the past 50 years in the field of corrections, particularly those that evolved from the work of Martinson. Shifting the focus to the community and to informal controls, while it appears to be appropriate, also opens up old wounds about the ability of people to change and the tolerance of the community for incremental change in behaviour. Much of the debate about treatment for offenders in the last 25 years has centred around the issue of whether offenders deserve such services. Maruna's (2001) recent study reinforces the earlier observations of Irwin (1970) that document the difficult steps that often result in do-loops or the recovery–relapse–recovery process that people go through as they change. While the community and natural systems may intellectually understand these processes, the question remains as to whether the support systems will persevere for the offenders who 'make good' and those who do not. History has shown that the implementation issues tend to muddy the waters, are difficult to overcome, stress the partnerships and programmes and, ultimately, dilute support. With the community and natural systems involved, the stakes are high – both in maintaining the interest in offender reintegration and in the individual offender(s) who pursue pathways towards desistance.

Acknowledgements

The original study was sponsored by the National Institute of Justice under grant 2000IJCX0045. All opinions are those of the authors and do not reflect the opinion of the sponsoring agency. The authors would like to acknowledge the contributions and efforts of each of the eight Reentry Partnership Initiatives (RPI) who provided a fruitful learning environment. We would also like to thank Ms. Julie Marshall for her assistance in preparing this document.

References

Altschuler, D.M. and Armstrong, T.L. (1994) *Intensive Aftercare for High-risk Juveniles: Policies and Procedures*. Washington, DC: Office of Juvenile Justice and Delinquency Prevention.

Bazemore, G. (2000) 'Community justice and a vision of collective efficacy: the case of restorative conferencing', *Policies, Processes, and Decisions of the Criminal Justice System, Criminal Justice,* 3: 225–97.

Beck, A.J. and Harrison, P.M. (2001) *Prisoners in 2000. Bureau of Justice Statistics Bulletin* NCJ 188207. Washington, DC: US Department of Justice.

Beck, A.J. and Maruschak, L.M. (2001) *Mental Heath Treatment in State Prisons, 2000. Bureau of Justice Statistics Bulletin* NCJ 188215. Washington, DC: US Department of Justice.

Bernstein, J. and Houston, E. (2000) *Crime and Work: What we can Learn from the Low-wage Labor Market*. Washington, DC: Economic Policy Institute.

Burke, P. (1995) *Abolishing Parole: Why the Emperor has no Clothes*. Washington, DC: National Institute of Correction.

Byrne, J. (1990) 'Reintegration community into community corrections', *Crime and Delinquency*, 35: 471–99.

Byrne, J.M., Taxman, F.S. and Young, D. (2003) *Emerging Roles and Responsibilities in the Reentry Partnership Initiative: New Ways of Doing Business*. Report submitted to NIJ. College Park, MD: University of Maryland.

Clear, T., Rose, D. and Ryder, J. (2001) 'Incarceration and the community: the problem of removing and returning offenders', *Crime and Delinquency*, 47 (3): 335–51.

Corbett, R., Beto, R., Coen, B., DiIulio, J., Faulkner, R., Fitzgerald, B., Gregg, I., Hinzman, G., Malvestuto, R., Paparozzi, M., Perry, J., Pozzi, R. and Rhine, E.

(1999) *Broken Windows' Probation: Then Next Step in Fighting Crime. Civic Report 7.* New York, NY: Manhattan Institute.

Duffee, D.E. and Carlson, B.E. (1996) 'Competing value premises for the provision of drug treatment to probationers', *Crime and Delinquency*, 42 (4): 574–92.

Farabee, D., Prendergast, M., Cartier, J., Wexler, H., Knight, K. and Anglin, M.D. (1999) 'Barriers to implementing effective correctional drug treatment programs', *Prison Journal*, 79 (2): 150–63.

Goldstein, H. (1990) *Problem-oriented Policing.* New York, NY: McGraw-Hill.

Gottfredson, M.R. and Hirschi, T. (1990) *A General Theory of Crime.* Stanford, CA: Stanford University Press.

Horney, J.D., Osgood, W. and Marshall, I.D. (1995) 'Criminal careers in the short-term: intra-individual variability in crime and its relations to local life circumstance', *American Sociological Review*, 60: 655–73.

Hughes, T.A., Wilson, D.J. and Beck, A.J. (2001) *Trends in State Parole, 1990–2000. Bureau of Justice Statistics Bulletin* NCJ 184735. Washington, DC: US Department of Justice.

Irwin, J. (1970) *The Felon.* Englewood Cliffs, NJ: Prentice Hall.

Karp, D. and Clear, T. (2000) 'Community justice: a conceptual framework', *Policies, Processes and Decisions of the Criminal Justice System, Criminal Justice*, 3: 323–68.

Laub, J.H., D.S. Nagin and Sampson, R.J. (1998) 'Trajectories of change in criminal offending: good marriages and the desistance process', *American Sociological Review*, 63: 225–38.

Laub, J.H and Sampson, R.J. (2001) 'Understanding desistance from crime', in M. Tonry (ed.) *Crime and Justice: A Review of Research. Volume 28.* Chicago, IL: University of Chicago Press, 1–71.

Lynch, J.P. and Sabol, W.J. (2001) *Prisoner Reentry in Perspective. Crime Policy Report. Vol. 3.* Washington, DC: The Urban Institute.

Martinson, R. (1974) 'What works? Questions and answers about prison reform', *The Public Interest*, 35: 22–54.

Martinson, R. (1979) 'New findings, new views: a note of caution regarding sentencing reform', *Hofstra Law Review*, 7: 243–58.

Maruna, S. (2001) *Making Good: How Ex-offenders Reform and Reclaim their Lives.* Washington, DC: American Psychological Association Books.

Mumola, C.J. (1999) *Substance Abuse and Treatment, State and Federal Prisoners, 1997. Bureau of Justice Statistics Special Report* NCJ 172871. Washington, DC: US Department of Justice.

National Institute of Drug Abuse (NIDA) (1999) *Principles of Drug Addiction Treatment.* Rockville, MD: National Institute of Health.

Petersilia, J. (2000) 'When prisoners return to the community: political, economic and social consequences', *Sentencing and Corrections*, 9: 1–7.

Pogrebin, M. (1978) 'Role conflict among correctional officers in treatment oriented correctional institutions', *International Journal of Offender Therapy and Comparative Criminology*, 22 (2): 149–55.

Rottman, D.B. (1996) 'Community courts: prospects and limits', *National Institute of Justice Quarterly*, 231: 46–51.

Sampson, R. and Laub, J. (1993) *Crime in the Making: Pathways and Turning Points through Life*. Cambridge, MA: Harvard University Press.

Sherman, L., Gottfredson, D., MacKenzie, D., Eck, J., Reuter, P. and Bushway, S. (1997) *Preventing Crime: What Works, What Doesn't, What's Promising*. Washington, DC: US Department of Justice.

Silverman, K., Higgins, S.T., Brooner, R.K., Montoya, I.D. Cone, E.J., Schuster, C.R. and Preston, K.L. (1996) 'Sustained cocaine abstinence in methadone maintenance patients through voucher-based reinforcement therapy', *Archives of General Psychiatry*, 53: 409–15.

Simpson, D.D. and Knight, K. (1999) *TCU Model of Treatment Process and Outcomes in Correctional Settings*. Washington, DC: National Institute of Justice, US Department of Justice.

Simpson, D.D., Joe, G.W., Broome, K.M., Hiller, M.L., Knight, K. and Rowan-Szal, G.A. (1997) 'Program diversity and treatment retention rates in the drug abuse treatment outcome study (DATOS)', *Psychology of Addictive Behaviors*, 11 (4): 279–93.

Simpson. D.D., Wexler, H.K. and Inciardi, J.A. (1999) 'Introduction', *The Prison Journal*, 79 (4): 381–83.

Stone, C. (1996) 'Community defense and the challenge of community justice', *National Institute of Justice Journal*, 231: 41–5.

Surgeon General (2000) *Mental Health: A Report of the Surgeon General*. Washington, DC: US Government Printing Office.

Taxman, F.S. (1998) *Reducing Recidivism through a Seamless System of Care: Components of Effective Treatment, Supervision and Transition Services in the Community* NCJRS 171836. Washington, DC: Office of National Drug Control Policy, Treatment and Criminal Justice System Conference.

Taxman, F.S. (1999) 'Unraveling "What Works" for offenders in substance abuse treatment services', *National Drug Court Institute Review*, II (2): 93–134.

Taxman, F.S. and Bouffard, J. (2000) 'The importance of systems in improving offender outcomes: critical elements of treatment integrity', *Justice Research and Policy*, 2 (2): 37–58.

Taxman, F.S., Byrne, J.M. and Young, D. (2003c) *Targeting for Reentry: Matching Needs and Services to Maximize Public Safety*. Washington, DC: National Institute of Justice.

Taxman, F.S., Soule, D. and Gelb, A. (1999) 'Graduated sanctions: stepping into accountable systems and offenders', *Prison Journal*, 79: 182–204.

Taxman, F.S., Young, D. and Byrne, J.M. (2003a) *Offender's Views of Reentry: Implications for Processes, Programs and Services*. Washington, DC: National Institute of Justice.

259

Taxman, F.S., Young, D., Byrne, J.M., Holsinger, A. and Anspach, D. (2003b) *From Prison to Pubic Safety: Innovations in Offender Reentry*. Washington, DC: National Institute of Justice.

Taylor, B., Fitzgerald, N., Hunt, D., Reardon, W. and Brownstein, H. (2001) *ADAM Preliminary 2000 Findings on Drug Use and Drug Market: Adult Male Arrestees*. Washington, DC: National Institute of Justice.

Warr, M. (1993) 'Age, peers and delinquency', *Criminology*, 31: 17–40.

Wexler, H.K., DeLeon, G., Thomas, G., Kressel, D. and Peters, J. (1999) 'The Amity Prison TC evaluation: reincarceration outcomes', *Criminal Justice and Behavior*, 261 (2): 147–67.

Young, D., Taxman F.S. and Byrne, J.M. (2003) *Engaging the Community in Offender Reentry. Report submitted to NIJ*. College Park, MD: University of Maryland.

Chapter 11

'Less than the average citizen': stigma, role transition and the civic reintegration of convicted felons

Christopher Uggen, Jeff Manza and Angela Behrens

Previous research in life-course criminology has shown how desistance from crime is linked to the successful transition to adult roles (Sampson and Laub 1993; Uggen 2000). In particular, offenders who establish a stable work history and a strong marriage appear to have better post-release adjustment than those who have yet to enter such work and family roles. More generally, the transition to adulthood is characterized by the assumption of age-graded roles and the attainment of specific behavioural markers. Completing formal education, obtaining a full-time job, marrying and voting are all markers signalling adult status, although their sequence and timing may vary over time and space (Shanahan 2000). Specifying the social-psychological process under-lying role transition among offenders has therefore emerged as a critical question for theory and empirical research on the desistance process (Shover 1996; Maruna 2001).

In this chapter we unite and extend these lines of research in two ways. First, in addition to work and family, we suggest that *civic reintegration* represents a third important reintegrative domain, one not examined by previous researchers. Following Maruna's contention that desistance is only possible when ex-offenders 'develop a coherent prosocial identity for themselves' (2001: 7), we specify the varieties of civic participation that contribute to such an identity and their subjective meaning to ex-felons. Secondly, building on the work of Matsueda and Heimer (1997), we show how a symbolic interactionist theory of role transition across socioeconomic, familial and civic domains is especially useful in explaining identity shifts over the life course. Although we do not attempt a rigorous empirical test of this theory in this chapter, we will elucidate the model using illustrative evidence taken from intensive interviews with a small sample of convicted felons. Based on these interview data and our conceptual model, we suggest that self-concept as a deviant or conforming citizen is the principal mechanism linking adult role transition and desistance.

A life-course model of role transition and desistance from crime

Symbolic interactionist theories of crime hold that a person's self-concept as deviant or law-abiding is developed through processes of role-taking and social interaction (Cohen 1965; Thornberry 1987; Matsueda 1992; Matsueda and Heimer 1997). For example, released offenders who are embedded in networks of criminal activity are likely to take the role of felon when considering illicit activity (Matsueda and Heimer 1997). When repeated over time this process increases the salience of a deviant identity and strengthens role commitment and social relationships with others in the network (see, e.g. Stryker and Burke 2000). As persons identify and commit to such roles, they become subject to informal social controls (Heimer and Matsueda 1994). To explain changes in offending with age, symbolic interactionists look to the different deviant and conforming roles that individuals are likely to take at each life-course stage – the 'socially recognized and meaningful categories of persons' it is possible to be at a particular age (Cohen 1965: 12). The choice of roles in a given situation is the product of the relative salience of deviant or law-abiding identities, which, in turn, are functions of social relationships and role commitments.

Symbolic interactionists emphasize adult work and family roles in explaining desistance and the transition away from crime (Matsueda and Heimer 1997). They call particular attention to the changing identities that accompany these new roles, and the stabilization of new identities through role commitments (Schwartz and Stryker 1970; Matsueda and Heimer 1997). In most cases, commitment to work roles (as co-worker, supervisor or employee) and family roles (as spouse or parent) reduces the likelihood of criminal behaviour, although precocious or 'off-time' events (Hagestad and Neugarten 1985) such as teenage pregnancy may solidify already marginalized identities and foster criminal behaviour.

Adding civic reintegration to a conceptual model of role transition

Much of the empirical research literature has similarly focused on work

(Sampson and Laub 1990; Uggen 2000) or family (Laub *et al.* 1998) roles. Civic participation and reintegration into community life, however, have received comparatively little attention, although the desire to 'be productive and give something back to society' appears to be critical to the desistance process (Maruna 2001: 88). Moreover, criminal offenders, and crime itself for that matter, are explicitly defined in relation to the state and its citizens. We suggest that civic reintegration and the citizen role, as well as work and family roles, may prove central to successful reintegration. In fact, we will argue that work and family roles may also be subsumed under a general 'law-abiding adult citizen' identity construct.

As we point out elsewhere (Uggen *et al.* 2000), criminal offenders are less distinguished by class or by social status than by their legal relationship with the state and their separation from their fellow citizens. The concept of citizenship is particularly relevant here. The diverse models of citizenship that have been developed in recent years have, broadly speaking, distinguished two central components (Shafir 1998; Manza 2001): citizenship as a set of entitlements that citizens acquire by virtue of membership in the polity (e.g. Marshall 1950); and citizenship as practice, something which is achieved through virtuous action or participation in the community in one way or another, as communitarians have argued (e.g. Oldfield 1990). In his famous mid-century writings on citizenship and social class, T.H. Marshall argued that 'citizenship is a status bestowed on those who are full members of a community. All who possess the status are equal with respect to the rights and duties to which the status is endowed' (1950: 28). Yet a felony conviction often strips the offender of the most basic rights of citizenship, including the right to vote, the right to hold elective office and the right to serve on juries. Moreover, the enduring stigma of a felony conviction imposes restrictions on parental rights, work opportunities, housing choices and myriad other social relationships, isolating ex-felons from their communities and fellow citizens. In short, both the *rights* and *capacities* of ex-offenders to attain full citizenship are threatened.

A model of role transition and reintegration

Adding civic reintegration to life-course models yields a new picture of how roles and identities interact with work, family and community to shape the prospects for desistance. Our provisional model of identity transformation across these domains is shown in Figure 11.1. Prior to formal sanctioning, many criminal offenders occupy marginal social

Figure 11.1 Roles and identity transformation of convicted felons across socioeconomic, familial and civic domains

	PRE-PUNISHMENT		PUNISHMENT		POST-PUNISHMENT	
Domain	Life-course markers	Common roles and resources	Trying on idealized adult roles	Barriers and marginalization	Role commitment	Identity salience and role choice
Socio economic	school completion, full-time employment	idle, unemployed, under-employed, 'stuck'	**Productive citizen:** getting a 'good' job going to work every day	occupational restrictions		
Familial	family formation	absent or dependent, a 'drain'	**Responsible citizen:** family man or woman, good parent, partner, son or daughter	loss of parental rights, extended absence from family		
Civic	voting, neighbouring, home ownership	inactive, negative, disfranchised, a 'taker'	**Active citizen:** participating, volunteering, 'giving back'	politically disenfranchised, housing restrictions, notification		

Box: Social relationships and personal resources

Identity salience and role choice

1. Reintegration and desistance stable commitment to conformist identity and behaviour

2. Reintegration without desistance adult role transition without conformist identity or behaviour

3. Desistance without reintegration no adult transition, nor criminal behaviour

4. Neither desistance nor reintegration stable commitment to deviant roles, identity and behaviour

positions and few have attained standard life-course markers of the transition to adulthood (see, e.g. United States Department of Justice 1993, 2000b; Uggen and Massoglia 2002). Many are idle or under-employed with few close family or community ties. Even when they have attained established markers, such as full-time employment or parenthood, their criminal histories suggest that they have not always taken the role of the 'good citizen'.

During the process of punishment, however, felons are often eager to establish or re-establish adult roles as workers, family men and women, and citizens. For example, a recent study of life narratives of 300 low-income fathers finds that many former prisoners experience incar-ceration as a period in which there is space for reflection and recommitment to rebuilding broken family ties (Edin *et al.* 2001). Although the felons we interviewed recognize the stigma of a felony conviction and the civil disabilities imposed on them, we will show how they have little difficulty taking idealized roles such as 'family man', 'good worker', or 'active citizen' in conversation.

Their desire to claim membership in such categories, however sincere, is not founded on a solid base of training or socialization for these roles. Trying on a conformist identity in prison, as a purely cognitive process, is much easier than establishing the role commitments that will elevate the salience of this identity and guide behaviour upon release. Offenders may lack both the personal resources and social relationships necessary to sustain an identity as a law-abiding citizen, as well as a realistic understanding of what the roles themselves entail. Nevertheless, in our view such expressions constitute more than fictive storytelling or 'fantasizing' (Snow and Anderson 1987). We believe that trying on the roles of productive citizen, responsible citizen and active citizen provides, at minimum, an imaginative rehearsal for their assumption upon release.

After release, however, establishing commitment to such pro social roles and thereby securing a conformist identity is undermined by the stigma of a felony conviction, as well as any pre-existing personal or social deficits. Ex-felons face additional barriers as collateral con-sequences of their felony conviction, including occupational restrictions, loss of parental rights or standing, political disenfranchisement and other formal and informal social stigma. Moreover, post-release adjustment is complicated by the abrupt discontinuity between pre-punishment and post-punishment roles and social positions.

Once offenders complete their sentence and bump up against their own limitations and the stigma of a felony conviction, the relative salience of deviant and law-abiding identities is likely to shift. Their choice of roles in given situations – and, ultimately, their likelihood of desistance from crime – is a product of identity salience and the role commitments they have established. Although we expect most persons who have established role commitments as law-abiding citizens to desist from crime, it is useful to distinguish between conceptions of societal reintegration and desistance from crime. Adopting the roles of productive, responsible and active citizen across work, family and community domains will generally increase felons' likelihood of behavioural desistance from crime because people seek to create and maintain stable and coherent identities (Schwartz and Stryker 1970: 15). We illustrate the greater probability of congruence in Figure 11.1 with solid lines for agreement between desistance and reintegration and dashed lines where they are in conflict. According to our model, the latter incongruent role choices and identities are likely to represent unstable or transitional states.

Albert Cohen once described the process of role commitment as becoming 'hooked' on a role (1966: 101). Once 'hooked', new identities are fashioned out of new roles. 'Whole bundles' of behavior inconsistent with the claims of the new self are cast aside, and new bundles that are expressive or supportive of that role are picked up (1965: 12–13). Prisoners may experiment with new roles and try on new identities, though they lack the network of social relationships and other resources necessary to establish commitment to them. The likelihood that a fragile pro social identity will strengthen and take root upon release is therefore a function of resources and role commitments: ex-felons must become a productive citizen at work, a responsible citizen at home and an active citizen in the community.

In short, work, family and community inhibit (or promote) crime by changing the way that offenders think about themselves as citizens. We do not view these role behaviours and reintegrative domains as fixed or isolated. To the contrary, each domain is mutually reinforcing, with work and family combining in the breadwinner role, work and community in the volunteer role, and community and family in the informal 'neighbouring' role. Following Schwartz and Stryker (1970), some of the fundamental assumptions of this model are that people seek stable and coherent identities, that these identities are motivational and can impel behaviour and that identities are fixed or stabilized by role commitments. Although identity shifts may appear to occur rapidly among convicted felons, role commitments and the relative salience of these identities will only change gradually after sustained social interaction.

Working hypotheses

From this model, we offer the following working hypotheses:

H_1: felons are likely to be delayed or 'off-time' with respect to standard life-course markers of the transition to adulthood (see, e.g. Uggen and Massoglia 2002).

H_2: the stigma of a felony conviction imposes additional barriers to establishing or maintaining successful adult roles.

H_3: felons link adult role behaviour to desistance from crime, both generally when talking about other felons and personally in discussing their own life histories.

H_4: the primary idealized adult roles within the socioeconomic, familial and civic reintegrative domains include the productive citizen at work, the responsible citizen at home and the active citizen in the community.

H_5: convicted felons may envision themselves in these idealized roles and express a sincere desire to assume them, but they often lack the resources and social relationships necessary to establish role commitments and solidify new identities.

H_6: the mechanism linking adult roles and criminal behaviour is one's generalized self-concept as a deviant or conforming citizen.

Data and sample characteristics

We conducted 33 semi-structured interviews with convicted felons in Minnesota during the spring of 2001. The interviews were undertaken as part of a larger project examining the consequences of felon disenfranchisement laws in the USA (Uggen and Manza 2002; Manza and Uggen forthcoming). Prisoners, parolees and felony probationers were asked about their voting behavior, their participation in political and civic life before and after conviction, and their attitudes about crime and community. Each taped interview lasted approximately one hour, with the printed transcripts ranging from 16 to 44 typed pages.

Overall, 10 female prison inmates, 13 male prison inmates, 7 male probationers and 3 male parolees were interviewed at two state correctional facilities and one county community corrections office. Although the interviews were conducted within these facilities, we arranged for a private room with a closed door so that correctional and administrative staff would not overhear the interview questions or responses. The volunteer respondents ranged from 20 to 54 years of age, with a racial distribution of 22 white respondents, 6 African-American respondents and 5 Native American respondents. To protect the participants' confidentiality, we do not identify their race or real names when quoting from the interview transcripts. All major offence categories were represented among the interviewees, although most had been convicted of at least one violent crime.

Elsewhere we have used survey data to explore the impact of a felony conviction on a range of measures of civic and political participation (Uggen and Manza 2000; Manza and Uggen forthcoming). However, the limited survey data available have some significant limitations: the underlying factors accounting for the relationship between variables (in this case felony convictions and civic participation) remain opaque; and the data on hand are limited to analysing a one-way causal flow, the impact of conviction on participation. The in-depth interviews we rely on in this chapter allow us both to probe more deeply into how different statuses are related to behaviour and simultaneously consider the impact of civic participation on desistance. To be sure, we cannot make strong claims about the reliability and external validity of the interview data, given our semi-structured interview format and the non-representative sample. Instead, we will use these data as illustrative evidence to elucidate the concepts and causal connections we hypothesize in our model of identity, citizenship and desistance. We organize the interview data around the three domains and role identities discussed above: socioeconomic reintegration and the productive citizen role; familial reintegration and the responsible citizen role; and civic reintegration and the active citizen role. We discuss the barriers to establishing role commitments within each domain, its connection to desistance from crime, and the resulting implications for the felon's identity as a law-abiding citizen.

Socioeconomic reintegration and the productive citizen role

Apart from their limited human capital and social networks, a felony conviction imposes additional barriers to employment for the ex-offender, such as employer reluctance to hire convicted felons and occupational licensing restrictions (Uggen 1999; Holzer et al. 2001; Pager 2003). The probationers and parolees interviewed were currently facing these problems while the prisoners interviewed were well aware of the work-related obstacles awaiting them upon release. Both current inmates and those under community supervision spoke about the dominance of the felon label when seeking employment. For example, Karen, a 39-year-old female inmate, described her experiences as follows:

> What is it, the fourth question of every job interview? 'Have you ever been convicted of a crime?' They ask you that before they ask you for your prior work history or your education. All that's on the second page, so they read 'felon' before they ever read that side.

Because of such resistance to hiring convicted felons and their resulting restriction to secondary sector or 'survival' jobs, many felt they had 'lost the right to get a good job that's not paying minimum wage' (Michael, male probationer, aged 23) and were 'forced to take [a] lower position' (Travis, male parolee, aged 27). Most of the interviewees who presently had jobs or had arranged employment from prison relied on their limited social networks: family members and a few close friends and, in one case, a well-connected fellow prisoner. Offenders generally have few 'weak ties' (Granovetter 1973, 1974) to acquaintances that would help them expand their limited social circle to access jobs of higher quality.

Felons who have been embedded in dense networks in the illegal economy may believe that their illegal opportunities exceed their legitimate earning potential (Sullivan 1989; Hagan, 1993; Bourgois, 1995). With illegal opportunities more readily available, such offenders may have only vague plans for non-criminal employment. Rita, a 41-year-old female prisoner, exemplifies these points:

> I don't know what I'm going to be able to do to make money unless I go out and sell drugs again ... And the easiest thing for me to do would be to go back out and go stay with my dope people. And I can make money, you know? And I mean I know how to make money illegally and do it good, but that will bring me back here ... I'm one of them that's pretty much doomed to fail unless I get really lucky out there and find a job right away ... I mean I'm gonna get a job that probably, if I'm lucky, I'll make $8 or $9 an hour, which I can go make a drug deal in a half-hour and make $300, you know?

Struggling to make ends meet, one probationer noted: 'You gotta survive, you need money. So a lot of people resort to crime ... So, you know, do what you gotta do' (Peter, male probationer, aged 24).

Lacking both legitimate networks and opportunities and hoping to

269

avoid returning to illegal activities, some of our interviewees expressed concern about recent policy debates over welfare reform. Sally, a 30-year-old incarcerated mother, explained:

> It's really gonna affect us. You know we get out, we're felons. It's hard to get a job for some of us … Even though we are willing to work, it's hard to get a job. We can get a job paying $7, $8 an hour, but that doesn't feed me, my child, and pay the rent and pay the bills.

Even the limited forms of social provision available to low-income families in the American welfare system can seem like lifesavers when opportunities in the legal job market are so severely constrained.

In addition to the structural constraints they identify, convicted offenders must also overcome the role symbolism embodied in the generalized felon label (Cohen 1965). Several of our interviewees recognized an explicit contradiction between their identity as a felon and their identity as a productive citizen by taking the role of potential employers. The over-riding dominance of the felon label, particularly in relation to the world of work, is especially painful for many ex-offenders. Karen catalogues her positive attributes in the excerpt below, but notes that her status as a felon will likely take precedence when she seeks employment:

> It doesn't matter what your felony conviction is, it's still there. So it doesn't matter what that says. I have to realize I am more than what is written on and in paper about me. *I am more than a felon.* I am educated, I am intelligent, I'm hard-working, I'm a good mother, I'm dependable, all of those things. I don't have to worry about parole telling me I'm a felon because there's gonna be a ton of other people that are going to say, 'You're a felon'. … You know, and without that, if you can't stand up for yourself and say, '*I understand that you're concerned about hiring me as a felon'*, it doesn't matter that I'm college-educated, graduated valedictorian of my class. None of those things matter because 'felon' is what matters. (Prisoner, aged 39, emphasis added)

Many of our interviewees spoke of their fatigue with 'street life' and a desire to adopt adult socioeconomic roles (see also Shover 1996). Despite his belief that a man his age should have a 'decent job' and should be 'going to work every day', Michael felt 'stuck' in street life:

Street life will catch up with you real quick ... I've been doing this since I was 13 and I am truly tired, and I'm 24, and I just feel like I'm just wore out. [I feel] like *I'm just stuck* in the middle [of street life]. Stuck in the middle. I don't want to be here, I don't want to be doing this, I want to get out, but there are certain things that will always be tied to you forever ... I caught a brand new case like three days ago, for narcotics. Now I've got to go to trial with that...so this could be a turning point. If I get convicted, I don't know how I'm going to do the time. For real. (Male probationer, aged 23[1], emphasis added)

Most of the jobs that ex-offenders with limited skills are able to obtain upon leaving prison are very poor (Uggen 1999). But even a low-paying job can be connected to the broader goal of shaking a felon identity if it evokes a sense of becoming a productive citizen and returning something back to the community. Consider the case of Lori, a 37-year-old prisoner. Working with children at a park in her community helped change the way she thought of herself and her identity as an addicted felon:

I worked at the parks board ... You take someone like me and you put me working with kids. I tell you kids can get a whole lot of guidance from some of us ... And the reason that I was working at [name of park] was because the person that was in charge of that park, he was at one of my [Narcotics Anonymous] meetings. And he said 'You'd be ideal at this'. ... I think that was the touchstone in my life when I knew that I was really in recovery. Because – you know what? Drug addiction – any kind of addiction you got going on is a real selfish situation. It's about you and your shit, and that's it. You know? The world can fall off, drop off, and quit breathing. I gotta get my money and get my dope or whatever, you know? It's really, really selfish ... I was able to start stepping outside of myself. ... When the healing really starts to begin within you, you feel you have something to give, and you know *you have something to offer this world.* And you want to put it out there ... As my sobriety got better and clearer, I was saying, you know what? *My identity as an offender didn't come into play.* It was like, 'Who cares? Big deal! It has nothing to do with me now'. And I'll tell you what – it won't have anything to do with me when I leave here. This is just something that's happening right now. (Emphasis added)

Lori's job is somewhat unique in that working with children reinforced the connection between work, community and a sense of self-worth that was not available as drug addict and petty criminal.[2]

Lori's comments exemplify the power of visible connections between the socioeconomic and civic domains. Other interviewees discussed the relationship between work and family life. For example, the reflected appraisals of children and other family members – and their perceived reactions to an ex-offender's socioeconomic role behaviour – may be especially important for role identities. Scott, a 26-year-old male probationer with children, discussed how becoming a 'family man' made legitimate work more attractive to him:

> I think being a family man has changed me in that [career] way. To want to be – to get my money right because *I don't want to look like a piece of nothing in front of my kids*. So stuff like that has to do with pride, too. That helps, man. That helps to have a family. (Emphasis added)

Familial reintegration and the responsible citizen role

Reintegration into family life also poses obstacles to convicted felons, as they are often separated from family members for extended periods of time (cf. Edin *et al.* 2001). This physical and emotional distance is experienced as a 'huge loss' (Pamela, female prisoner, aged 49); several asserted that while their crimes may have appeared to be 'victimless,' their families were victimized by their absence:

> You know they say my crime is a victimless crime, okay? Because it's conspiracy to commit, it's nothing that I overtly did. It was not an action that I committed. But you know what? There is victims: my parents, my father-in-law, my mother-in-law, my four children. There are victims because I'm not there to help them through any education. I'm not there to give them their loving, nurturing that children deserve at tender ages. Even at 21, 22, they still need mom's guidance. And, you know, my parents depended on me to do a lot of things. (Mary, female prisoner, aged 40)

Even more extreme than the temporary separation all inmates experience, however, some offenders may be permanently severed from their families after their parental rights are legally terminated. For many of the female inmates, this process 'shatters' (Mary, female prisoner, aged

40) their identities as mothers. It is possible for incarcerated parents to maintain legal custody of their children, but the general consensus among inmates was that, 'it's pretty near impossible' (Lori, female prisoner, aged 37). One woman felt fortunate that her father was able to adopt her son once her rights were terminated, and another remarked that 'if my ex-husband knew about them laws, he'd probably have me lose my parental rights' (Rita, female prisoner, aged 41).

The legal termination of rights and the perceived finality of this act strip away felons' claims on the title, if not the role or identity, of parent. Unmarried women, in particular, are at great risk of losing parental rights (Hagan and Dinovitzer 2000). For many of the women interviewed, the termination of parental rights, and even the temporary separation from their children, was an extremely sensitive subject that was difficult to discuss with a male stranger. Several female respondents established verbal distance in talking about their children, shifting from the first person 'I' to the third person of 'women', 'they', or 'she', or by talking about specific women besides themselves. Lori related her reaction to losing custody of her son and her subsequent breakdown before directing the conversation away from herself and towards women in general:

> It's so aimed at hurting people's hearts and souls that they're not getting – I remember when they took my son from me. Let me tell you something – I was literally nuts for two years. I didn't give a shit. I did as I pleased when I pleased, and I didn't give a shit about the consequences. I was literally nuts for like two years, you know? … After six months if you ain't got your shit together here – I think the women with kids, that's such a key component of their life, and then you take that away. I mean *a lot of these women, their children are like their sole identity*. (Prisoner, aged 37, emphasis added)

Mary, another incarcerated mother, offered similar comments:

> And it crushes a lot of women. I mean *their whole world gets totally shattered in here because they don't have their children* nearby. Or their children are in different homes and things like that. There's a lady here who has four children, and they're each in a different foster home. When she gets out is she going to be able to collect her children back? I don't know. (Female prisoner, aged 40)

The acute pain experienced by the temporary or permanent suspension of parental rights has been reported by other analysts, and is one of the hidden social costs of high incarceration rates (Smith and Goretsky Elstein 1994; Gabel and Johnston 1995; Amnesty International, 1999; Hagan and Dinovitzer 2000; US Department of Justice 2000a; Enos 2001). Additionally, however, our interviews underscore the very strongly expressed desire of many offenders with children to be good role models – and the conflict between family roles and deviant roles emerged repeatedly in the interviews. Several respondents emphasized becoming a conforming role model for their children:

> Otherwise what's gonna happen? Your children are going to end up where you've been. You know that's the last thing you want. You want them to learn from your mistakes. You don't want them to copy your mistakes. (Mary, female prisoner, aged 40)

Despite a sincere (if abstract) desire to become a responsible parent, however, offenders may not have experienced the anticipatory socialization that would ease their assumption of parental roles. Thomas, a 23-year-old parolee who described his father as a 'pimp' and 'player', stressed how his childhood experiences made it difficult for him to assume a responsible parental role, but noted that fatherhood was changing him none the less:

> *Because you can't be a father in jail.* But I ain't never had a father. I never had a father, was out doing God knows what. And I don't want my children to have to go through that … 'Cause you can party 'til your head fall off, but you know it ain't all about that. I wanted to live the fast life, but it ain't all about that anymore. There's consequences to that. There's consequences, and I paid them. I paid for that. I have been shot at, I have been in prison … so that's where my mind was set at … [Having a family] changes a lot of things. It changes my opinions [and] views, my belief system, things like that. (Emphasis added)

Such reflections on emerging family roles as responsible citizens – as parents, partners, adult children or siblings – are representative of the interviews and appear to be central to a developing identity as a conforming citizen. For most of the men interviewed, this change was either relatively recent, still occurring or a change that they foresaw in the future as they step into familial roles (Edin *et al.* 2001). In fact, while few male felons discussed their children, several described fatherhood in terms of idealized role behaviour. Scott, the young probationer quoted earlier, planned to show his children his court papers when they reached adolescence to document his failures, as well as his later efforts to assume a law-abiding paternal role:

> I got two kids. And I always wanted to be that neighbor who *takes the kids to soccer* and stuff like that. Or the guy who *comes home from work and plays ball with his son*. And there was a couple neighbor kids, you know, take them all to a game or something … But it just takes time, doing the right thing … I've got a life and I'm doing things for myself. I go to this domestic abuse project thing because I was involved in some other problems with my fiancée so I'm almost completed with that. And I went through alcohol treatment 'cause I used to drink alcohol and smoke marijuana. I completed that, it's been almost a year now. So some changes I've made in my life, I feel like I'm going towards the right thing. (Emphasis added)

One additional aspect of family ties is important to mention. Our respondents often expressed a new or renewed appreciation for their importance and gratitude that their parents, partners or children remain in their lives. Pamela, an incarcerated mother who retains legal custody of her daughter but is currently incarcerated over 1,000 miles away from her, expressed gratitude for what is left in her life:

> Yes, I'm in prison, and yes, I lost my daughter and that comes up, but I still have a lot that God's left me to work with. You know? And I focus, I choose to focus on that. And those are resources that I can lean on when – you know go to a nursing home, there's people that have no one. *I have my family.* You know I have God. I have a lot to give people. (Emphasis added)

As this excerpt illustrates, the chance to reunite with their families may provide motivation and social support for offenders facing an otherwise uncertain future.

Civic reintegration and the active citizen role

In addition to socioeconomic and familial reintegration, convicted felons are expected to return to their communities and either resume or begin their lives as active and law-abiding citizens. Their prior behaviour and stigmatized current status as ex-felons, however, often limits participation. As one male noted, 'there's too many sanctions against me for me to be an active part of the community' (Paul, male prisoner, aged

37). Some sized themselves up from the perspective of others in their communities:

> They say, 'Okay, I want you back into the community', and then you point your fingers at them and keep your fingers pointed at them and say, 'This guy did a bad thing'. … Make it easier to come back into society instead of saying, 'We're accepting you back, but you can't do this and you can't do that, and you can't do this. You can walk around our streets, but after 9:00 at night, *I want you to be out of sight so the good people of, you know, Pleasant Acres won't see you'*. (Roger, male probationer, aged 54, emphasis added)

> For you to make a transition from prison and come out here and they expect you, *'you need to do this' and 'you need to do that'*. You know, you're telling me to do so much, and there's only so much that I can do. I don't have too many options. I'm a felon. (Thomas, male parolee, aged 23, emphasis added)

> People just look at you like, 'I can't believe you. I can't believe you. *Look at her. Oh my God, she went to prison'*. (Rachel, female prisoner, aged 20, emphasis added)

> 'You broke the law, you bad. You broke the law, bang – *you're not a part of us anymore'*. (Henry, male parolee, aged 25, emphasis added)

The felons we interviewed often cited loss of privacy and concern for personal safety as an additional barrier they face in the community 'because it's on record. It's public information. So …it's really difficult to get somewhere' (Scott, male probationer, aged 26). Susan, a 31-year-old inmate, discussed how her public identification as a murderer makes it difficult for her to establish an identity as anything other than a murderer:

> It's kind of scary now for felons, with the internet … if I'm going to be on there, you know, if people can know my address and stuff. That kind of makes me want to go back underground in a criminal element. I mean, *I was, I'm a, I committed a murder. I'm not a murderer 'cause that's not what I am*. But I did do a big mistake once, and, you know, a lot of people like to judge you on your past mistakes. And they like to label you and not see you, but that's not the totality of my being, you know? I'm, I'm a really good person. I have a good heart, and a lot of people are like, 'Yeah, right.' *But what if it's true?*

... You're going [to] squelch that, you're not going to let that happen, you're not going to let me be good because you have these labels on me? And you're going to make it hard for me to get a job, and you're going to make it hard for me to get a place to rent? And if my address is on the internet, what if some local renegade kind of, I don't know, people, just want to go kill an ex-con, or something or go harass them? I mean ... I mean, that's scary to me. (Emphasis added)

Such concerns about privacy and public exposure are particularly acute for offenders formally classified as sex offenders, or for one of our interviewees, as a 'sexually dangerous predator' under Minnesota law. Their situation raises unique concerns because registration laws give them an extra 'black mark' (Alan, male prisoner, aged 38) and hyper-stigmatized status. 'They notify everybody – your community, all the schools, all businesses, everything. They just blurt you out there to everybody. And it really screws your chances up' (Dennis, male prisoner, aged 23). They face further scrutiny in comparison to other felons because the stigma of their crime is so powerful that 'a person would rather have a murderer living next-door than me' (Alan, male prisoner, aged 38).

The reaction felons receive when re-entering the community may instil an ongoing sense of punishment that goes beyond anything court imposed. Their hostile reception in the community may restrict informal neighbouring and other civic participation, but felons must also contend with formal sanctions that literally disenfranchise them. At present, 48 of the 50 US states bar some or all convicted felons from voting – in most cases including those on probation or parole (as is the case in Minnesota). At least nine of those states also bar ex-felons from voting, two other states permanently disenfranchise recidivists and three more states require a post-release waiting period (Uggen and Manza 2002). Losing the right to vote incited a range of emotion because 'on top of the whole messy pile, there it was. Something that was hardly mentioned, and it meant a lot' (Steven, male probationer, aged 52). One prisoner described how the loss of voting rights is part of a larger package of restrictions that make it impossible for her to become a 'normal citizen':

I think that just getting back in the community and being a contributing member is difficult enough ... And saying, 'Yeah, we don't value your vote either because you're a convicted felon from how many years back', okay? ... But I, hopefully, have learned, have paid for that and *would like to someday feel like a, quote, 'normal*

citizen', a contributing member of society, and you know that's hard when every election you're constantly being reminded, 'Oh yeah, that's right, I'm ashamed.' ... It's just like a little salt in the wound. You've already got that wound and it's trying to heal and it's trying to heal, and you're trying to be a good taxpayer and be a homeowner ... Just one little vote, right? But that means a lot to me. ... It's just loss after loss after loss. And this is just another one. Another to add to the pile ... When I said salt in the wound, the wound's already there. Me being able to vote isn't going to just whip up and heal that wound ... And I am looking forward to and trying to prepare to be that productive member of society that I've always wanted to be. I have this wound and it's healing ... But it's like it's still open enough so that you telling me that I'm still really bad because I can't [vote] is like making it sting again. It's like haven't I paid enough yet? ... You can't really feel like a part of your government because they're still going like this, 'Oh, you're bad. Remember what you did way back then? Nope, you can't vote'.
(Pamela, prisoner, aged 49, emphasis added)

These sentiments were echoed throughout our interviews. Many suggested in one way or another that the right to vote was fundamental to citizenship and a pro social identity, even if they had never exercised that right in the past. Voting is 'part of being a citizen and being an adult' (Lynn, female prisoner, aged 38), with franchise restrictions leaving felons feeling 'exiled' from their fellow citizens. Paul, a 37-year-old inmate, declared:

I have no right to vote on the school referendums that will affect my children. I have no right to vote on how my taxes is going to be spent or used, which I have to pay whether I'm a felon or not, you know? So basically I've lost all voice or control over my government ... And this system, once you're a felon you're punished for life. And you don't have a voice ... People don't want to recognize that *we can still be citizens and still be patriotic* even though we made a mistake. And that's a hard pill to swallow ... I can't say anything because I don't have a voice. Or 'cause I can't vote about it ... I'm not saying give back gun rights or anything like that to people that definitely don't deserve them. But giving back voting rights is another way to make a person feel part of that community. How can you feel that you're giving back to a community that you're a part of when you're *exiled* from it by not being able to vote and have a voice in it? (Emphasis added)

Other respondents described their disenfranchised status as 'outsiders', stating that they were 'less than the average citizen' (Rachel, female prisoner, aged 20) or that their citizenship was currently 'put on hold' (Dennis, male prisoner, aged 23). As Karen, a prisoner who had been an active voter prior to her conviction, told us:

> I voted every single solitary year from the day I was granted voting privileges when I was eighteen until I was convicted … For me it's important because I like to know that when I leave here, I will start – I will continue my life because I won't start it over – *although there's a whole new part of me coming out of here – I will continue my life*, and I would like to have that position back. To be able to vote. (Emphasis added)

For Karen, the restoration of the right to vote provides a clear marker of civic reintegration, while the loss of voting rights is a visible symbol of the costs of a felony conviction.

Although their civic participation is limited in many ways, ex-felons often express a desire to volunteer their time or 'give back' to their communities in other ways. While most of the felons interviewed said they planned to volunteer, coach youth sports, speak publicly about their crimes or engage in some other form of civic participation, their motivation for doing so differed. Susan believed that criminals 'kind of have a responsibility. You can't always undo what you've done, but you can try to promote harmony in another area' (female prisoner, aged 31).

To be sure, the rhetoric about 'giving back to the community' is not universally shared. Henry, a young parolee, disagreed with the idea of restitution or 'earned redemption' (see, e.g. Bazemore 1998):

> [The concept of prisoners saying 'I want to give back to my community' is] something that they were taught in treatment. They got a therapist that installs that inside of their head. That if you take something or hurt somebody around your neighborhood, which is your community, don't you think you should give back? *'Cause only a bad person wouldn't*. So they make a person think maybe they should feel that way. They should give back if they took something or harmed somebody… I don't feel I owe anyone anything. I owe myself something. I owe myself a better life, you know? I owe myself a chance to do better. That's what I owe. (Male parolee, aged 25, emphasis added)

Scott affirmed his commitment to an identity as a law-abiding citizen, but resisted the role of the contrite ex-felon:

> I don't feel guilty, man, after spending five years in the joint. I'm sorry, I just don't ... I feel like I repaid my debt. I don't feel guilty at all for it. All the people that are smoking drugs and do that, yeah, I did help them get high. I helped them hurt their body, yes, I did. But when you're talking about my freedom, the price of my freedom? I already paid for it ... And to me that'd be really selfish to say that I didn't hurt anybody, I don't feel bad about it. But as far as me feeling guilty about it like I owe somebody something else – what I owe society is to not get in trouble no more. *To be law-abiding.* I've got that brand already, you know. I fucked up. (Probationer, aged 26, emphasis added)

If such brands are indeed permanent, offenders will never be 'delabeled' as deviants (Trice and Roman, 1970). Such beliefs make it difficult for offenders to envision themselves rejoining their com-munities as active citizens. Paul, a convicted sex offender, explicitly resented the idea of 'giving back' to the community that cast him out:

> I really get kind of peeved when people say 'give back to the community' because *I'm not a part of the community anymore* as far as I can see it ... And so when they [say], 'What are you going to give back to the community for this and for that?' I'm like well, *hey, community doesn't want a damn thing to do with me*, why should I go back and give anything to do with the community? (Prisoner, aged 37, emphasis added)

The bitterness underlying these comments shows the flip side of the power of community reintegration: when stigma and rejection are the dominant experience, the potentially restorative benefits of civic participation are lost.

In spite of such concerns about community rejection on the part of some interviewees, almost all said they planned some form of participation as active citizens in the future, with several specifically linking civic participation with their desire to stay away from crime. Pamela provided volunteer services by making blankets for children and spoke of the letters she had received from the recipients:

> I'm doing it for kids I'll never see and they'll never see me. But that makes me feel so good that I'm doing something here that's not

about me. You know that's not selfish … And it is so fulfilling for them and that's just a small example of the same thing on the outside. If you start filling yourself up. It's the same principle of sponsorship in AA and NA. You start helping other people who have less time than you clean and sober, *you stay well, too.* Because there's a connection there and there's people relying on you. (Prisoner, aged 49, emphasis added)

One of the most common ways in which felons expressed a desire to give something back is through public speaking or sharing their stories with others. Alex, a 37-year-old male inmate who killed his brother while intoxicated, hoped to solidify his identity as sober and law-abiding upon his release by communicating his personal experiences with alcoholism:

When I leave [prison], I want to go maybe going around to juvenile detention centers. Speaking about alcoholism … from the first time I started drinking to my incarceration and what I went through in prison. And just sharing that with younger kids around the community … will *keep me aware of what I want* … it would just remind me of what could happen, what I could go back to. (Emphasis added)

Some ex-felons envisioned themselves in an idealized role as an active citizen by sharing their insights with young people. The desire to impart hard-won knowledge about crime and punishment is often voiced. Dylan, a 29-year-old male inmate, spoke of his volunteer work and public speaking in some detail:

Well, the first thing I'm going to do, even when I'm on work release someday, there's an extension of the [city] Youth Services Bureau. We work with them here where they bring in their repeat offenders, and we talk to them. But once I'm on work release, or even once I'm paroled, you can go to schools, you can go to community centers, all kinds of places and talk to kids … I'm in here for murder, and I can't ever get that person's life back. I can't return him to his family, I can't balance that scale any way, but I can keep trying for the rest of my life … We have a Toastmasters Club here. And I've been involved with that for the last two and a half years, so that's definitely helped my communication skills of being able to articulate myself so I want to be able to use that when I go out, too. Actually go give talks, not – *I watch the legislators talk sometimes on*

281

[channel] 17, and I can see myself actually, as … It seems probably unrealistic right now. A friend of mine who got out, he was a doctor before came in. He's up in [city] now and he's given a talk to a criminology class … So I'm like, 'If you can do that …' I mean I'd love to go to criminology classes or talk in front of the legislators about all kinds of issues. (Emphasis added)

However much these plans seem 'unrealistic right now,' offenders such as Dylan express commitment to civic-minded role behaviour that may help solidify identities as conforming citizens: 'I've done everything I could since I've been in here to try and do that [contribute something]. I've started youth groups to try to talk to youth, and tried to get as much of an education as I could, get as many job skills as I can.' Similarly, one woman whose drug use and criminal activities were widely discussed in her small town was eager to rejoin that community and establish a new role as an active citizen. Lynn said that 'people seen that I changed' and had written her with offers of employment and other support:

When I get out I'll be home in time to do whatever I can to help out with [my hometown] centennial. The last two years I've been on house arrest so I couldn't be involved. I had to sit at home. So this will be my first year not [on house arrest], and I plan on, you know, whatever day if they need me to clean up the streets, whatever, I plan on doing it. (Prisoner, aged 38)

Paul, who had a high level of community involvement prior to his conviction, wished to resume his former role as an active citizen:

I get *Sessions Weekly* and *Senate Briefly* every week, and I follow along on what's going on in the legislature and committee reports … I was really involved in my community. There was a community group in our area that I was involved in that was having to do with [business name] and businesses and gun shops moving in too close to our parks and stuff like that. You know all the business people in the area and the residents kind of teamed up and we had the ear of the government because we were such a forceful group. [I plan to get involved again] to a degree that I can. I'm going to be limited in what I can and can't do. If there's an open mike at some committee hearing, I may well be down there voicing my opinion. I've been known to do that in the past. (Prisoner, aged 37)

Despite prior community involvement and a willingness to involve themselves, ex-felons face a multitude of barriers that prevent full participation. Whether it is the enduring 'felon' label or the formal loss of citizenship rights, these restrictions send messages that lead many to question whether they truly belong – 'not being able to vote kind of says you don't matter, and you're not really a part of this community. But then here I am, your next-door neighbor' (Susan, female prisoner, aged 31).

Stigma, citizenship and identity

While the preceding sections focus on the socioeconomic, familial and civic domains in isolation, felons often experience stigmatization across all three reintegrative domains simultaneously. The pervasive generalized 'felon' label that defines the relationship between ex-felons and society complicates problems of adjustment upon re-entry. Many considered their status as felons to be a scarlet letter, leaving them permanently marked or 'branded' (Scott, male probationer, aged 26). Thomas, a young parolee, referred to the 'F' on his record:

> You are labeled as a felon, and you're always gonna be assumed and known to have contact with that criminal activity and them ethics. And even when I get off parole, *I'm still gonna have an 'F' on my record*. I can have twenty million dollars just sitting in an account. I'm still gonna be a felon. (Male parolee, aged 23, emphasis added)

Moving from an environment in which 'felon' is simply a 'term' to one in which it is a generalized label with wide-ranging consequences induces a sense of role discontinuity. As Karen stated:

> When I leave here it will be very difficult for me in the sense that I'm a felon. That I will *always* be a felon … Being a felon is *a term* here, obviously it's not a bad term. Being a felon in this environment, everyone is – this is acceptable. [Outside prison] I don't have a single, solitary friend who has a speeding ticket, let alone a criminal record, you know? So for me to leave here, *it will affect my job, it will affect my education, … custody, it can affect child support, it can affect everywhere – family, friends, housing* … People that are convicted of drug crimes can't even get housing anymore … So I know that when I leave here, I have to be a whole lot

stronger than I have ever been … yes, I did my prison time. How long are you going to punish me as a result of it? And not only on paper, I'm only on paper for ten months when I leave here, that's all the parole I have. But, that parole isn't going to be anything. *It's the housing, it's the credit re-establishing,* uh… I mean even *to go into the school*, to work with my child's class – and I'm not a sex offender – but all I need is one parent who says, 'Isn't she a felon? I don't want her with my child'. Bingo. And you know that there are people out there like that. (Prisoner, aged 39, emphasis added)

Susan characterized her loss of citizenship rights as tantamount to losing the 'right to belong':

Right now I'm in prison. Like *society kicked me out*. They're like, 'Okay, the criminal element. We don't want them in society, we're going to put them in these prisons'. Okay, but once I get out – then what do you do? What do you do with all these millions of people that have been in prison and been released? I mean, *do you accept them back? Or do you keep them as outcasts?* And if you keep them as outcasts, how do you expect them to act? (Prisoner, aged 31, emphasis added)

Seeing themselves as 'outcasts' from the perspective of their communities calls felons' identities as citizens into question: if society rejects them no matter what they do, the incentive to transition into a law-abiding citizen role is correspondingly reduced. Moreover, most of the felons interviewed were significantly 'off-time' with respect to the standard life-course markers of adult status. In taking stock of their current circumstances, many respondents lamented that they had not gotten further in life, building careers, forming families, purchasing houses and taking on other adult roles. This sense of being behind schedule further exacerbates feelings of isolation and separation from community norms:

[I] have so much to make up for like lost time, and I have nothing to show for it. I'll get out when I'm 34. I have no house, no car, no anything. (Dylan, male prisoner, aged 29)

I'm about 25 now, and *I need a decent family, decent job, car, going to work every day* … the way I'm going, I need to slow down and do something positive. So I can show my little brothers, 'cause they know I'm in the street, they in Chicago, too, though. My main focus really though is to get everything right so I can have them move up here with me and go to school and college. I don't want them growing up in Chicago, like I did. (Michael, male probationer, aged 23, emphasis added)

Conscious of the enduring stigma of their felony convictions, most respondents were careful to separate their criminal act from their overall sense of self. Roger, a middle-aged probationer, drew from his Gambler's Anonymous experience, declaring that 'it's the person who did something bad, but they're not a bad person'. Rachel, a young female inmate, asserted, 'I'm not a criminal. I mean I'm guilty of what I did, and I'm here, but my crime – I'm twenty, I'm almost twenty-one, but my crime was committed when I was eighteen'.

Even as they stress their own intrinsic worth, however, felons attach great importance to the perceived reaction of others in their communities: 'I just want them to say, "You're not a bad person" … *It's just weird to me that it means so much to me that society thinks of me in a certain way'* (Susan, prisoner, aged 31, emphasis added). Finding ways to manage stigma and establish an identity as a law-abiding citizen thus becomes a primary concern for offenders upon release, imposing additional barriers to reintegration. Thomas, who had already been released from prison twice at 23, explained how the ability to deal with stigma is important in avoiding recidivism:

I'm a felon. And I'm on parole. So what choice do you have? You either deal with this [stigma], or you go back to prison … They say that when you first get out, you shouldn't let someone know if you just got out. You should try to hold it low until you can be sure. But you also have to be confident. You got to be comfortable and it will all be right. And *it'll all float away* … The second time I got out [of prison], I changed myself, my surroundings, the people I was with. A lot of things, but at the same time I wasn't gonna allow myself to be put down, and I was gonna be persistent. I was gonna show that I can do that, you know? I was gonna show that I can do, more or less, *the same that any man can do.* (Parolee, emphasis added)

Given such concerns, the extremely modest goal of simply being perceived the same as 'any man' or woman in their social relationships was paramount for several of the felons interviewed.

Regardless of the imminent barriers, many looked to the future and saw a chance to salvage what is 'left' and to contribute something as citizens. The following comments from Scott and Dylan show both recognition of potential for change and a 'generative' (Erikson 1968; Maruna 2001) concern for the well-being of others:

> I'm *very appreciative* right now. I feel like I've got another chance. I feel like somebody somewhere, something didn't want me to just fall in the cracks and die and do nothing. So I feel grateful that I have the opportunity to make myself better, to try to move my children into what they need to be to survive. To not only survive, *but to make a mark. A positive mark.* I have a lot of hopes. (Scott, male probationer, aged 26, emphasis added)

> And once I wound up here looking ahead in my life and *saying this is what I have left when I walk out.* I can either be like the rest of these guys and get out and come back, get out and come back, and basically amount to nothing my entire life, or I can *try to make the best of what I've got left and try and contribute something.* (Dylan, male prisoner, aged 29, emphasis added)

Summary and conclusions

In this chapter we have drawn from symbolic interactionist theories of crime over the life-course and some original interview data to develop a life course model of role transitions and desistance. We hypothesized that ex-felons are likely to be off-time with respect to standard life-course markers of the transition to adulthood and that the stigma of a felony conviction imposes additional barriers to successful adult role transition. Although our small sample of felons can only provide illustrative evidence on these points, the interview data demonstrate how the stigma of a felony conviction creates new obstacles to assuming adult roles and exacerbates pre-existing barriers. Karen summarized the impact across different domains: 'it will affect my job, it will affect my education ... custody ... child support ... housing ... credit re-establishing,' and even the ability to 'go into the school, to work with my child's class'.

We also hypothesized that felons would link successful adult role transition to desistance from crime, both generally when talking about other felons and personally in discussing their own life histories. Although the majority of our sample remains incarcerated, it is clear that they had already established a connection between desistance and their roles as workers, 'family men' and women, and citizens. Some viewed themselves as 'stuck' in street life and 'pretty much doomed to fail' until they established commitment to adult roles, whereas others attributed changes in offending to taking on roles as a 'family man' or obtaining a 'decent job'.

Unlike previous work on role transitions and desistance, we hypothesized that such idealized roles could be organized around the concept of *citizenship* – the productive citizen at work, the responsible citizen at home and the active citizen in the community. Citizenship themes were most pronounced in discussions of voting rights and volunteer experiences, but were also evident in the way felons spoke of their work and family lives as a 'good taxpayer' and 'productive member of society', or as wanting to 'be that neighbor' who takes the kids to ballgames. As with the social science literature on citizenship, our interviewees collectively expressed both a desire for the rights of citizenship and willingness to involve themselves in civic life.

In response to our questions, the interviewees frequently provided detailed and thoughtful responses to the hurdles they faced in the three reintegrative domains we had identified. Additionally, many respondents linked these domains in ways that we had not foreseen – connecting family roles with socioeconomic and civic roles in particular.

We also observed some clear differences between prisoners and felons living in the community. Those who were currently incarcerated were more likely to envision themselves in idealized roles, such as becoming model parents, speaking to schools and legislators or assuming leadership positions such as co-ordinating transitional housing programmes. The expressed goals of probationers and parolees, in contrast, were tempered by their recent experiences in their communities. After presenting himself in an idealized family role, for example, one ex-prisoner said: 'I don't know if I could do it. I don't want to put myself that high, you know?' (Scott, male probationer, aged 26). This is consistent with our expectation that convicted felons may express a sincere desire to assume these idealized roles, but they often lack the resources and social relationships necessary to establish role commitments and solidify new identities. For those supervised in the community, the struggle to establish such commitments was an immediate concern, as many considered themselves 'branded' as a felon with a permanent 'F' on their records.

Finally, we hypothesized that the primary mechanism linking adult role transition and crime is a generalized self-concept as a deviant or conforming citizen. Although we cannot provide definitive evidence on this point, the interview data are generally consistent with this interpretation. For example, Lori noted that her 'identity as an offender' no longer came into play once she began working in a park with children. Of course, levels of civic participation and conceptions of citizenship vary among felons as they do in the general population.

Almost all respondents spoke of how their felony convictions made them outsiders, occupying a status that is 'less than the average citizen'. The increasing availability of public information about their crimes, however, made many feel especially marked and vulnerable. Although the most stigmatized respondents distanced themselves from 'the good people of Pleasant Acres' who do not want a 'damn thing' to do with them, they consistently defended their rights and embraced their responsibilities as citizens.

Perhaps most surprisingly, we found that barriers to establishing or re-establishing adult roles appear to engender a new or renewed sense of their importance. Offenders are eager (if sometimes naïvely optimistic – see, e.g. Maruna 2001: 97) to establish or re-establish their roles at work, home and in the community and to capitalize on 'what's left' for them in each of these domains.

Caveats and remaining questions

Our analysis was designed to illustrate a conceptual model of role commitment and identity transformation among convicted felons rather than to provide a critical test of competing hypotheses. We should note that our sample is unlikely to be representative of the felon population and that we cannot address behavioural desistance from crime because many of our respondents remain incarcerated. We have also emphasized a general model of identity transformation without attention to potentially important subgroup differences. For example, it is possible that the criminal history, race and gender of the respondents may condition the processes we describe.

An important remaining question for research and policy concerns the societal management of stigma. At present, communities are ill-prepared to accept felons as fellow citizens. Prohibitions on ex-felons' occupational licensing, parental rights and ownership of firearms may serve a needed societal interest in minimizing the risk associated with their release in the community. Our interview data suggest that many felons support some of these restrictions in principle (though they are *not* supportive of disfranchisement and housing restrictions), but argue convincingly that such restrictions should be much more narrowly tailored and limited in duration. For example, the felons we interviewed believed that voting restrictions should be limited in scope (to election crimes) and duration (for the term of imprisonment); firearms restrictions should be limited to violent offenders; and restrictions on parental rights should be exercised with greater concern for families' individual situations.

A related question concerns the potential for deviant decertification or reintegration ceremonies (Braithwaite and Mugford 1994). As Kai Erikson observed in the 1960s (1964: 16–17), one is 'ushered into the deviant position by a decisive and often dramatic ceremony, yet is retired from it with hardly a word of public notice. And as a result, the deviant often returns home with no proper license to resume a normal life in the community'.

In our view, the skills training and role commitments necessary to overcome stigma and adopt a law-abiding identity must begin long before release from correctional supervision. The felons we interviewed needed assistance or anticipatory socialization to turn their idealized role conceptions into workable commitments that would foster identities as law-abiding but imperfect citizens. Although many correctional programmes provide such socialization in the socioeconomic domain and, increasingly, the family domain, felons are currently ill-prepared to re-enter their communities as participating citizens. Creating avenues of participation that reinforce, rather than limit, citizenship would appear likely to enhance the possibilities of successful reintegration. This restoration of citizenship should entail both the customary bundle of social rights citizens possess and the creation of opportunities to participate in communal life.

Partially to address this concern, one inmate suggested establishing a civics curriculum in the prison. We second this idea by suggesting voluntary pilot projects that would provide goal setting, planning and preparation to resume or establish civic participation. These might include opportunities for community projects before release that would begin to activate the nascent desire for active participation many felons articulate in different ways. We can speculate that a well structured programme would be very likely to increase intermediate outcomes such as voter turnout and, potentially, to influence long-term desistance patterns. If the argument of this chapter is correct, the challenge for policy is to provide those links in meaningful ways during and after incarceration. In addition to their policy importance, we believe that evaluations of such programmes could dramatically increase scientific knowledge of the desistance process.

To date, most research and policy efforts on reintegration have emphasized juvenile offenders (Braithwaite and Mugford 1994) and those convicted of minor crimes, such as soliciting prostitution (see, e.g. Bazemore 1998 for examples of current programmes). In our view, the assumption of greater malleability among youth and minor offenders may be mistaken. In particular, we believe that older offenders with more serious criminal histories may ultimately be those most amenable to policy efforts that promise to facilitate their transition to adult roles (Uggen 2000).

Conclusion

When criminologists refer to 'citizens', they generally use the term in opposition to criminal offenders, placing criminals on one side of the street and law-abiding community residents on the other. Our research demonstrates that felons think of *themselves* as citizens, assuming roles as taxpayers, homeowners volunteers and voters. As they develop socioeconomic, familial and civic role commitments, the salience of their identities as law-abiding citizens rises and the salience of their identities as felons recedes. With this gradual shift in the identity salience hierarchy, their actions will more consistently meet the expectations of the citizen role. We therefore suggest that civic reintegration and establishing an identity as a law-abiding citizen are central to the process of desistance from crime.

Acknowledgements

This research was supported by grants from the National Science Foundation (# 9819015) and the Individual Project Fellowship Program of the Open Society Institute. We thank Melissa Thompson and Kathryn Edin for especially helpful comments and the Minnesota Department of Corrections and Hennepin County (Minneapolis) Department of Community Corrections for their cooperation and assistance with data collection. These individuals and departments have neither endorsed nor approved this chapter and the authors assume sole responsibility for any errors.

Notes

1 Although this respondent's age is recorded as 23, he stated that he is 24 and 25 at different points in the interview.
2 It is worth noting that a felony conviction would often preclude the opportunity to work in job that involves extensive contact with children. Lori was able to get the job through a surprising 'weak' tie established by meeting her future job supervisor at a Narcotics Anonymous meeting.

References

Amnesty International (1999) *'Not part of my sentence.' Violations of the Human Rights of Women in Custody*. New York, NY: Amnesty International.

Bazemore, G. (1998) 'Restorative justice and earned redemption: communities, victims, and offender reintegration', *American Behavioral Scientist*, 41: 768–813.

Bourgois, P. (1995) *In Search of Respect: Selling Crack in El Barrio*. Cambridge: Cambridge University Press.

Braithwaite, J. and Mugford, S. (1994) 'Conditions of successful reintegration ceremonies: dealing with juvenile offenders', *British Journal of Criminology*, 34: 139–71.

Cohen, A.K. (1965) 'The sociology of the deviant act: anomie theory and beyond', *American Sociological Review*, 30: 5–14.

Cohen, A.K. (1966) *Deviance and Control*. Englewood Cliffs, NJ: Prentice Hall.

Edin, K., Lein, L. and Nelson, T. (2001) 'Taking care of business: the economic survival strategies of low-income non-custodial fathers', in F. Munger (ed.) *The Low Wage Labor Market*. New York, NY: Russell Sage Foundation.

Edin, K., Nelson, T. and Parnal, R. (2001) 'Fatherhood and incarceration as potential turning points in the criminal careers of unskilled men.' Paper presented at the 'Effects of incarceration on children and families' conference, Institute for Policy Research, Northwestern University, May.

Enos, S. (2001) *Mothering from the Inside: Parenting in a Women's Prison*. New York, NY: SUNY Press.

Erikson, K. (1964) 'Notes on the sociology of deviance', in H.S. Becker (ed.) *The Other Side*. New York, NY: Free Press, 9–22.

Erikson, E. (1968) *Identity: Youth and Crisis*. New York, NY: Norton.

Gabel, K. and Johnston, D. (eds) (1995) *Children of Incarcerated Parents*. San Francisco, CA: Jossey-Bass.

Granovetter, M.S. (1973) 'The strength of weak ties', *American Journal of Sociology*, 78: 1360–80.

Granovetter, M.S. (1974) *Getting a Job: A Study of Contacts and Careers*. Cambridge, MA: Harvard University Press.

Hagan, J. (1993) 'The social embeddedness of crime and unemployment', *Criminology*, 31: 465–91.

Hagan, J. and Dinovitzer, R. (2000) 'Collateral consequences of imprisonment for children, communities, and prisoners', *Crime and Justice*, 26: 121–62.

Hagestad, G.O. and Neugarten, B.L. (1985), 'Aging and the life course', in E. Shanas and R. Binstock (eds) *Handbook of Aging and the Social Sciences*. New York, NY: Van Nostrand Reinhold.

Heimer, K. and Matsueda, R. (1994) 'Role-taking, role commitment, and delinquency: a theory of differential social control', *American Sociological Review*, 59: 365–90.

Holzer, H., Raphael, S. and Stoll, M. (2001) 'Perceived criminality, criminal background checks, and the racial hiring practices of employers.' Paper presented at the conference 'Incarceration and families', Northwestern University, 5 May.

Laub, J., Nagin, D. and Sampson, R. (1998) 'Trajectories of change in criminal offending: good marriages and the desistance process', *American Sociological Review*, 63: 225–38.

Manza, J. (2001) 'Citizenship and the right to vote: some hidden problems of American democracy.' Unpublished paper, Department of Sociology, Northwestern University.

Manza, J. and Uggen, C. (forthcoming) *Locked Out: Felon Disfranchisement and American Democracy*. New York, NY: Oxford University Press.

Marshall, T.H. (1950) *Citizenship and Social Class*. Cambridge: Cambridge University Press.

Maruna, S. (2001) *Making Good: How Ex-convicts Reform and Rebuild their Lives*. Washington, DC: American Psychological Association.

Matsueda, R. (1992) 'Reflected appraisals, parental labeling, and delinquency: specifying a symbolic interactionist theory', *American Journal of Sociology*, 97: 1577–611.

Matsueda, R. and Heimer, K. (1997) 'A symbolic interactionist theory of role-transitions, role-commitments, and delinquency', in T. Thornberry (ed.) *Developmental Theories of Crime and Delinquency*. New Brunswick, NJ: Transaction Publishers, 163–213.

Merton, R. (1938) 'Social structure and anomie', *American Sociological Review,* 3: 672–82.

Oldfield, A. (1990) *Citizenship and Commuity: Civic Republicanism and the Modern World*. New York, NY: Routledge.

Pager, D. (2003) 'The mark of a criminal record', *American Journal of Sociology*, 108: 937–75.

Sampson, R. and Laub, J. (1990) 'Crime and deviance over the life course: the salience of adult social bonds', *American Sociological Review*, 55: 609–27.

Sampson, R. and Laub, J. (1993) *Crime in the Making: Pathways and Turning Points through Life*. Cambridge, MA: Harvard University Press.

Schwartz, M. and Stryker, S. (1970) *Deviance, Selves and Others*. Washington, DC: American Sociological Association.

Shafir, G. (1998) 'Introduction: the evolving tradition of citizenship', in G. Shafir (ed.) *The Citizenship Debates*. Minneapolis, MN: University of Minnesota Press, 1–28.

Shanahan, M.J. (2000) 'Pathways to adulthood in changing societies: variability and mechanisms in life course perspective', *Annual Review of Sociology*, 26: 667–92.

Shover, N. (1996) *Great Pretenders: Pursuits and Careers of Persistent Thieves*. Boulder, CO: Westview Press.

Smith, B.E. and Goretsky Elstein, S. (1994) *Children on Hold: Improving the Response to Children whose Parents are Arrested and Incarcerated*. Washington, DC: ABA Center on Children and the Law.

Snow, D.A. and Anderson, L. (1987) 'Identity work among the homeless: the verbal construction and avowal of personal identities', *American Journal of Sociology*, 92: 1336–71.

Stryker, S. and Burke, P. (2000) 'The past, present, and future of an identity theory', *Social Psychology Quarterly*, 63: 284–97.

Sullivan, M. (1989) *Getting Paid: Youth Crime and Work in the Inner City*. Ithaca, NY: Cornell University Press.

Thornberry, T.P. (1987) 'Toward an interactional theory of delinquency', *Criminology*, 25: 863–92.

Trice, H.M. and Roman, P.M. (1970) 'Delabeling, relabeling, and Alcoholics Anonymous', *Social Problems*, 17: 538–46.

Uggen, C. (1999) 'Ex-offenders and the conformist alternative: a job quality model of work and crime', *Social Problems*, 46: 127–51.

Uggen, C. (2000) 'Work as a turning point in the life course of criminals: a duration model of age, employment, and recidivism', *American Sociological Review*, 65: 529–46.

Uggen, C. and Manza, J. (2002) 'Democratic contraction? The political consequences of felon disenfranchisement in the United States', *American Sociological Review*, 67: 777–803.

Uggen, C., Manza, J. and Thompson, M. (2000) 'Crime, class, and reintegration: The socioeconomic, familial, and civic lives of offenders.' Paper presented at the American Society of Criminology Annual Meeting, San Francisco, CA, November.

Uggen, C. and Massoglia, M. (2002) 'Desistance from crime and deviance as a turning point in the life course', in J.T. Mortimer and M. Shanahan (eds) *Handbook of the Life Course*. New York, NY: Plenum.

US Department of Justice (1993) *Survey of State Prison Inmates, 1991*. Washington, DC: Government Printing Office.

US Department of Justice (2000a) *Bureau of Justice Statistics: Incarcerated Parents and their Children*. Washington, DC: Government Printing Office.

US Department of Justice (2000b) *Survey of Inmates in State and Federal Correctional Facilities, 1997* (computer file). Ann Arbor, MI: Inter-university Consortium for Political and Social Research.

Index